# individualized instruction-programs and materials

# individualized instruction—programs and materials

James E. Duane, Editor
University of Utah

**selected readings and bibliography**

educational technology publications
englewood cliffs, new jersey 07632

Library of Congress Cataloging in Publication Data

Duane, James E        comp.
   Individualized instruction—programs and materials.

   Includes bibliographies.
   1.   Individualized instruction.   I.   Title.
LB1031.D77        371.39'4        72-11990
ISBN 0-87778-043-9

Printed in the United States of America.

Library of Congress Catalog Card Number:
72-11990.

International Standard Book Number:
0-87778-043-9.

First printing.

# PREFACE

This book is designed for teachers, media specialists and administrators who are interested in learning about effective methods of planning, designing and implementing individualized instruction programs. All of the readings present practical and easily understood approaches concerning a particular area of individualization.

The selected readings have been organized into four sections. Part 1 deals with the problems encountered in making the transition from traditional group oriented instruction to individualized instruction. Part 2 surveys several of the established and successful individualized instruction formats presently in use throughout the country. Part 3 outlines the characteristics of various types of media, and suggests methods for integrating media into individualized instruction programs. Part 4 is concerned with the evaluation of individualized programs and presents some generalized criticisms of existing programs. A bibliography is provided at the end of each section for those who desire more information related to the section headings.

An introduction to each section is included, which describes the central theme of each article in that section. These introductory segments are provided to allow the reader to choose articles most relevant to his particular needs. Since individualized instruction procedures have changed drastically in the last few years, the articles and bibliographic references in this book are limited to those that have been written within the past four years.

Three appendices are included. Appendix I contains an annotated bibliography of books dealing with individualized instruction. Appendix II contains an annotated bibliography of commercially available media on various individualized instruction topics. Appendix III contains four sample individualized instruction packages.

James E. Duane, Ed.D.
Division of Instructional Systems
    and Learning Resources
University of Utah

September, 1972

# CONTENTS

Contents

# THE CONTRIBUTORS

|  | Page |
|---|---|
Howard E. Blake
Professor of English Education
Temple University
Philadelphia, Pennsylvania 19122 — 7

Ann W. McPherson
Associate Professor of Math Education
Temple University
Philadelphia, Pennsylvania 19122 — 7

Gerald C. Ubben, Associate Professor
Department of Educational Administration
 and Supervision
University of Tennessee
Knoxville, Tennessee 37916 — 17

Richard W. Burns, Professor
Department of Curriculum and Instruction
University of Texas at El Paso
El Paso, Texas 79968 — 25

John O. Bolvin, Director of IPI
Learning Research and Development Center
University of Pittsburgh
Pittsburgh, Pennsylvania 15213 — 33

William P. McLoughlin                                    47
Professor of Education
St. John's University
Jamaica, New York 10457

Gail L. Baker, Program Specialist                        61
National Clearinghouse for Mental
 Health Information
Chevy Chase, Maryland 20015

Isadore Goldberg, Director                               61
Education and Training Departments
Computer Applications Incorporated
Silver Spring, Maryland 20907

Richard V. Jones, Jr. Chairman                           73
Department of Education
Stanislaus State College
Turlock, California 95380

Roger Tunks                                              87
Vice-Principal, Curriculum
Thomas Jefferson High School
Portland, Oregon 97217

Robert G. Scanlon, Project Director                     109
Research for Better Schools, Inc.
Philadelphia, Pennsylvania 19103

Alice Hosticka, Project Director                        117
Learning Research and Development Center
Pittsburgh, Pennsylvania 15213

John C. Flanagan, Director                              125
Project PLAN
American Institutes for Research
Palo Alto, California 94302

Robert A. Weisgerber                                          251
Senior Research Scientist
American Institutes for Research
Palo Alto, California 94302

Paul R. Daniels                                              257
Instructional Consultant
Prince George's County Public Schools
Upper Marlboro, Maryland 20870

R.S. North                                                  261
Dean of Instruction
Oklahoma Christian College
Oklahoma City, Oklahoma 73111

Richard Hooper                                              269
Centre for Educational Development Overseas
Tavistock House South, Tavistock Square
London, WC1H 9LL

O.L. Davis, Jr.                                             289
Professor of Education
University of Texas at Austin
Austin, Texas 78712

Paul W. Kirby, Professor                                    289
Department of Curriculum and Instruction
University of Texas at Austin
Austin, Texas 78712

Robert E. Keuscher                                          299
Director of School Services
International Center for Educational Development
Encino, California 91316

Margaret C. Wang                                            307
University of Pittsburgh
Pittsburgh, Pennsylvania 15213

John L. Yeager      307
University of Pittsburgh
Pittsburgh, Pennsylvania 15213

C.M. Lindvall, Associate Director of IPI      313
Learning Research and Development Center
University of Pittsburgh
Pittsburgh, Pennsylvania 15213

John O. Bolvin, Director of IPI      313
Learning Research and Development Center
University of Pittsburgh
Pittsburgh, Pennsylvania 15213

John M. Flynn      325
Associate Professor
Nova University
Fort Lauderdale, Florida 33314

Clifton B. Chadwick      325
Research Associate
Department of Educational Research
Florida State University
Tallahassee, Florida 32306

Judith R. Steward      341
Assistant Professor
Department of Psychology
Nova University
Fort Lauderdale, Florida 33314

W.A. Love, Jr.      341
Assistant Professor
Department of Psychology
Nova University
Fort Lauderdale, Florida 33314

Russ Mouritsen                                          Appendix III
Boyd Bronson
Steven Streadbeck and
Kristeen Fjeldsted previously were students, Division of
      Instructional Systems and Learning Resources,
      University of Utah, Salt Lake City.

# PART 1

## THE TRANSITION FROM GROUP TO INDIVIDUALIZED INSTRUCTION

# PART 1

# The Transition from Group
# to Individualized Instruction

The selections in Part 1 expose and analyze the problems encountered in making the transition from traditional group organization and methodologies to a learner centered, individualized instruction program.

Blake and McPherson begin this section by presenting a brief history of individualization. The article describes the current trends in individualized instruction, emphasizing the advantages for both the teacher and the learner.

In the second article, Ubben stresses the need for establishing a system that will pace each learner according to his individual needs. He also discusses the basic approaches to individualized instruction, using a matrix developed by Jack V. Edling. This matrix is a guide for categorizing individualized instruction programs in terms of the degree of student control over content and resources. The Edling matrix provides a handy reference for comparing and contrasting the various approaches to individualized instruction.

In the third article, Burns views individualized instruction from the standpoint that no two learners are identical. He lists nine ways in which individuals differ. Burns further breaks down individualized instruction into the variables of objectives, study habits and time. He goes on to present a flow chart for implementing a modular individualized system, and provides suggestions for activities required for the transition to individualized instruction.

Individualized instruction must be considered in terms of its effect and demands on the curriculum, the staff and the student body. To help clarify some important distinctions, Bolvin clearly defines and differentiates curriculum design, instructional design and instruction. He emphasizes behavioral objectives and ordering processes in curriculum design. He breaks down instructional design, discussing evaluation and environmental conditions for learning. He states four basic assumptions underlying the implementation of individualized instruction that have implications for materials design.

McLoughlin takes a critical look at some of our so-called individualized programs. He lists and warns of programs that do little more than change *the name* of previous programs. He emphasizes that instructional programs must be developed to deal with individual differences, and not group similarities. To help develop a program of individualized instruction, McLoughlin outlines a basic plan to follow, and he enumerates specific procedures to be considered for achieving the goal of individualization.

Baker and Goldberg, after a brief discussion of the fundamentals of individualized instruction, focus attention on eight areas which must be considered when implementing individualized learning systems. Each of these areas is integrated into a model which the authors have designed to diagrammatically show the interrelationship of concepts and procedures in an individualized learning system.

Jones provides a well-organized argument for the transition to individualized instruction, placing the primary emphasis on the role of the administration. He describes several of the fundamental qualities of a school district which tend to support and nourish innovative programs, the necessary elements in developing this type of change, and the effects of an individualized learning package program in other areas of the educational system. Included in his article is a workshop program, which he maintains is essential for the orientation of the teachers. With the adaptation of individualized instruction, all other systems in the school will be affected, and the author discusses effects on curriculum, materials, community, students and the staff.

Tunks, in his advice for individualizing learning package use, gives attention to factors which enhance learning and minimize clerical responsibilities. He describes simple student-accessible record keeping and package dissemination. He lists guidelines in developing programs with student appeal and evaluation procedures which remove the threat of testing. Tunks emphasizes the vital importance of teacher enthusiasm and student involvement.

# 1

## Individualized Instruction—
## Where Are We?

### Howard E. Blake and Ann W. McPherson

A question that has been of continuing concern to teachers throughout most of the history of education, and particularly of interest to American educators, is that of how to meet the individualized needs of pupils in a school operation which is geared to masses of students. Despite the magnitude of this problem, it is still largely unsolved. The consensus of those who have given serious attention to it seems to be that its solution will require rather massive and long range research effort.

Looking back to the pre-Christian era, we find that Confucius, Aristotle, Plato and even Socrates recognized the existence of human variabilities in the education process. Confucius adapted his teachings to the needs and capabilities of individual students. Socrates emphasized self-knowledge as the basic idea, and he wanted people to live meaningful lives within their own capacities. Plato suggested that the philosophers should attempt to educate each person only so far as his limitations would permit.

During the early middle ages, Charlemagne called a teacher to his high court to teach because he had heard that this person paid particular attention to individualized differences. During the Renaissance in Italy and the Reformation in England, various interests of students were recognized. Students were encouraged to apply themselves to do anything for which they had natural inclination. Teaching at that time was mostly by group instruc-

Reprinted from *Educational Technology*, Vol. 9, No. 12, December 1969, pp. 63-65, by permission of authors and publisher.

tion. The masters assigned work to students and then worked with small groups of children in order to take care of individual differences. Comenius, who wrote school textbooks in the seventeenth century, formulated rules for teaching. Interestingly enough, many of his rules are applicable today. For instance, he suggested that education should appeal to the child's natural interest, that education should fit the comprehension level of the child and that children should learn by doing.

The direction of modern education was strongly influenced during the eighteenth century by Rousseau. He criticized teachers of his day for giving the same exercise to all the children, thus destroying any special individuality which might exist in the classroom. Pestalozzi expressed his belief in individuality thusly: "Since each child is an individual and possesses capabilities for individual power, the method of teaching must be so individualized and individualizing that each child's capabilities will develop." He used visual aids in instruction.

We have benefited from some influences from abroad during the twentieth century. For instance, Alfred Binet gave tremendous recognition to individual differences by his invention of a scale for measuring individual capacities. He was the first person to develop a test for measuring intelligence—the "IQ" test. He believed that the aptitude of children was the greatest business of instruction and education and that it was according to children's abilities and aptitudes that they learned.

Another educator of this period in Italy, Maria Montessori, believed firmly that the first duty of every human being was to be himself and that anything which checked this development did him serious injury. She also encouraged students to work at their own rate of speed, to concentrate on what interested them at the moment and to use school materials in ways which best served their needs. In her teaching techniques, or rather, approach to education, she made every effort to adapt what she had to say to each child. Often, she taught pupils individually to get the greatest possible adaptation from her technique.

Now let us look at our own nation. In America, we find that this country was established on two basic principles—equality and individuality. The stirring words of the Declaration of Independence begin: "We hold these truths to be self-evident . . . that all men are created equal." We are especially concerned with the problem of equality of opportunity in education. The individual's schooling is the best gateway for a just society.

If we look at the history of instruction in the United States, we see that individuality has always been emphasized. Formal learning from its beginning in this country was an individual affair. That is, pupils came to school to receive instruction individually from the teacher. For example, in the one-room school, pupils proceeded on an individual basis, rather than in intact groups. Each child learned at his own rate of speed, and he was allowed to learn as much as he possibly could.

As educational advantages were offered to a larger section of the growing population, it became necessary to deal with pupils in "grade-level" groups, and individualized instruction began to vanish. American schools from this point on became predominantly "textbook schools." Textbooks became more influential in determining what was to be taught than the course of study itself. The basic assumption underlying textbook teaching is that the child be classified into homogeneous groups and taught the material uniformly by standardized procedures. We have moved toward group instruction rather than in the direction of caring for the individual differences of children. It appears that in our country we have given up the idea of caring for the individual and are more concerned about structuring our classroom organization so that we can take care of pupils in groups. In a sense we have been trying to organize schools so as to get rid of individual differences.

**What Is Individualized Instruction?**

Individualized instruction means that the learning program for each curriculum area is organized in such a manner as to allow each child to move at his own pace under the guidance of his teacher. Instruction is non-graded, enabling each child to go as far in each subject as his ability permits. Careful records are kept on each child's progress.

Individualized instruction does not mean the child works alone at all times. It does not mean that the teacher relinquishes his responsibilities to some sort of machine or other teaching materials. While the child works alone more than in traditional classrooms, the teacher has to diagnose his progress frequently and to offer him, as well as small groups or the entire class, supplemental instruction where there is a common need.

Children cannot learn effectively through individualized instruction simply by being told to proceed at their own pace through the study of traditional materials. Specially prepared materials are essential. Present experience indicates that a series of projects, worksheets or lessons are necessary, commencing at the very beginning of each subject and proceeding sequentially until all the content of the subject has been completed.

## Current Trends in Individualized Instruction

For about the past ten years there has been a concerted effort to do something about individualizing instruction. Major efforts in this direction have been increasing, and several factors have strengthened this movement:

1.  Education and industry have joined forces to provide technology as well as teaching materials that will enable the teacher to organize his classroom on an individualized basis.

2.  We have learned much more in recent years about the process of instruction itself. We have developed experience in producing programs of materials that teach a subject in relation to its basic structure and according to the best ways through which children learn. We know that children must be involved in their learning and not merely "told"; that pupil interest is a great factor in learning; that reinforcement and immediate feedback of answers aids learning rate; and that children learn best when allowed to learn at their own pace.

3.  Our country has realized that local school districts cannot provide all the financial support necessary for a

quality educational program and has significantly in-creased its financial support of schools. Among other actions it has created the Office of Economic Opportu-nity, has expanded the functions of the United States Office of Education and has passed the Elementary and Secondary Education Act of 1965. This support has enabled school districts to increase their efforts to experiment and innovate and to purchase teaching materials which they could not possibly have afforded before.

4.  Teacher-education institutions are preparing a "new breed" of teachers who are committed to making schools more challenging for children.

5.  The current emphasis on community involvement in schools has led parents to question the value of group-teaching and to demand that their children be provided instructional programs that individualize learn-ing for all children.

6.  There is a growing feeling among teachers themselves that they want to individualize instruction, but they do not have the time to prepare all the materials needed.

**The Teacher and Individualized Instruction**

Some educators take the point of view that individualized instruction programs—both the hardware and the software—will some day take the place of the teacher and eventually make the teacher's role unnecessary. Another frequently heard reaction is that prepared materials dehumanize learning. It is interesting to remember that teachers in the fifteenth century felt the same threats when the printing press was invented. Individualized instructional programs, if used wisely, will eventually enhance the role of the teacher in the same respect as the printing press.

Individualized programs, although many are quite thorough in nature, are but a start in what children must learn. They cannot possibly replace the teacher. Instead, they will take the load off the teacher for teaching much of the basic skills and content, leaving him valuable and much-needed time to humanize learning—leading discussions, raising challenging questions, diagnosing, working with individuals, conferences, examining materials, planning, listening to children. Teachers seldom feel they can find enough time to devote to these matters and this makes teaching a frustrating matter. What better way can we give attention to these important concerns than by finding a way to be relieved of the teaching of a large portion of the basic skills and content?

Not only will individualized instructional programs give the teacher a new status and role in the classroom, but they will bring a new excitement into teaching and learning, making it a truly creative experience for teachers and children. They will not increase the teacher's work load but will free him to use more of his time on the often neglected dimensions of teaching. Good teachers will seek good individualized instructional programs and will develop a philosophy that will enable them to use this approach in their classrooms, for these programs offer the greatest assurance of raising the quality of both teaching and learning.

**Current Practices in Individualized Instruction**

Schools throughout the nation are currently testing numerous individualized instructional programs of one kind or another. The most notable of all these is the project in Individually Prescribed Instruction (IPI), developed at the Learning Research and Development Center, University of Pittsburgh. Offered at the elementary school level in three subjects—mathematics, reading and science—numerous worksheets or lessons have been developed for children to study on an individualized basis. Frequent diagnosis of a child's progress is made by the teacher, who then writes a "prescription," telling the child which lessons he is to do next. Children study at their own pace and may proceed as far in the study of each subject as they can. In a given classroom some children might be studying at the first grade level while others might be at the tenth grade. A child might be studying at one grade level in one subject but at a lower or higher grade level in another subject. In mathematics, for example, a first grade pupil might be studying at fifth grade level for addition but at first grade level for fractions. IPI is currently offered in many selected schools throughout the nation. The Oakleaf Elementary School in Pittsburgh is its demonstration-pilot school.

The Duluth, Minnesota, school system has developed its own curriculum for individualization. In that program, each subject area is broken down into a series of sequential contracts which children undertake and complete at their own pace. Other school systems throughout the nation—Dayton, San Francisco, San Mateo, Philadelphia, Washington, D.C.—are engaging in various experimental projects to individualize instruction.

Interest in individualized instruction is not limited to the United States, however. Japan, for example, which is recognized for the quality of its educational program, organizes nearly all its schools on an individualized basis. A recent UNESCO report revealed that children in Japan scored significantly higher on mathematics achievement than those in fifteen other major countries in the world, including the United States. Many educators attribute this difference to the influence of individualized instruction.

## Advantages of Individualized Instruction

The experience gained from all these and other programs indicates that individualized instruction has advantages for both the teacher and the child not found in other kinds of teaching.

*For the Child:*
1. It enables him to proceed at his own pace through the study of each subject.
2. There is a one-to-one relationship between him and the subject he is studying.
3. It permits him to get an immediate response to his answers; immediate satisfaction is gained.
4. It enables him to understand better the structure of the subject he is studying.
5. It enables him to study in greater depth those aspects of the subject which diagnostic tests indicate he needs, and to move with greater speed on those materials with which he is more familiar.

6.    Instruction is non-graded; each child can proceed in a subject as far as his ability will permit.

*For the Teacher:*
1.    It frees the teacher from teaching many of the routine basic skills of a subject.
2.    It enables him to meet more accurately the instructional needs of each child.
3.    It furnishes him with diagnostic devices.
4.    It allows him to spend more time with students who need the most help.
5.    It enables him to bring a structured, carefully thought out program to his pupils.
6.    It brings about a higher degree of job satisfaction.
7.    It helps the teacher to serve not only as a lecturer but also as a guide to the pupil in his efforts to increase his knowledge of a given subject.

**Hardware versus Software**
    The development in recent years of a great amount of technological equipment has made it possible for a different kind of instruction to be offered in schools. The difficulty is that the present machines are much more sophisticated than the available teaching materials for them. Some people are saying there is an overabundance of "hardware" and not enough "software." Computers are the most glamorous of the available technology but there are very few instructional programs prepared for use on them and, also, they are too expensive for the average school.
    A number of educational and industrial institutions are currently developing instructional materials—the "software"—that are going to have a great impact on teaching in the immediate future. Technology will be better harnessed to be of more help to the classroom teacher.

**Looking Ahead**
    In the 1970s more schools will be organized on an individualized basis. No more will the child who is considered "slow" today

become a failure. There will be fewer C, D and F pupils, because children will be able to spend all the time needed to understand concepts. They will not fall behind as they do in present group teaching practices and there will be fewer drop-outs because of failures.

No more will the teacher have to spend countless hours preparing stencils and individual activities for his pupils. There will be available to him a large number of tested instructional programs from which to choose. The materials will be well prepared and will be of better quality than most individual teachers working alone can possibly produce within the limitations of all their responsibilities.

No more will the teacher be a lecturer, an assignment-giver and a drill master. Instead, he will become a tutor, diagnostician and discussion leader. Through individualized instruction the teacher can truly teach and can reach levels of achievement and satisfaction that were not possible in other curricular organizations. Individualized instructional programs will relieve the teacher of the routine drill that requires so much classroom time. These new programs show high promise not only of providing better education for children but also of improving the teaching process itself.

# 2

# The Role of the Learning Package
# in an Individualized Instruction Program

Gerald C. Ubben

The learning package in today's classroom is intended to serve as a means to individualize instruction. As educators we have had the bits and pieces of an individualized instructional system for some time. We have long talked of multi-text and multi-media approaches to instruction, but as teachers, most of us have failed to implement these ideas. Instead, we have talked of providing the appropriate instruction for the individual child, while as teachers we have continued to retain the group presentation as the major method of instruction, basically treating most of the children in the group alike.

What has been needed is a system of individualized instruction that will not depend on mass verbal presentation but that can be designed and paced for each child according to his individual needs. This system must be designed so that the instruction may be managed on a one-to-one basis for each youngster in the school. Teachers need to be recast in the role of instructional managers, prescribing learning experiences for the student on an individual basis, managing the learning process and evaluating the results.

To accomplish this, the educator is desperately in need of an instructional management system which will make it possible to preplan an infinite number of lessons to achieve an infinite number of behaviors. This system can be called upon by the teachers in the form of a prescription after appropriate diagnosis

Reprinted from *Journal of Secondary Education*, Vol. 46, No. 5, May 1971, pp. 206-209, by permission of author and publisher.

of the individual student's needs.

## An Instructional Management System

The learning package offers a beautiful design for an *individualized management system.* Learning packages can be sequenced in a logical order for continuous progress learning, or particular packages can be identified to help the child with remedial work if the diagnosis has determined that the child needs additional help in particular skills. If the materials have been appropriately designed in a self-instructional nature, the majority of the teacher's time is free to work with individual students. While children are working on learning packages there is no need for a large group of children to be working on the same material in order for the teacher to appropriately manage classroom instruction. A truly individualized program cannot be achieved in this way.

The learning package, because of its self-instructional nature, can be administered in the classroom on an individual prescription basis. Theoretically, in a classroom of 30 children, work on as many as 30 different packages could be underway at the same time. In practice, however, it can be expected that the children will cluster around fewer packages. If, however, in a given classroom, all 30 children were working on the same package, it would *not* seem that the packages were being used to their best advantage as a means of individualization.

Properly used, there are four basic approaches that can be used for package selection that fit into the general construct of the individualized instruction. A well-designed package system consists of multiple packages covering a range of skills, ideas and/or concepts appropriate for the particular group of youngsters in a learning area. This allows for great latitude as to which packages or objectives might be undertaken by the student. Likewise, a well-designed learning package should have within it multiple resources and activities, each resource being directed toward the achievement of the objective stated in the package. These resources and activities should, most desirably, be diverse in nature, including reading, viewing, doing and listening tasks as well as covering an appropriate range of learning levels for all those students who might possibly work in that package. This combination of the availability of multiple packages or objectives and the availability of multiple resources within each package allows for a number of options as to how the package prescription system might be administered.

Borrowing an idea presented by Jack Edling* in his material on individualized instruction, the following table illustrates the options available.

**Objectives**

|  | Teacher Selected | Student Selected |
|---|---|---|
| **Resources — Teacher Selected** | A | C |
| **Resources — Student Selected** | B | D |

The question to be answered is "Who is to make the decisions regarding the selection of objectives and the assignment of resources to be used in the achievement of those objectives?"

*Option A.* The teacher retains all decision control over the child by prescribing both the package to be studied and the resources within that package to be completed.

*Option B.* The teacher prescribes to the student a particular learning package but then allows the student freedom in choosing the resources most appealing to him. Under this option the student needs to complete only enough resources to adequately prepare him for the behavioral performance called for in the objective.

*Option C.* Assuming there exist within the package system

*Edling, Jack V. *Individualized Instruction: A Manual for Administrators.* Corvallis, Oregon: Continuing Education Publications, 1970.

numerous packages, the student is allowed to select a package of his own choosing. After he has determined the package which he is going to work, the teacher assigns the resources for the child within that package.

*Option D.* The student not only selects his own package from those available but also has freedom to choose his resources within that package.

Practical application in the classroom probably will entail the use of all four options at some time—depending on the nature of the package, the adequacy of the resources and the independence of the particular child. However, greater involvement on the part of the child in making his own educational decisions will most often result in greater commitment on his part.

Additional freedom on the part of the learner in the design of his instructional program could be obtained only with a learner designed package. The objective would not be one predetermined by the teacher but would be one created by the student and stated in behavioral terms. The student would then identify those resources necessary for the achievement of that objective. This, again, can be the achievement of a single objective or it could be represented by a more complex learning package including multiple objectives, ideas and concepts. This last category approaches the ideal concept of individualized instruction with learner initiated objectives and activities. It is very closely related to some concepts of independent study or quest activities.

### The Effect of Learning Packages on School Organization

The six major organizational components of the school—instruction, curriculum, student grouping, staffing patterns, scheduling and facility design—are very closely related and function in an interlocking organizational pattern within the school. When a major modification is made in one of these six components, it inadvertently has repercussions as to the organization of the other five. Therefore, when a major component—that of instruction—is radically modified, as it is when an individualized package system is initiated, it is necessary to review the organization of the other five components to identify those places where it is necessary or desirable to adjust organizational structure.

An individualized instructional system through learning packages allows for and, in fact, demands a greater amount of organizational flexibility within the school program. In the area of curriculum an individualized program demands a truly continuous progress system if it is to become operational. Each student must be allowed to proceed through the program at a rate which is appropriate for him. The group no longer can become the determining factor as to the pacing of the individual. This individualization not only allows the curriculum to become self-pacing, but also makes possible a personalized curriculum with the individual student having greater freedom to pursue his own interests regardless of the availability of an appropriately sized group to also study the subject.

In an individualized program, the decision-making regarding that program needs to be brought closer to the level of the student. Since the decisions are no longer to be made on a group basis, or since, in order to keep flexibility in the program, they can no longer be made once for the entire year, the level of the principal is no longer the appropriate location for many of the decisions to be made. Rather, teachers need to make many of the decisions regarding the instruction of children and in many cases in an individualized program these decisions should be made by the individual student himself. For example, the Option B or D from the previous section of learner selected objectives means, in the broad sense, that the student is making his own choices in the selection of curriculum. This same freedom of choice on the part of the student in many cases also becomes the determining factor as to how the student may be grouped. The student may, and appropriately so, select a particular learning package because it will determine the group with whom he will be working rather than just the content which he will be learning. Grouping, therefore, in an individualized program becomes a daily or even hourly operation with many of the decisions being made by the students themselves.

With many of the sub-grouping decisions in the hands of the

students and teachers, the principal many times can best facilitate appropriate grouping by placing students together in large enough numbers to make many different combinations possible within the space available.

The decisions regarding scheduling in an individualized package system also need to be brought closer to the level of the student. It is most appropriate in programs of this type to allow the student to in fact build his own schedules where he can decide, on the basis of package assignment, whether one hour was an appropriate length for science that day or whether he would rather spend a half day on science and pick up some of his other work at a later time. Even primary children can very quickly be taught to assume responsibility for this particular task, and many of them do an excellent job of designing their own series of activities on a day-by-day basis.

These modifications of instruction, curriculum, grouping of students and scheduling force reconsideration of the staffing patterns within the school. Schools that have gone to package systems have found most often at both the elementary and secondary levels that staffing patterns modified to either team teaching or differentiated staffing seem to serve the individualized instructional system more adequately than the self-contained classrooms. There are many reasons for this, including: the need for teacher specialization in package development (usually by subject area); the desirability of providing a larger number of students than normally found in self-contained classrooms in order to obtain maximum utilization of the materials necessary in a package system; the need for people with different types of specialization within the instructional area to carry out diagnosis and prescription tasks, classroom management functions, clerical functions and technical functions related to media. A common staffing-grouping pattern is for the school staff to group students in blocks of 100 or 200 or more, assigning them to an appropriate complement of teachers. This group of teachers then becomes the decision-making team for grouping, scheduling, teacher assignments, etc. Quite often this staff in an individualized system, in turn, passes much of the decision-making regarding certain aspects of instruction, curriculum, scheduling and staff selection directly on to the student.

All of the organizational components, of course, have a drastic effect on facility utilization and design. It becomes immediately obvious that for many types of instruction a large open-space school would provide the maximum amount of flexibility and continuity between the several program elements mentioned.

# 3

# Methods for
# Individualizing Instruction

Richard W. Burns

Teachers frequently inquire about individualized instruction—they intuitively feel (and rightly so) that as a method it has a lot to offer in improving classroom learning. However, with present facilities, materials, curricular organization and administrative constrictions, it is difficult to achieve little other than token individualization of learning. In practice, there are degrees of individualized instruction (hereafter designated as I-I) ranging from idealized methods to the use of single operating features which are a start in the right direction.

The basis for believing that I-I is educationally desirable resides in the nature of man. *No two living organisms are alike.* If this statement is true, and all evidence appears to support it, then basically we are led to the assumptions that:

1.  No two learners achieve at the same rate.
2.  No two learners achieve using the same study techniques.
3.  No two learners solve problems in exactly the same way.
4.  No two learners possess the same repertoire of behaviors.
5.  No two learners possess the same pattern of interests.
6.  No two learners are motivated to achieve to the same degree.

Reprinted from *Educational Technology*, Vol. 11, No. 6, June 1971, pp. 55-56, by permission of author and publisher.

7.  No two learners are motivated to achieve the same goals.
8.  No two learners are ready to learn at the same time.
9.  No two learners have exactly the same capacity to learn.

Coupling these nine assumptions with variations in city, home and school environments, it is easy to see how learning for the individual must be, to some degree, unique. Perhaps in reality, small differences between individuals may not demand I-I; however, in many cases the differences are not small, and hundreds of years of educational experience have repeatedly confirmed the futility of looking for the *one* method which, if used by teachers, will reach the learner. No one textbook has been found which will adequately serve a given classroom, no one explanation of a concept reaches each learner, and so on, to each classroom feature of practice. All evidence seems to support the idea that learning is a unique process.

What then is I-I? Earlier it was indicated that there is an ideal concept and, in practice, there are degrees of individualization which do not take into account all the features of the ideal. *Ideally, individualized instruction is a system which tailor-makes learning in terms of learner needs and characteristics.* This is to say, I-I concerns itself mainly with the three variables:

a.  objectives;
b.  study habits;
c.  time.

In relation to the first variable, objectives, I-I is based on the learner: his needs, desires, wishes, skills and motives. Learners need to achieve different goals or objectives in the various areas of their learning. Ideally, I-I attempts to give the learner the opportunity to achieve uniquely in relation to what he already knows and what he is attempting to learn. To provide this type of "tailor-made" instruction for the learners, there must be a minimum of two instructional features present:

a.  learner diagnosis;

   b.    a variety of curricular units (modules, lessons, etc.).

If the learner is to profit (achieve faster, achieve more or remember longer) from I-I, then whatever instruction he receives *must take into account present behaviors and some idea of his objectives.* The student must be given some latitude in selection of his learning objectives. A diagnostic analysis is necessary to establish the subject matter proficiency or subject readiness of the learner. Has he achieved (acquired the proper behaviors) to some minimum level which will permit him to profit from the coming instruction? Also, is the ensuing instruction related or necessary for his (the learner's) education? This implies that what he is to learn is known to be necessary by adults, experts in the field, or is desired by the learner. Some objectives may be attained solely because the learner "wants" to attain them for his own personal reasons. Since each learner will *need* and/or *want* different learnings, a variety of things to be learned must be available. First, there must be rich curricular offerings by way of different subject matter to learn; and second, each learner should be permitted to achieve as far (or deeply) into a subject as his talents permit.

The second variable, study habits, also demands two instructional features, namely:

   a.    learner diagnosis;
   b.    a variety of teaching materials and aids.

If the learner is to profit from I-I, then the instruction he receives must take into account his strengths and weaknesses as far as study habits and ability to learn are concerned. His reading level; reading rate; preference for visual, auditory or tactile learning; ability to conclude; ability to summarize; ability to compare; ability to translate; ability to abstract; ability to infer; ability to express himself orally; ability to express himself in writing; and possibly other skills, or lack of them, must be taken into account. In order to effectively implement the results of such a diagnostic analysis of the learner, a variety of teaching materials and aids must be available. Tapes and recorders, filmstrips, film loops, reading materials designed for a variety of levels, maps, charts, drills and dozens of other types of aids need to be readily accessible for learner use. In addition, many teaching strategies should be employed.

Time, the third variable, must be flexible for I-I. Some learners proceed slowly and others rapidly because of a variety of reasons, such as: (1) intelligence, (2) study habits, (3) prior learning, (4) motivation, (5) competitive pressure, (6) social/ family pressure, (7) physical/physiological status and (8) additional causes.

Synthesizing these three variables into an effective I-I program takes considerable instructional insight, effort and cooperation. The learner must cooperate with the instructor (guider of the learning process), and the instructor must receive administrative support. I-I implies more guidance of learners as they learn and less emphasis on the traditional role of teaching, the imparting of knowledge.

Implementation of this idealized concept of I-I in the classroom is enhanced if the program is subdivided into small, manageable parts and a systematic method for dealing with the parts is established. One common method is to provide the learning sequences in the form of *modules.* Modules are difficult to define, as they vary greatly in their length, composition and degree of organization. Generally, however, and as the term is used here, modules are short (1-3 hours), organized learning sequences. Each module develops one, or at most a very few, terminal behaviors.

A flow chart of one unit in a modular system is depicted in Figure 1. The learner (L) enters the system and is given a diagnostic test (DE) to determine if he has the necessary behaviors required to profit from the planned instruction. If he does not have the prerequisite behaviors, he is sent for remedial instruction so that he can acquire the entering behaviors. If he has the prerequisites, he then is given the criterion test (CT) for the module to determine if he already has the terminal behaviors (TB) the module is intended to develop. If the learner already has the behaviors, he goes to the next module; but if he does not, he

## Figure 1

### Flow Chart of Performance Based Module System

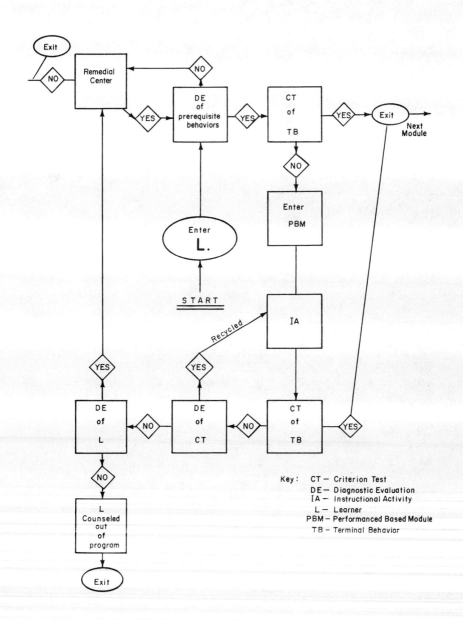

Key:  CT — Criterion Test
      DE — Diagnostic Evaluation
      IA — Instructional Activity
      L — Learner
      PBM — Performanced Based Module
      TB — Terminal Behavior

enters the performance based modules (PBM) for instruction. After the learner has participated in the instructional activities (IA), he takes the criterion test (CT) again to determine if he has acquired the behaviors intended. If the learner does not pass the criterion test, the test results are examined to see if there is a clue to his problem. If it is thought that the learner can profit from going back through the module (or parts of it), he is recycled. However, if the analysis of his CT shows that he is having great difficulty, another diagnostic analysis is made to try to determine the reason for his failure to learn. If the diagnostic evaluation of the learner (DE of L) points to a cause which can be remedied by instruction, the learner is referred to the remedial center. If the evaluation turns up nonremedial causes, the learner is counseled out of the program (the set of modules).

The system just described obviously tries to tailor-make the instruction to the learner and allows him to progress at his own pace. If properly designed, the modules can also provide for differences in learning modes or habits through the appropriate choice and application of learning activities.

The modular system presented above was not described to *sell* it *in toto*. That is, do not make the mistake of thinking that I-I is an all-or-nothing concept. Remember, we said earlier that there are degrees of I-I, and anything you can do in teaching which is in the direction of I-I should be helpful to the learner. Here are some suggestions of things that can be done quite easily, either alone or in combination.

1. Provide alternate reading materials at a variety of levels of difficulty.
2. Provide for a variety of topics to be studied.
3. Let learners select some topics they want to study.
4. Let learners help set the goals of instruction.
5. Let learners study using their own preferred study habits.
6. Encourage learners to hunt and locate their own sources of information.
7. Provide for a variety of modes for learning (auditory,

visual, tactile).

8. Let learners proceed at their own pace (fast or slowly).
9. Provide tutorial help.
10. Devise and administer diagnostic pretests to determine what learners already know.
11. If it is known that the learner has already acquired the desired instructional behaviors, excuse him from the instruction, but provide alternative things to learn.
12. Encourage learners to select and pursue related topics of learning on their own.
13. Provide for supplementary and concurrent projects for students to pursue.
14. Encourage students who are having difficulty in learning to try new, alternative methods of study, until they find study techniques which work for them.
15. Devise and administer diagnostic pretests to ensure that learners possess the prerequisite knowledges, understandings and skills needed to achieve the next set of things to be learned.
16. Provide a variety of visual, auditory and tactile materials to aid learners.
17. Provide remedial instruction for learners who need it before they attempt to learn new sets of materials.
18. Provide remedial instruction during the learning of the new set of materials.

Individualizing instruction really is nothing more than applying logic to the learning act, and then, by careful planning and organization, providing an efficient method whereby learners have the opportunity to acquire behaviors in their own way at their own rate.

In addition to individualizing the instruction in terms of the three main variables—objectives, study habits and time—it is helpful to consider other factors which will enhance learning. One such factor is response confirmation—feedback and reinforcement; another is application or practice (preferably distributed); a third is readiness.

Methods and teaching strategies also are closely related to I-I. The utilization of team teaching, nongraded instruction, discussion seminars and small group techniques can enhance and contribute to an I-I system. More closely related are micro techniques, flexible scheduling, continuous progress systems, contract methods and independent study. Each of these methods and strategies can contribute in some way to implementing the 18 suggestions for I-I, as listed previously.

In summary, I-I appears to be a natural way of learning, and in the long run it may be the answer to part of the problems currently facing school systems. I-I is not a single thing in practice, which is done or not done, but a concept of instruction which takes into account learners' needs, habits of study and time. With a little effort, each teacher can find some way and time to provide one or more methods, strategies or applications of opportunity pointing in the direction of I-I.

# 4

# Implications of the Individualization of Instruction for Curriculum and Instructional Design

John O. Bolvin

One of the basic themes permeating the educational reform movement today is the individualization of instruction. Granted, this is not a new theme in education; however, the intensity of interest in it is far greater today than ever before. Some of the factors underlying this emphasis would have to include (1) the introduction of programmed instruction, (2) the development of nongraded and team-teaching programs, (3) the wider application of the use of computers, (4) the changing technology and its application to educational problems and (5) the recent involvement by subject matter scholars and behavioral scientists in the more practical problems of education.

One major problem, the discussion of individualization of instruction, centers around the variety of types of school programs that are identified as providing for individualization. Some educators interpret individualization as simply providing tutorial assistance for pupils and/or providing for independent study. At the same time, there are a few interpreting individualization to mean the planning and implementation of an individualized program of studies tailored to each student's learning needs based on his competencies and his characteristics as a learner. It is this latter definition of the term that has more implication for the application of technology in curriculum planning. What then does this definition of the individualization of instruction mean to the

Reprinted from *Audiovisual Instruction*, Vol. 13, No. 3, March 1968, pp. 238-242, by permission of author and publisher.

curriculum director? Approaching this problem systematically requires the application of task analysis and of systems analysis. This means that one begins by defining the objectives, analyzing the input and output of the system, determining ways of measuring these factors, and defining and describing all the relevant conditions affecting the system. Since individualized instruction involves the interaction of persons, procedures and materials, the necessary system is quite complex.

For clarity in discussion, a differentiation should be made between curriculum design, instructional design and instruction. Curriculum design relates to the determination of the behavioral objectives selected on the basis of the philosophy of education and the structure of the subject matter under consideration. Instructional design is that portion of the educational system relating to factors that facilitate the learning of content, processes, etc., as specified in the statement of objectives. Elements of the instructional design would include diagnostic and evaluative instruments, materials, hardware and environmental conditions necessary in assisting the learner to acquire the desired behaviors. Instruction is the total function of providing an integrated program of learning experiences for each student.

**Curriculum Design**

*Objectives.* A point of departure in attempting to individualize instruction is a statement of the philosophy of the educational program. Of particular importance here is the specification of level as either stated or implied in this philosophy. Generally these goals should reflect the subject matter to be included, the types or kinds of learning desired, and the learner characteristics to be included or emphasized. For the goals to be in agreement with the definition of individualization applied here, they should include such statements as: each pupil makes continuous progress toward mastery of instructional content; every student continues to mastery of content at his own rate; every pupil is engaged in the learning process through active involvement; the pupil views the learning process as primarily self-directed; every pupil is able to evaluate the quality, extent and rapidity of his progress toward mastery of successive areas of the learning continuum; the pupil develops a favorable attitude toward school and learning in general; the pupil may develop interest in specific academic subjects; the pupil manifests increased motivation toward academic subjects; different pupils work with different learning materials adapted to individual needs and learning styles, etc.[1] It is from these goals that the plan, operation and eventual assessment of the program must develop.

To implement these goals, the curriculum designer must first determine the content areas to be included in a total educational program. For each of the specific areas noted it is then necessary to analyze the subject matter domain for structure, including competencies desired, conceptual hierarchies and operating rules. For instance, in mathematics there might be counting, addition, subtraction, multiplication, division, fractions, etc. In science there might be classification, discrimination, biological measurement, inferring, etc. In the social studies there may be social relationships, time relationships, economic relationships, etc.[2] Generally speaking, this is a task that would involve subject matter specialists, teachers, curriculum designers and social scientists. Whether it is necessary or even desirable for every school or school district to become individually involved in all aspects of this stage of curriculum design is very much open to question.

Once a possible framework for a particular subject area has been selected, the next step is to begin specifying behavioral objectives. The specifying of educational objectives is fundamental in developing an individualized system of instruction since it provides a real basis for (1) determining materials and learning experiences needed, (2) developing diagnostic instruments to measure each learner's competencies, (3) setting up each student's program of studies and (4) analyzing teacher functions and activities. Precisely stated objectives permit the analysis of the behaviors required as prerequisites to a given objective. This analysis serves as a guide to the curriculum designer in sequencing and ordering the objectives. Regardless of the way a subject matter is structured, there is usually some hierarchy of objectives that indicates certain performances must be present before learning subsequent performances. Clearly stated behavioral objectives are of assistance to the curriculum designer in establishing this hierarchy of subobjectives. Since the statement of an objective refers to a behavior which is some performance by the student, the more precise the behavioral objective, the more likely the measurement is to be valid and reliable.

In relation to the development of materials and learning experiences in an individualized setting, it is necessary, at least to some degree, to provide self-instructional materials. It is only through the use of self-instructional materials that individualization will be manageable within the context of an operating school situation. This means that when behavioral objectives are clearly stated, then the persons involved in materials development are better able to develop self-instructional materials that can lead the child to the performance of the desired behaviors. From the point of view of teacher functions, it is the responsibility of the teacher to determine whether materials and procedures assigned enable the student to reach the desired level of performance for a particular task. To evaluate this, the teacher must know precisely what it is that the child is able to do after he has had this learning experience. It is important to note here the distinction between the behavioral statement and the process to be used in obtaining the behavior. In the first situation, you may have a sequence of objectives relating to "learning to inquire," while in the second situation, you may require the student to attain the behavioral state by inquiry. In either case, it is important that the teacher know what is expected on the part of the learner.

Techniques for writing behavioral statements have been described by Mager,[3] Lindvall[4] and others, and may be useful to those initiating such a program. The development of any curriculum requires hundreds of such statements reflecting the generic goals of the learning process. The eventual interaction between curriculum design and instructional design provides a basis for a redefinition, reordering and identification of additional objectives as the curriculum is implemented.

*Ordering.* The next major task in curriculum design is the ordering process. An essential characteristic of an effective instructional program is that it permits the student to acquire the necessary skills and competencies before moving to a next hierarchical step for which the present learnings are prerequisites. Since the structure of most subject matter does not follow a single linear pattern, it is necessary to make several kinds of ordering decisions based upon the structure of the subject matter and the goals of the program. The technique of task analysis can serve two useful functions at this stage. In the first instance, it serves as a guide to determining what objectives are useful in attaining another objective. For instance, addition is helpful in learning multiplication. A second use of task analysis is related to what critics characterize as a weakness of this procedure—that of cutting the learning experiences into smaller and smaller steps with the possibility of leading to less and less meaningful experiences. An analysis of the separate tasks involved in attaining each objective can provide a basis for establishing sets of objectives that can be organized as a unit. By grouping these related tasks together under general characteristics it is possible for the teacher and the student to focus both on the individual objective and the larger and more integrating experiences.

The end product of such an analysis is a scope and sequence chart divided into levels, units and objectives. A level in this case consists of a set of operational tasks grouped into categories and represents a level of achievement at the end of a large sequence of work. Each category within a level would be the unit or unifying set of behavioral objectives.

Having established this scope and sequence chart, the next major question related to individualization is whether a different sequence or ordering is necessary for each learner, for groups of learners or for selected learners, and if the developed sequence can permit such variations. At present, most individualized instruction programs provide for some degree of variation of routes through the curriculum. In the case of the IPI program as operating in the Oakleaf Elementary School, there are a limited number of variations existing which do provide a number of alternate routes for each learner over the period of a year or so. To illustrate this, it is necessary to briefly describe one of the curricula.

Mathematics is divided into subtopics such as numeration, place value, addition, subtraction, multiplication, geometry, etc. The sequencing and ordering of the objectives for the mathematics program was done separately for each of the subtopics going from the simple to the more complex. Once this was done, rather arbitrary decisions were made as to when to interrupt the pupil's progress in numeration to begin place value, when to move the place value to addition, etc. Each of these subsets of objectives, then, constitutes a unit, and the combination of units constitutes a level, labeled A, B, C, etc. in Figure 1. The numbers in each cell refer to the number of objectives grouped together for the particular unit.

*Figure 1*

*Number of Objectives in Each Unit*
*(a Given Topic at a Given Level)*
*in Individually Prescribed Instruction Mathematics*

| | | | Level | | | |
|---|---|---|---|---|---|---|
| **Subtopic** | A | B | C | D | E | F |
| Numeration | 9 | 9 | 7 | 5 | 8 | 3 |
| Place Value | - | 2 | 5 | 9 | 7 | 5 |
| Addition | 2 | 11 | 5 | 8 | 6 | 2 |
| Subtraction | 1 | 4 | 4 | 5 | 3 | 1 |
| Multiplication | - | - | - | 8 | 11 | 10 |
| Division | - | - | - | 7 | 13 | 8 |
| Combination of Processes | - | - | 6 | 5 | 7 | 4 |
| Fractions | 2 | 4 | 5 | 5 | 6 | 14 |
| Time | - | 3 | 5 | 10 | 9 | 5 |
| Money | - | 4 | 3 | 6 | 3 | 2 |
| Systems of Measurement | - | 4 | 3 | 5 | 7 | 3 |
| Geometry | - | 2 | 2 | 3 | 9 | 10 |
| Special Topics | - | - | 1 | 3 | 3 | 5 |

The general procedure for a student to follow in this program is to move vertically through all the objectives in A level, beginning with the nine objectives in numeration, going to the two objectives in addition, then to the two objectives in subtraction, etc., continuing through A-special topics. However, a student having mastered the objectives of A-numeration, which in this case relates to learning to count to ten, could continue to progress by going to B-numeration, which is counting to 100, thus providing one type of variation, vertical or horizontal movement. Student movement in the horizontal direction is usually the result of his own interests and desires in pursuing a topic he has found interesting or challenging.

Another variation that exists is the assignment of the order of the objectives within a given unit. Generally, the students follow the sequence of objectives within a unit in the numerical order that they appear. However, there may be situations in which the individual student might move from objective (1) to objective (7) with the materials for the other objectives available to him if and when he desires to use them. In this case, mastery of all the objectives is generally a requirement before going to the next unit.

A third variation is that of selecting certain objectives and ignoring others for a particular student. This differs from the second technique in that the student may or may not be required to return to the omitted objectives as a part of his program. This selective process is the most difficult to operate and should only be instituted after one is thoroughly familiar with the particular curriculum and relevant characteristics of the learner. In this process, the teacher is actually saying that this particular child does not need to know or is not capable of learning some particular content.

These are only a few of the ways that the curriculum can be modified to provide for individual interests, abilities, desires, etc. As more becomes known about the learning process and perhaps as computers become available for providing the teacher with up-to-date data, more and more variations can be built into a given program by the designer. In the early stages of development it is probably wise to consider a limited number of alternate sequences so that information relative to the alternatives can be assessed and additional alternatives can be built empirically into the design. An important consideration here, however, is the implication that this requirement has for instructional design.

**Instructional Design**

Once the work of the curriculum design has established the scope and sequence of objectives, the tasks of instructional design begin. In the initial stages of development, the tasks to be considered are the development and specification of evaluation and diagnostic instruments, materials and related instructional techniques.

*Evaluation.* A key aspect of individualization of instruction is that each student should be permitted to work at the places in the learning sequence most appropriate for him with amounts and kinds of instruction adapted to his individual needs. Implicit in this statement is the necessity for information related to (1) what the student has already mastered; (2) the extent to which he has already acquired some of the things to be learned in his next sequential step; (3) the extent to which he has acquired the necessary prerequisites in the same content field, other content fields, and certain motor, sensory and other skills required in learning the new behaviors; and (4) the extent to which he has had sufficient experiences related to a behavior to be able to move to the next point in his program.

Instruments to provide this information must be keyed to the sequence of a given set of objectives. Since the primary use of these instruments is to provide information to the teacher and the student for deciding the next instructional step, the information reported will be in terms of criterion-referenced scores rather than norm-referenced scores. This means that the information reported will tell how well Johnny can do a particular task, not how he compares to others in doing the task.

The first type of tests falls under the heading of placement tests. These instruments provide a profile for each student for each of the subject areas, indicating for which units the student has reached the desired criterion and for which he has not. This information can then be used to determine the first unit of study for each student. The second set of instruments provides information as to how much the student already knows about the assigned unit before he actually begins work in it. It is obvious that instructional decisions should differ for those who already know most of what is desired. These instruments are referred to as pretests. Pretests should also provide information relative to needed prerequisites specific to the learning of any desired behaviors which may not have been measured previously.

Once the student begins working in the selected areas, information relative to progress of the student and appropriateness of the prescribed materials and techniques should be available as an integral part of the system. Since one of the goals of individualized instruction is to permit the instruction to be geared to individual learner characteristics, this information as to appropriateness of assigned techniques is a must. In any case, the student should not work for long without assessment being possible. Finally, the student and the teacher need feedback of information for assessing the nature and kind of knowledge achieved in terms of the criterion that has been established. Instruments for this purpose are referred to as posttests.

The next major set of tasks in instructional design consists of those tasks necessary in assisting the student in going from the preinstructional state (measured by placement tests and pretests) to the desired level of competence of behavior. This requires the availability of instructional materials, instructional devices, and teachers competent to use a variety of tutorial techniques. It also requires the availability of information concerning learning styles, interests and attitudes of the learner that can be used in developing individualized lesson plans.

There are several basic assumptions underlying the implementation of individualized instruction and several goals associated with the individualizing of instruction that have implications for materials development. Examples of these assumptions are as follows: (1) for individualization to be economically and operationally feasible, much of the instructional materials must be self-instructional, (2) the student should be actively involved in the learning process, (3) not all students require the same amount or kind of practice to achieve mastery of a given objective and (4) different styles of learning require different techniques of instruction. The goals of individualized instruction that have implications for materials design are as follows: (1) a pupil can proceed to mastery at his own rate, (2) every pupil is able to evaluate his own progress, (3) different learning materials are available to accommodate different learning styles and (4) pupils are able to become self-directed and self-initiated learners.

In general, the implications are that self-instructional materials must be available for those students able to use them, the self-instructional materials must accommodate various learner characteristics (e.g., the child that is advanced in math but not in reading must have materials that can be self-instructional without requiring reading skills beyond his competencies), and the materials must provide for varying paths and branchings. Two factors that make this new instructional designer's role possible are (1) the emphasis on the detailed statement of behavioral objectives, and (2) the availability of such aids to individualization as new low-cost, easily operated technical devices such as tape and disc recorders, single-concept film projectors, other combination audio-visual machines and computers to assist instruction.

Once the specification of the behavioral objective and its placement within the curriculum have been decided, the instructional designer can determine what minimum competencies can be expected of the learner, approximate age level for most of the students working with the materials and the criterion level expected as a result of the instruction. Information of this kind can assist in the identification and coding of materials that are already available. For instance, in the IPI mathematics curriculum, the first objective at C-fractions reads: "Divides a whole object into halves, thirds, or fourths, and identifies an object divided into halves, thirds, or fourths."[5] An analysis of the A and B level fraction units indicates the child can divide into halves. Next, since this objective appears at the C level, students encountering this task will be primary age children (6-9) with limited reading skills. Finally, since there are no other indications shown, all children are to be vertically 100 percent competent in doing this at the time of being posttested. Knowing these points and recognizing that this is an individualized program requiring these materials to be self-instructional for many students, the instructional designer would probably begin his search by looking at commercial films or filmstrips which can demonstrate these concepts to the students. He would probably rule out most commercially available text-books and workbooks as introductory materials since these generally rely on a great deal of teacher explanation and demonstration. However, having decided upon the techniques to introduce the vocabulary, concept and manipulations, the instructional designer may wish to identify materials for practice and could then code available workbook-type materials requiring the child to discriminate between objects divided in halves, thirds, or fourths.

When the package of materials for this set of tasks has been assembled, the designer should appraise its appropriateness by how well it meets the criteria of the system.

In the case of C-fractions, Objective 1, the criteria may be:

1. Can it be used by readers and nonreaders alike?
2. Can it accommodate students who cannot readily go to the abstract route of pencil-paper?
3. Can it provide varying sequences for those with varying amounts of knowledge of the behavior before beginning, e.g., the student who can identify objects divided into halves, thirds and fourths, however cannot divide whole objects into thirds and fourths?
4. Are the materials organized so that students requiring more and less practice can be accommodated?
5. What provisions are made for providing a variety of objects that can be divided or manipulated by the learner?
6. What are the alternative ways that the learner can demonstrate to the teacher that he can perform these tasks and are they known by the teacher?
7. What provisions for checking the retention of these concepts are built into the curriculum?

The actual evaluation of the effectiveness of the materials of instruction must always await the ultimate test, which is that of usage. As more and more schools adopt individualized instructional systems, the technique of developing materials and the design for evaluating the effectiveness of materials will require more vigorous treatment than given in the past.

**Summary**

The concern of educators for adapting instruction to the needs of individual students is placing more and more demands upon those involved in curriculum and instructional design. The role of the teacher in such a system makes it mandatory that he be provided with well-defined outcomes to be achieved by the learner, information as to what learner characteristics are related to what kinds of learning, sufficient information about each learner in order to assess his abilities and a well-defined set of alternatives from which to select the means of assisting a learner to attain the goals desired. This would seem to suggest that those responsible for providing the necessary tools and information to the teacher must begin by defining the objectives of the system, then analyzing the inputs in terms of learner characteristics, determining ways of measuring these factors and defining and describing all the relevant conditions related to the system. In this way only will we be able to generate information to feed back into the system to assist in its improvement.

**Notes**

1. Examples taken from goals stated for the Individually Prescribed Instruction Project, Learning Research and Development Center, University of Pittsburgh, Pennsylvania.

2. For more information, see R. Glaser. "The Design of Instruction." *The Changing American School.* Sixty-fifth Yearbook, Part II, National Society for the Study of Education. (Edited by John Goodlad.) Chicago: University of Chicago Press, 1966. Chapter 65, pp. 215-242.

3. Robert F. Mager. *Preparing Objectives for Programmed Instruction.* San Francisco: Fearon Publishers, 1962.

4. C.M. Lindvall (Ed.). *Defining Educational Objectives.* "A Report of the Regional Commission on Educational Coordination and the Learning Research and Development Center." Pittsburgh: University of Pittsburgh Press, 1964.

5. *Individually Prescribed Instruction Project's Mathematics Curriculum.* Experimental edition. Working Paper No. 26. Pittsburgh: Learning Research and Development Center, University of Pittsburgh, September 1, 1967.

# 5

## Individualization of Instruction
## Vs. Nongrading

### A Review of the Basics of
### Viable Individualized Instructional Programs

William P. McLoughlin

Articles on individual differences and individualization of instruction are frequently written as if these were new educational problems. Of course they are not. Nearly every prominent educator from Plato to the present has commented on the implications of human variability for instruction.

We are prone to forget that American schools began as *ungraded* schools. Children of different ages met in one room with one teacher and progressed at their own rate through the few instructional materials available. I do not mourn the passing of the one-room schoolhouse nor opt for its return. I merely wish to point out that even in the one-room school the instructional implications of individual differences were recognized.

As enrollments grew and the inability of the one-room school to deal effectively with individual differences became increasingly apparent, the graded school seemed a more effective way of dealing with these problems. By 1871 virtually every school in America, even the one-room rural school, was a graded school. But by the end of the nineteenth century efforts were already under way to "break the lockstep approach to education" found in the graded school. The emotional and psychological carnage left in the wake of relentless conformity to procedures developed by the graded school to reduce learner variability screamed out for more viable and humane alternatives. In 1888, for example, Preston

Reprinted from *Phi Delta Kappan*, Vol. 53, No. 6, February 1972, pp. 378-381, by permission of author and publisher.

Search was developing procedures for the individualization of instruction in the schools of Pueblo, Colorado, and by 1911 Frederick L. Burke and his associates at the San Francisco State College Training School were individualizing instruction in all curriculum areas requiring the least amount of group contact. This was the precursor of a number of "laboratory approaches to education" like the Winnetka Plan.

After the floodgates for "plans" for individualizing instruction were opened, American education soon became inundated with such propositions. The St. Louis Plan, the Dalton Plan, the Batavia Plan, the Elizabeth Plan—and plans far too numerous to list—became *the* educational innovations of the late nineteenth and early twentieth centuries. More than a decade ago, Harold Shane identified 35 such attempts at individualizing instruction.[1]

All these efforts, and many which followed, had two things in common. First, they were not thoroughgoing rejections of the basic approach of the graded school for individualizing instruction through group teaching of children assumed to be similar. At best they were well-intentioned but faulty attempts at vulcanizing the holes in such an approach for coping with individual differences. Second, each of these plans sought new organizational devices for adjusting the child to the instructional offerings of the school but never looked for ways of adjusting the instructional offering of the school to the child.

### The Nongraded School

Perhaps the most viable alternative to the graded school has been the nongraded school. Unlike the other educational propositions purporting to recognize individual differences and individualize instruction accordingly, the nongraded school does not seek to bolster the sagging graded school. Rather, it begins by suggesting that children's progress through school should be continuous and devoid of artificially induced skips or lags.

Though this approach was first tried in Bronxville, New York, in 1925,[2] it did not receive critical acclaim until the late 1950s. While well-intended, the message of the nongraded school is at best vague and its translation into practice leaves much to be desired. Almost without exception, converts to the nongraded school rely on one or more of the organizational schemes mentioned by Shane. Also, and again virtually without exception, *no substantial changes in instructional procedures accompany contemporary plans to nongrade the graded school.* Reliance is placed on *group instruction* as the method of ministering to individual differences. Viewed from this vantage point, most efforts made to nongrade the elementary school are little more than tired reruns of inefficient and ineffective administrative gambits at grouping away the influence of individual differences on instruction.

A casual analysis of the characteristics of most efforts at nongrading reveals a hierarchy, not of quality but of organizational complexity, in the schemes developed to individualize instruction:

1. Without altering so much as a grade level, some schools simply announce they are henceforth nongraded. Teachers are instructed to take children where they find them and bring them as far as they can go during the year. Visitors to these nongraded programs frequently observe no differences from the typical graded school. Class organization, teacher and pupil assignments, and, lamentably, instructional practices are unchanged. This approach, I suppose, simply verifies the adage that a graded school by any other name surely smells.

There is something inherently reprehensible in such an approach to educational change. Essentially, it maintains that teachers all along have the ability to individualize instruction under the present educational arrangement but simply withhold this type of instruction until they receive administrative approval. I do not believe this to be the case, any more than I believe programs founded on this approach to the individualization of instruction are effective.

2. The next procedure used for nongrading a school and individualizing instruction is only modestly more complex. The basic design of the graded school is retained—one teacher for one self-contained class for one year—except that children of similar achievement and/or ability are grouped for instruction. Utilizers of

this procedure are vehement in their denials that their nongraded plan is homogeneous grouping revisited. They justify such an arrangement of children by observing that it greatly reduces the range of differences within the class, eases the teacher's job, and makes individualization of instruction not only feasible but attainable.

It may be graceless to observe that the major purpose of nongrading and other respectable efforts to individualize instruction is not to ease the job of instruction for the teacher but to facilitate learning for the child. They are not designed to mask individual differences among children by bringing children of assumed likenesses together for instruction but to create an instructional setting which will magnify each individual's uniqueness bigger than life, so that something may be done to capitalize on those differences. Additionally, these efforts, which are at best thinly disguised homogeneous grouping schemes, have been exquisitely distinguished in the past by their failure to influence either student achievement or adjustment. Even more discouraging, however, is the fact that those espousing this brand of nongrading seem marvelously unaware that what they have done is introduce into their schools in the name of nongrading an organizational scheme developed to preserve the graded school from complete collapse.

3. Large schools frequently use "cross-class grouping" to produce nongrading and individualize instruction. Essentially, the grade structure is preserved and children "on the same level" are regrouped for instruction in reading and sometimes in arithmetic in these subjects. These procedures are obviously more concerned with *group* learning needs than with *individual* learning needs; they are simply another effort to individualize instruction within the framework of group instruction.

4. Smaller schools use an adaptation of cross-class grouping to nongrade their schools and individualize instruction. Typically, the primary grades are viewed as a single instructional unit. During the day children from these classes are regrouped for instruction in reading and sometimes in arithmetic. Again, the single requirement for inclusion in any group is similar achievement in reading and/or

arithmetic. It goes without saying that a mere willingness to transgress established grade lines to form classes for instruction in reading is a poor guarantee that instruction in these classes will be individualized.

Even if this were an effective way of organizing children for individualized instruction, few schools would be willing to undertake the massive reassignments of children such a plan dictates. If in grade five, for example, a class of 34 pupils is to be formed so the range of reading achievement falls between 5.1 and 5.4, the class would probably contain: eight second graders, eight third graders, seven fourth graders, nine fifth graders, and two sixth graders. Furthermore, it is educational folly to pretend such rearrangements of children accomplish anything. About the only way a homogeneously grouped class can be kept homogeneous is to teach them nothing, for the differences in learning rates alone assure us that children will differ greatly after instruction is begun.

5. Lastly, interage grouping—assigning children of different chronological ages to one teacher in a self-contained classroom for more than one year of instruction—is also found in nongraded schools. This, of course, is the condition that prompted the conversion of the pre-1850 ungraded schools into graded schools. Remember, while this organization of children may teach teachers a considerable amount about child growth and development, it in no way provides them with additional instructional resources for coping with these differences. At best, such procedures do little more than complicate the instructional problems faced by most teachers.

The affinity for the graded structure of those who would nongrade is reminiscent of the problem faced by the Australian bushman who received a new boomerang—he couldn't throw the old one away. The nongraded school, while an agreeable enough educational idea, is so vague and chameleonic that it makes a poor blueprint for building a thoroughly new instructional program. The answers to the instructional problems produced by individual variabilities are not to be found in unique groupings of students but in unique instructional practices. This article is intended to suggest the banning of innovations that simply rediscover past educational failures. Too many innovators are little more than educational archeologists who delight in resurrecting moldy plans for individualizing instruction. Without a doubt education would be better off if these schemes had been left to mold in peace.

## Planning for Individual Instruction

Hastily conceived programs for individualized instruction will probably rediscover many of the ineffectual educational practices detailed above. Viable individualized instructional programs emanate from carefully planned strategies for educating each individual to the fullness of his potential. Basic to such planning are these goals:

1. The individual instructional programs must be developed to deal with individual differences, not group similarities.

2. The individual instruction program is at least a schoolwide program, and hopefully a districtwide program. Most homegrown educational innovations are underplanned and oversold and eventually die from an acute attack of administrative jitters. Apparently administrators fear direct confrontations with incompetent instruction and justify their "hands off" approach to educational improvement by pointing to anticipated adverse teacher reactions. More often than not they simply meet the instructional problems produced by individual learner differences by pledging support to any teacher willing to try to individualize instruction in his classroom. Effective programs of individualization of instruction must be considerably more than a *tour de force* for an occasional willing and competent teacher, a random, uncontrollable occurrence available to a limited number of children on an unpredictable schedule in an indeterminable number of classes.

3. A basic recasting of the role of the teacher in the instructional process is necessary for development of effective and durable programs for individualized instruction. In such a program increasing responsibility and accountability for learning must be placed on the instructional materials used. It is clearly impossible for a teacher, even the most dedicated teacher, to satisfy all the individual learning requirements of all of the children in all

learning areas of the school curriculum. We must demand much more teaching effectiveness from the instructional materials in use and require teachers to become increasingly proficient in recognizing and supporting the learner's expanding capacity to become an independent learner.

4. *Systematic* development of individualized instructional programs must relate the purposes of instruction, the instructional procedures developed for realizing these purposes, and the evaluation employed to assess the adequacy of instruction and the scope of learning.

Implicit in this systematic approach is the interchangeability of instructional materials, a requirement that should discourage schools from undertaking the production of these materials. The question, "Why can't teachers produce these materials?" assumes that the teachers have both the expertise and the desire to do this job. But such undertakings require the use of rather sophisticated constructs about teaching and learning, constructs which the typical teacher has not developed.

More mundane reasons for discouraging teacher production of these instructional materials include cost (teachers often demand and receive compensation for the work done to produce instructional materials) and the inability to integrate such materials into the school's instructional program. Administrators know that teachers, even beginning teachers, are hesitant to use instructional materials developed by other teachers. The discouraging legacy of local efforts to develop materials for an individualized instructional program is an enormous, disorganized, underutilized collection of ditto masters that are considerably more trouble to locate and run off than they are worth.

5. A carefully developed and continuous in-service program for introducing teachers to individualization of instruction must be an integral part of the school program. Too often schools undertake pervasive educational changes without developing procedures for the preservation and refinement of these innovations. The schools cannot assume that the staff which plans the innovation will implement and operate it. If the typical school has a 70 to 80 percent turnover in a 10-year period, it means that

teachers with little of the understanding of the programs as developed by their creators are expected to operate these programs. Lack of effective and efficient indoctrinating procedures is one of the most serious shortcomings of most innovative efforts.

6. Detailed evaluation procedures should be formulated concurrently with program development. Too often the intense desire to put an educational idea into practice is so overpowering that little or no attention is given to developing procedures for evaluating the efficacy of the innovation introduced. Programs worthy of introduction into schools should also be worthy of the best possible evaluation available, not an unsystematic, uninterpretable collection of teacher and administrator opinions about the presumed merits of the program. This requires ongoing and pervasive evaluation of all aspects of the innovation.

**Some Specific Procedures**

I hope that what I have been giving the reader is a tall order and not simply a tall story. Here is a list of specific references to procedures helpful in filling this order:

*Behavioral Objectives*—Virtually every serious effort at individualization of instruction uses behavioral objectives. The works of Mager[3] or Vargas[4] or Vimcet[5] materials developed for group instruction are useful guides for the purposes and preparation of behavioral objectives. Other sources include the 4,000 or so behavioral objectives developed for PLAN (Program for Learning in Accordance with Needs); they are available from the Westinghouse Learning Corporation for under $60. The Instructional Objectives Exchange of UCLA's Center for the Study of Evaluation sells numerous lists of behavioral objectives in a wide range of instructional areas at minimal cost.

*Commercially Prepared Programs*—Schools seriously considering individualizing instruction should look carefully at commercially prepared programs. IPI (Individually Prescribed Instruction), from the University of Pittsburgh and Research for Better Schools in Philadelphia, and PLAN, the Westinghouse Program, are perhaps the two most ambitious works in this area. Programs of this type are not giveaways. PLAN, for example, costs a school district approximately $100 a year per child to operate after initial fees have been paid. A complete breakdown of the costs looks like this:

|  | *Annual Charges for a School of 400 Pupils* |
|---|---|
| Teaching Learning Units<br>*($6/child/month)* | $24,000 |
| Computer Control<br>*($2.80/child/month)* | 11,200 |
| Computer Line and<br>Terminal Charges<br>*($2/child/month)* | 8,000 |
| Total | $43,200 |
| | |
| Initial Sign-up Charges<br>*(one time only)* | $ 5,000 |
| Supervisor Training Chart<br>*(one-time-only charge)* | 500 |
| Teacher Training Chart<br>*($300/week/teacher)* | 4,800 |
| Total | $10,300 |
| Support Material Charge<br>*(varies with amount of<br>equipment and utilization<br>patterns of the school)* | $53,500 |

Some educators seeing these program costs for the first time think, "My board will never buy it." Possibly we are overquick to diminish the efforts made to support education and even use our fiscal woes as reasons for doing nothing. We point with almost masochistic pleasure to the fact that in a recent year the world only spent $100 per child on education but $7,800 per soldier. While allocating $110 billion of its resources to education, it invested a whopping $159 billion in armament.[6] We are quick to conclude from these and similar data that schools are not getting their fair share of the tax dollar.

This is far from the whole story of educational support. In the past two decades education spending in the U.S. increased fivefold[7] while personal consumption merely doubled.[8] In the same period school enrollments increased 88 percent, but school expenditures, in *constant dollars*, increased 350 percent.[9] While employment in private industry increased 38 percent, employment in public education increased 203 percent.[10] The public has not been unwilling to support education.

Taxpayers may be justified in digging in their heels to resist school tax increases, for there is virtually no relation between the money spent on education—per-pupil expenditures, community tax rates, teacher salaries, pupil-teacher ratios, number of administrators per 100 pupils—and educational attainment.[11] Even the feeble relation between grade six reading achievement and educational expenditures virtually vaporizes by the tenth grade. About all that increases in staff size and salaries seem to do is increase the size of the educational tax bill.

I have no desire to dazzle the reader with fancy statistical footwork. I merely wish to replace the conjecture and wishful thinking that shroud discussions of the efficacy of increased educational spending on education attainments with hard data on this point. Traditionally, the public has been led to believe that money was the cure-all for instructional ills and that the yellow brick road to educational excellence is paved with smaller classes and larger and better-paid staff. Taxpayers once endorsed this solution but are now disappointed with its attainments. Most of them, too, do not necessarily demand more bang for the buck; they would gladly settle for an occasional pop.

Suggesting the merits of the "big package" of commercially developed instructional materials as the starting point for a local effort to individualize instruction is often characterized and rejected as the impossible educational dream. Solutions short of this are solicited. Inherent in this quest is tacit recognition of the merits of the big package approach but a willingness to make do

with second-best solutions. I do not countenance reckless educational spending, but I suggest that those coveting educational
innovation be innovative themselves. I feel the time may have
come when we must stop asking boards of education what they
can do for our instructional program and start asking ourselves
what alternatives to increased spending we can develop for these
programs.

Innovation, like charity, begins at home. In the days of tight
money, unique solutions should be developed for obtaining the
innovations desired, and creative use of resources placed at our
disposal is imperative. I know one administrator, for example, who
filled one first grade teacher opening with two half-time teachers.
Besides providing valuable opportunities for using unique staffing
patterns, this departure from tradition saved money which
otherwise would have gone to auxiliary compensation, retirement
funds, medical insurance, etc. The money saved was used to
purchase additional instructional supplies and services. Boards of
education must be presented with alternatives to the funding
needs of innovative schools. They simply cannot be asked
regularly and relentlessly to dig deeper and deeper into the
taxpayer's pocket for more dollars for these programs.

*Taxonomies for Education*—Essentially, most available solutions to the instructional problems resulting from individual
differences focus on a single aspect of learner differences—
differences in learning rates. Qualitative differences are known to
exist among learners, too. Space does not permit a critique of
available references, but I would like to draw attention to the
works by Bloom and Krathwohl.[1,2] Together with other relevant
studies, these taxonomies could provide a framework for assessing
the scope of the learnings provided by the school curriculum.
They will not provide cures for ills plaguing a school but may help
explain what is killing the school's individualized instructional
program.

*Systems for Evaluation*—Because evaluation is related to the
goals and procedures used to achieve specified outcomes, it is not
possible to provide a system for evaluation prior to program
development. However, CAM (Comprehensive Achievement Moni-

toring) has an overall assessment design which may provide schools interested in individualizing instruction with a framework for developing a sound procedure for program assessment.[13]

### Elixir for the Individual

The discussion of individual differences and individualization of instruction has come full circle. While the instructional difficulties produced by individual learner differences are clearly not new educational problems, viable solutions to these problems are still urgently needed. What has been learned about individual differences from earlier efforts to deal effectively with the instructional problems they produce fills many volumes. The yet-unanswered questions about individual differences, however, would fill many more. If indeed the past is truly prologue, it must be scrutinized, for educators can ill afford to accept its errors as their truths. The time for stockpiling outmoded organizational gimmicks and empty dictums about individual differences has passed. Both the public and the professional have drunk too long and too deeply of this old wine in new bottles to mistake it as an elixir to cure the instructional problems produced by individual differences. A brave new world of procedures for working effectively with individual differences is being built; it could decline and fall for want of brave new educational leadership.

### Notes

1. Harold G. Shane. "Grouping in the Elementary School," *Phi Delta Kappan,* April 1960, pp. 313-319.

2. William P. McLoughlin. *The Nongraded School: A Critical Assessment.* Albany: New York State Education Department, 1967, p. 2.

3. Robert F. Mager. *Preparing Instructional Objectives.* Palo Alto, California: Fearon Publishers, 1962.

4. Julie S. Vargas. *Writing Worthwhile Behavioral Objectives.* University of West Virginia, undated.

5. Vimcet Associates. *Vimcet Filmstrip-Tape Programs,* Vimcet Associates, P.O. Box 24714, Los Angeles, California 90024.

6. "The Cost of World Armaments." *The UNESCO Courier,* January 1970, p. 13.

7. U.S. Office of Education, *Digest of Educational Statistics,* 1970 ed., Table 25.

8. *President's Economic Report.* January 1971, pp. 197-198.

9. U.S. Office of Education, *op. cit.*

10. Office of Business Economics. *The National Income and Product Accounts of the United States, 1929-1965,* p. 100.

11. California State Department of Education. *California State Testing Program, 1968-1969: An Analysis of Reading Test Scores and Other School Factors.* Sacramento, 1970.

12. Benjamin S. Bloom. (Ed.). *Taxonomy of Educational Objectives, Handbook I: Cognitive Domain.* New York: David McKay, 1956; and David R. Krathwohl. (Ed.). *Taxonomy of Educational Objectives, Handbook II: Affective Domain.* New York: David McKay, 1964.

13. William Gorth. *Comprehensive Achievement Monitoring (CAM).* Amherst: University of Massachusetts Press, 1970.

# 6

# The Individualized Learning System:
# What It Is and How to Use It

Gail L. Baker and
Isadore Goldberg

As the demand for qualified individuals to serve in business, industry, government and academic institutions increases, so the need for educating and training these people becomes greater and greater. In recent years, numerous attempts have been made to develop methods and techniques and to prepare new materials which will meet this need. But the methods, techniques and materials have been incorporated into existing educational and training systems and, because the systems themselves are now inadequate, this incorporation has not been successful. And a consideration of the problems which this situation presents brings us to a consideration of individualized learning.

## Each Learner an Individual

The major problem has not been due to the inappropriateness of any particular method or technique, or to the poor quality of any particular materials. Rather, the difficulty has lain with the failure of the existing systems to deal with the differing abilities and requirements of today's students.

A learner is an individual, and must be taught accordingly. Innovations such as small group work, audio- and videotape lectures and demonstrations and teaching machines and programmed instruction materials have all helped, to a degree, to improve education and training. Yet what is needed is a system

Reprinted from *Educational Leadership*, Vol. 27, No. 8, May 1970, pp. 775-780, by permission of authors and publisher.

which permits the selection of both the curriculum and the manner in which it will be presented for each individual learner. Individualized learning systems have been developed to accomplish just this.

## What Is Individualized Instruction?

Before individualized instruction is described and discussed, it should first be defined. An individualized learning system is a highly flexible system of multiple materials and procedures, in which the student is given substantial responsibility for planning and carrying out his own organized program of studies, with the assistance of his teachers, and in which his progress is determined solely in terms of those plans.

The individual system is a total educational program incorporating all useful concepts known to enhance the learning process. Its success depends upon an optimal balance between the student's own self-appraisal and the teacher's counsel—the student does not progress autonomously in his learning program.

In planning an individualized learning system, the distinction between individualized learning and independent study must be remembered. The two terms are not synonymous. Individualized learning is a more structured program than independent study, while at the same time remaining very flexible. To individualize instruction in a subject area, the student and his teacher select from a variety of materials and media and determine the sequence of study that appears most effective in terms of the student's abilities and needs. A student may choose to work independently in an individualized learning program, but merely working by himself does not mean that a student is participating in an individualized learning program.

In *Educational Leadership* in 1968, Frazier[1] discussed individualized instruction in general terms and presented a rationale for curriculum redevelopment incorporating the concepts of individualization. It is important now to understand just what these concepts are specifically, since the development of an individualized system of instruction involves the consideration of a number of variables. These include student features, teacher features, behavioral objectives, multiple activities, study requirements and student evaluation. Any system of instruction is individualized only to the extent that certain criteria for these variables are experienced and demonstrated by the students and by their teachers.[2]

*Student features.* To as great an extent as possible, the abilities and requirements of each student must be considered in planning his overall program of instruction and each of its component parts. These abilities and requirements must be specified in terms of entry level behaviors, with regard to the student's weaknesses and strengths. The characteristics of each student play a major role in the selection of objectives, the sequence of study and the choice of materials and procedures. It should be emphasized, however, that, regardless of the importance of the student in the individualized learning system, the teacher is no less important.

*Teacher features.* Teachers serve in varied roles—as members of the systems analysis, curriculum development and evaluation team, as diagnosticians and evaluators and as counselors. The individualized learning system provides for a significant amount of teacher-student interaction. Among other approaches, the teacher spends more time answering questions of individuals and small groups than lecturing to an entire class. In general, the teacher is concerned with reinforcing the behaviors appropriate for each of the individual students.

*Behavioral objectives.* Well-defined sequences of progressive objectives in various subject areas are established as guidelines for setting up an individual student's program of study. Each of the objectives is specified in terms of observable competence—either a particular behavior, or a particular product of the behavior. The student has available, in writing, the objectives toward which he is working which define what he is to learn. All of the students work toward a variety of objectives and this is encouraged by the teacher.

*Multiple activities.* To enable the students to better achieve their objectives, the teacher encourages students to help determine the materials they work with and the procedures they follow.

Each student uses a variety of materials and procedures. He moves freely about from place to place and talks freely with others, doing, with the teacher's approval, whatever is necessary to achieve the objectives. A student pursues his objectives individually, with small groups of classmates, or with his teachers, depending upon the requirements of each objective.

*Study requirements.* Each student proceeds through his program at his own pace. The time he spends in a given subject area is determined by his performance, rather than by an arbitrary time allotment. This flexibility permits the slower student additional time for review and the faster student opportunity either to pursue his regular course work in greater depth or to explore new areas of interest. Individualization does not, however, completely eliminate working together in groups, where such effort would be mutually advantageous to the several students involved.

*Student evaluation.* The progress of each student is continuously measured by comparing his performance with his own specific objectives, rather than with the performance or the objectives of other students. Testing and evaluation milestones, with adequate methods and instruments for assessing the student's abilities and accomplishments, are an integral part of the individualized program. A diagnostic placement test is given each student in any subject matter area to determine that point in the program at which he is qualified to begin. Pretests and posttests accompany each segment of an individualized learning system and frequent self-evaluation tests are given to provide the student both reinforcement and knowledge of his own progress.

## Implementing Individualized Instruction

Only recently have concepts and procedures for implementing such a truly schoolwide individualized learning system evolved. The supervisor of curriculum development can initiate such a program throughout the entire school system, or he can begin with one model school or experimental demonstration center. In any case, there are a number of points which must be considered in the implementation of an individualized learning system.

*Subject areas.* A school need not individualize instruction in all subject areas at the beginning. There are other alternatives which can also be effective, such as individualization by a few subject areas, or by a single department. In fact, it is often preferable to start with one or two subject areas which would have the greatest impact on improving the school's entire program. These might be core subjects, or more advanced subjects or certain specialized subjects. Regardless of the subject areas chosen, however, there must be long range commitment on the part of the staff which would be involved in the individualized program decided upon, so that curriculum development, staff training and program management plans can be made.

*Teaching-learning vehicle.* One of the first requirements for the implementation of an individualized learning system is that a basic instructional vehicle be chosen for the presentation of the individualized program. The vehicle simply refers to the basic methodological format which will be used by the teachers and other staff members in providing learning assignments to guide the students in planning and pursuing their own individual programs.

*Materials and media.* Perhaps the most important requirement for individualization is the availability of a wide variety of instructional materials and media from which to select. An individualized learning system must include alternative modes, or learning procedures, by which any particular objective can be reached. Because of the flexibility of the system, new developments in media and materials can be incorporated easily and quickly.

This is one of the distinct advantages of the systems approach—it allows adoption of the best features of new curricula and techniques as they are developed. That sufficient funds must be made available for design and development and purchase of the necessary materials and media required by the individualized program cannot be overemphasized. If all of the diverse components are not provided for the students to select and use, the very concepts of variety and flexibility on which individualization depends are undermined.

*Learning centers.* Learning centers are a desirable feature of

individualized learning systems. These centers vary from centralized facilities associated with library-audiovisual departments, to
decentralized facilities associated with teaching departments, to
specialized facilities such as science laboratories. Individualized
learning is fostered through adequate staffing and up-to-date
materials and equipment in these learning centers.

*Research and evaluation.* Research and evaluation continually
improve the quality of the instructional system. Unlike the
practice in more traditional systems, the burden for learning is
placed on the individualized system rather than on the student—if
the student does not learn, the curriculum, and perhaps also the
teacher's and the student's roles, must be revised.

For example, an alternate choice of materials and media, or
perhaps a different sequence of study, could be tried by the
student. Another option might be to give the student more, or
possibly less, freedom in deciding upon his own program. In
addition to the evaluation of the system which is provided by such
information as these observations, some individualized programs
also undertake basic research in the learning process and in the
development of specific uses of particular media, materials and
methods.

*Differentiated staffing.* In an individualized learning system,
there must be trained personnel at more than one level of
teaching. Included are regular teachers, teacher aides, master
teachers and possibly some specialized staff members. Pre-service
or in-service programs, or a combination of both, can provide the
training necessary for the school personnel to perform adequately
at different levels within the system. Each staff member must be
given sufficient time to accomplish the tasks required to organize
instruction for individualized learning, as contrasted with total
class management of learning.

*System management.* The critical requirement for individualized instruction is the establishment of school situations adaptable
to individual differences. The conventional boundaries of grade
levels and arbitrary time units for subject matter coverage need to
be redesigned, to permit each student to work at his actual level of
accomplishment in any subject matter area and to permit him to

move ahead as soon as he masters the prerequisites for the next level of advancement.

*Computer assistance.* Individualized learning systems are usually supported by computer-based flexible scheduling programs. Individualized instruction requires more record keeping than other methods of instruction, and provisions must be made for handling this requirement on a daily basis. Computerization of the schedule reduces the inordinate clerical load otherwise encountered by the school staff in assigning students and teachers to classrooms and other facilities. Computer-based instructional management systems show great promise for handling functions like testing, diagnosing student deficiencies, maintaining continuous and detailed records of student progress, and providing individual schedules and study assignments.

**Examples of Individualized
Learning Systems**

In specific individualized learning systems, broad curriculum priorities and decisions must be delineated and related to the individual students in the general target population. Systems analysis techniques are used for planning and development and for evaluation and improvement of the individualized program.

There are a number of demonstrations of individualized education which can be seen throughout the country. One is Individually Prescribed Instruction, begun in a suburb of Pittsburgh, Pennsylvania.[3] A second is the Milton Project in Central Pennsylvania.[4] A third is the Duluth, Minnesota, Chester Park Project.[5] A fourth is the Wisconsin Research and Development Center for Cognitive Learning's Individually Guided Education in the Multiunit Elementary School.[6] A fifth is the Project PLAN teaching-learning units, or TLUs, developed by the American Institutes for Research in Palo Alto, California.[7] A sixth is teacher-written UNIPACs, developed by the Kettering Foundation Project /I/D/E/A/.[8] A seventh is Learning Activity Packages, called LAPs, developed initially at the Nova Schools in Fort Lauderdale, Florida.[9] All of the approaches to individualized learning programs, in addition to some less structured approaches,[10] are discussed at length in a publication prepared by Computer Applications Incorporated.[11] An annotated bibliography of selected publications on individualized instruction has been issued by ERIC at Stanford.[12]

Let us now consider a specific organizing model for an individualized learning system. We might call this hypothetical model the Module for Individualized Education. Of course, you should keep in mind that the adoption of a particular individualized learning system will depend almost completely on the particular student population which will use it. But from this brief description you will have some idea of how the system might operate.

Each Module for Individualized Education—a MInE—is designed to strengthen the student's understanding of a single major concept or principle. To establish firmly the primary idea, each module includes secondary ideas. A complete structuring of ideas for each subject area results in a congruent sequence from preschool through college. The module is a map of the student's pathway through the system. At certain crossroads, the student meets with small groups for conceptualizations, or confers with the teacher on a one-to-one basis to decide on the activities he should undertake. The student participates in all decisions that affect him, assesses his own progress and helps design quest activities, which range from supplementary research, to work in industry, to creative experiences.

*Components of MInEs.* Each module includes eight basic components. The rationale is a statement justifying the inclusion of the subject matter, and integrating it with related topics in the total program. The statement of the primary and secondary behavioral objectives includes the skill or concept to be learned, the conditions under which the learning must be demonstrated and the criteria for and means of evaluating the learning. The pretest may cover either the entire module or individual objectives, depending upon the nature of the material or the length of the total module.

The list of activities provides options, with regard to media and mode, based on the results of the pretest, on learning styles and on preference. Self-testing devices measure the learner's achievement of the objectives and they help him decide on subsequent steps to follow. Teacher-made posttests take several different forms and come in different batteries. Recycling activities are provided for those students who need or want additional practice. Depth study opportunities are provided for those students who wish to pursue the subject matter in detail.

Additional components, such as special situations and contingencies, are included by standard inserts and special handouts.

*Levels of MInEs.* The modules are prepared with variations to accommodate various levels of learning. The objectives are organized into larger units or courses, or into a curriculum scope and sequence. The type of learning desired is frequently specified for an entire unit or sequence of units, from the most basic skills to the most advanced.

*Media in MInEs.* Since the major functional requirement of an individualized system is a wide variety of instructional materials, the role of media in providing this variety is extremely important. The media of instruction best suited to presenting a set of objectives are identified. Differentiated learning materials and media provide alternative learning paths to common objectives. Modules use oral communication, printed materials, videotapes, audiotapes, slide programs, filmstrips and films. Since much material is presented in more than one medium, a basic goal is accommodation of a broad range of learning styles and preferences, and several alternatives of instructional media are included in each module.

*Modes in MInEs.* The five basic instructional modes which make up a laboratory environment are large group, small group, tutorial, directed independent study and independent self-study. The large group mode, or lecture, is most useful at the beginning because commonalities of need and progress exist at this time. General interest and the introduction of new material are the uses for this mode as the student continues in his program. The small group mode is useful in certain aspects of the program from the beginning, such as discussions and project activities. The small group mode becomes a scheduling tool as commonalities arise during the course of a program. The tutorial mode, or one-to-one teaching, plays perhaps the largest role in an individualized program. This mode is built into the modules as a critical process. Directed independent and independent self-study procedures are dictated by modules on a systematic basis, and form important structural components of the program.

The interrelationship of the concepts required of an individualized learning system and the procedures required for implementing it can be thought of diagrammatically, as shown in Figure 1.

*Figure 1*

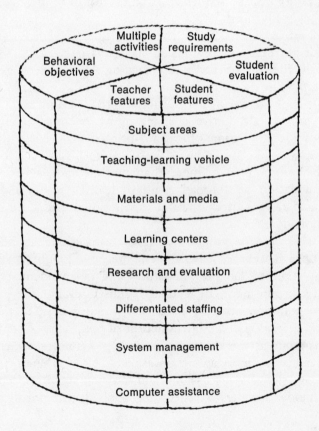

In summary, an individualized learning system is developed and implemented; then it is carefully observed, evaluated and improved. The evaluation-revision cycle, the basis for the internal self-improvement of the total system, may occur a number of times over a period of years. The system never ceases to adapt to the ever-changing abilities and needs of the students and it is the quality that makes individualized learning an absolute necessity in our schools of today and tomorrow.

## Notes

1. Alexander Frazier. "Individualized Instruction." *Educational Leadership,* Vol. 25, No. 7, April 1968, pp. 616-624.

2. The following description of identifying criteria expands substantially the guidelines given on the "Identification Card for Individualized Instruction" issued at the National Laboratory for the Advancement of Education sponsored by the Aerospace Education Foundation in Washington, D.C., November 18-20, 1968.

3. *Individually Prescribed Instruction: Education U.S.A. Special Report.* Washington, D.C.: National Education Association, 1968.

4. Hugh F. McKeegan. "What Individualizing Instruction Means to the Curriculum Director." *Audiovisual Instruction,* Vol. 13, March 1968, pp. 232-237.

5. Thomas J. Ogston. "Individualizing Instruction: Changing the Role of the Teacher." *Audiovisual Instruction,* Vol. 13, March 1968, pp. 243-248.

6. Herbert J. Klausmeier, Richard Morrow and James E. Walter. *Individually Guided Education in the Multiunit Elementary School: Guidelines for Implementation.* Madison, Wisconsin: Wisconsin Research and Development Center for Cognitive Learning, 1968.

7. Robert A. Weisgerber and Harold F. Rahmlow. "Individually Managed Learning." *Audiovisual Instruction,* Vol. 13, October 1968, pp. 835-839.

8. *What Is a UNIPAC?* South Laguna, California: Institute for Development of Educational Activities Materials Center, 1968.

9. Richard V. Jones, Jr. "Learning Activity Packages: An Approach to Individualized Instruction." *Journal of Secondary Education,* Vol. 43, April 1968, pp. 178-183.

10. Dwight W. Allen. "How You Can Individualize Instruction—Right Now." *Nation's Schools,* Vol. 81, April 1968, 43ff.

11. Isadore Goldberg, Norman J. Murray, Ronald E. Dozier, Gail L. Baker, Julie Kisielewski, C. Glenn Davis, Jane Bottorff, Thomas P. Ryan, *et al. Final Report: Model Secondary School for the Deaf—A Study of Instructional Methodologies.* Prepared for Gallaudet College and the Program Design Subcommittee of the Model Secondary School for the Deaf Coordinating Committee, National Advisory Committee on Education Applications Inc., Education and Training Division, 1968.

12. Serena E. Wade. *Individualized Instruction: An Annotated Bibliography.* Stanford, California: ERIC Clearinghouse on Educational Media and Technology at the Institute for Communication Research, Stanford University, 1968.

# 7

## Getting Started into
## a Package Program

Richard V. Jones, Jr.

The number of schools utilizing Instructional Packages to individualize their instructional program is increasing at a rapid rate. More are ready to go, but . . . well . . . where is the starting line? How does the faculty proceed? Who initiates the process? What are the pitfalls? What has "worked" to develop the program in these schools?

This essay will attempt to discuss these questions and, hopefully, suggest a few answers. The comments are derived from the experiences of those who have started down the Package path and are designed to aid those faculties and administrators who are convinced that an alternative to the lock-step instructional program is not only desirable, but vital.

In the experience of the author, those schools which have implemented package programs demonstrate both uniqueness and similarity. That is, while different in size, location, organizational design, etc., each school experienced similar problems as the package approach grew. Further, each of these programs had some characteristics which tended to have a similar effect on the instructional change.

In order to deal properly with the basic purpose of the article, described below will be some "foundational qualities," or those underlying characteristics of a school district which tend to support and nourish innovative programs; the necessary elements

Reprinted from *Journal of Secondary Education*, Vol. 46, No. 5, May 1971, pp. 218-226, by permission of author and publisher.

in developing this type of change in the instructional program; and finally the effects of a package program on other areas of the educational system.

### Foundational Qualities for Change

The implementation of an instructional package program is the work of many people: professionals, staff and community. Prior to the development of an instructional package system, an atmosphere must be developed at the school which will support the change process. This organizational condition is difficult to describe, but obvious if present. In the schools that tend to support change, there is a belief that change itself is natural and newness is expected. The fear of failure is therefore replaced by a feeling that effort expended toward improvement will be recognized and reinforced.

One way that administrators have developed this kind of an aura is through systematic planning: the goals and objectives were explicated; the major activities to achieve the goals were ordered; and the total staff was involved in those decisions which affected them.

A basic premise of planning is that the principal is a manager of educational resources. As managers, principals are responsible for the development of planning systems which allow for the maximum participation of all staff members in a sequential, organized fashion. An assumption of most educational planning systems is that the responsibility of the manager is not to direct professionals, but rather to facilitate the self-directed growth of these people toward predetermined, agreed-upon goals and objectives. Without some type of planning system, the principal finds himself evaluating random solutions to unspecified problems and dealing with short-range techniques, rather than helping a staff to clarify its overall purpose and thrust.

In one California school district with which the author was associated, all of the teachers were involved in a workshop to write Instructional Packages. After a day of intensive work, one of the teachers raised a question as to the purpose of using packages in that particular school system. With that question, the discussion of goals was opened for the entire group. After some three hours of interaction, a subgroup was appointed to write some overall goals for the instructional program; brainstorming sessions were held and a set of program goals and objectives were adopted by the total group. Once these goals were adopted, the work of writing the packages and implementing them seemed to make a lot more sense to the teachers.

Not only must a plan be developed in an atmosphere which tends to support productive change, but also the professionals involved must be allowed to develop procedures that most clearly represent their style of teaching. The major point is that if individualized instruction is an appropriate *modus operandi* for the learners, it also seems to be a most appropriate instructional approach for the teachers who must develop new skills, new understandings, and reexamine long-held values. Teachers have different teaching styles and it seems absurd to ask them to individualize their teaching without individualizing their learning of this new approach. Likewise, if the teacher is to motivate learners, then it would seem to follow that the principal should be motivating teachers toward instructional improvement. Principals who have facilitated successful package programs have encouraged teachers to develop alternate ways for moving toward the predetermined goal of individualized instruction. Typically, teachers are encouraged to try different methods and techniques, alternate grouping patterns, a variety of materials and media, etc., all designed to individualize instruction, rather than to find the "one best way" to instruct some particular classroom of students.

Teachers have become disenchanted with the idea of Packages when they unfortunately begin to see Package development as an end itself, rather than the means to the end. This has resulted from a lack of clearly defined goals and objectives. For example, rather than using packages, a teacher might decide to implement a contract system, or simply to sit down with each student and work out an individual learning plan. That teacher should be encouraged in his efforts, however, as long as the process chosen seems to be directed toward the goals of the program.

Another fundamental quality necessary to develop an effective Package program is the development of a cohesive spirit within the faculty. In every case where the author has worked with a total school or departmental faculty, a unifying comradery comes into being in those instances where the change was effective and lasting. Sometimes this kind of a positive professional relationship is limited to a single department, but if the package system is going to take a toe hold and spread throughout the school, the ability of the whole group to work together under difficult circumstances must be present. If it is the responsibility of the principal to facilitate those individuals who must work together within the school, then it should be his duty to assess and sharpen his abilities in interpersonal relations. Rather than developing this point here, the interested reader is directed to the literature presently available on group dynamics and interpersonal relations.

### Elements of Change

In addition to the fundamental qualities of change, a set of major elements which tends to support the change to Instructional Packages has been identified.

In the more than two dozen innovative educational systems with which the author has been actively involved in the past four years, a common characteristic has been the presence of strong leadership at the school. Typically, this instructional leader has been a member of the teaching staff, rather than an administrator. These people have been the innovative individuals who carried the main thrust of the change. The administrator in these instances has been most effective as a reinforcer and supporter to these teacher-leaders and has opened organizational "doors" for them.

In one small high school the principal is deeply committed to the goals of continuous progress education and the use of Instructional Packages as a vehicle toward this end. No change toward this goal has been achieved, however, in spite of many workshops, visits by teachers to other schools using Packages, the distribution of articles on such programs and other such encouragement from his office. The one element that seems to be missing is that of teacher leadership. Some teachers are interested, some are even trying to use Packages, but none seemed to be defined by their peers as leaders. To date, no major change in the instructional program of that school has been made.

The source of these vital educational leaders is varied. New teachers trained in these new processes should be of assistance, but the informal, on-the-job apprenticeship through which each beginning teacher must pass seems to blunt the initial enthusiasm of many to innovate. Therefore, by the time novice teachers have achieved a position of status within their peer group, these potential change agents have adopted the goals and values of their more traditional colleagues.

Innovative leadership can also be generated from summer and in-service workshops. Many teachers have developed an enthusiasm to write instructional packages in workshops and have maintained this motivation when they returned to school. These teachers can spark the interest of other teachers, and a program will begin. This procedure has been particularly effective when school-teams of teachers worked together in these sessions.

Experienced teachers have indicated, however, that some administrators have stifled this small degree of interest with a smothering blanket of "why-it-won't-work-here" and "but-have-you-considered-this" isms. These killer-phrases suggest another major element which tends to support change: administrative support.

In every situation where the Package system has been successfully adopted, there has been positive, active and interested support from the on-site administrator. At Hughson (California) High School the presence of a strong, dynamic, innovative administrator was instrumental in the development of one of the most unusual school programs in the country.[1] By freeing the teacher leadership within the faculty, that administrator was able to provide the kind of protective support that seems necessary to implement this kind of change.

An important aspect is that this administrative leadership must be organizationally close to the teaching staff. Certainly boards of education and central office staffs must be informed and have general positive orientation towards the development of

Instructional Packages, but the growth of lasting educational change seems more dependent upon the efforts of the local school principal and his assistants than upon the exhortations of those in central office administrative positions.

The most successful principals in terms of instructional improvement are those who become deeply involved in instructional matters and find ways that they can uniquely support the development of individualized instruction. The individual techniques employed by these administrators vary, but the effect is the same: a staff willing to move, and an educational program that is growing.

Another element that has been found to be significant is the clarification of the "next logical step" in the change process. When the faculty has identified the need for instructional improvement and the goals they wish to achieve, then the necessary skills can be outlined for the teachers to consider. The workshop model has been used extensively here to provide teachers the time and expertise to develop these skills. A typical weekend workshop[2] is described below:

*Workshop objectives:*

1.   Given a participant-selected topic, each would produce an Instructional Package which met all published requirements, and which could be used in the participant's classroom.

2.   Given a Package, the participant would be able to describe several ways it could be adopted to his instructional area.

A.   *First Day*

20 Minutes          —Large Group (Required)
                          Overview of the Workshop Objectives

45 Minutes          —The Need for and Characteristics

of Continuous Progress Education

| | |
|---|---|
| 60 Minutes (Including Break) | —Survey of Learner Needs  (Here, participants are asked to indicate their interest in the following areas.) |

a)   Higher Levels of Objectives
b)   Question-Asking Skills
c)   A Problem-Solving Curriculum
d)   Needs of Learners
e)   Finding a Variety of Activities
f)   Small Group Processes
g)   Writing Learning Objectives

55 Minutes          —The Outline of Instructional Packages

B.   *Second Day*

15 Minutes          —Large Group (Required)
Organization of Work Groups
Review of Learner Needs
Plans for the Remainder of the
Workshop

90 Minutes          —Large Group (Optional) or          *Work Group*
Overview of Instructional          Begin Writing
Package Elements          Package
Writing the Package (Techniques) 1)   Scope & Sequence

45 Minutes          —Large Group (Optional)          2)   Behavioral Objectives
Writing Learning Objectives          3)   Alternate Learning

45 Minutes          —Large Group (Optional)          Path
A Problem-Solving Curriculum

30 Minutes          —Large Group (Required)
Feedback on Progress          End

C. *Third Day*

| | | |
|---|---|---|
| 20 Minutes | —Large Group (Required)<br>Plans for the Day<br>Feed-Ahead on Progress | |
| 60 Minutes | —Special Group<br>Meeting with Facilitators<br>to Determine Progress and<br>Problems | *Work Group*<br><br>*Continue* |
| 60 Minutes | —Large Group (Optional)<br>Small Group Processes | |
| Lunch | | *Writing* |
| 45 Minutes | —Large Group (Optional)<br>Variety of Activities<br>(Instructor works with each<br>work group during afternoon<br>to assess and comment on<br>written materials.) | *of*<br><br>*Packages* |
| 30 Minutes | —Large Group (Required)<br>THE NEXT STEPS | |

Experience has shown that at least a two-week workshop is needed to develop the initial set of Packages to start a program. The basic skills, however, can be learned in a twelve- to fifteen-hour workshop, if a number of experienced Package writers are included in the group. A longer period is needed if these experienced teachers are not available.

Encouraging teachers to spend the time at the start of the process, in the clarification of a scope and sequence, will save them time in the writing phase. That is, if they decide on "what-is-to-be-taught," dovetailing it with other subject areas as appropriate and identifying the basic materials that will be used by the students, then the writing of the package itself will be done more efficiently.

In addition, novice Package writers are encouraged to start with their "best area," or that part of the subject matter that is of the greatest interest to them, or for which they have the greatest amount of learning materials available. As the package is designed to encourage alternative ways to learn, teachers many times have difficulty thinking of alternatives unless they are in a subject for which they have located a multitude of materials and approaches.

Teacher-writers also need the opportunity to try their "package prose" on others during the workshop. While student reactions are difficult to simulate—if not impossible!—a valuable critique can be obtained by asking a "process evaluator" to read the Packages for clarity, specificity and readability. Other teachers at the same grade level or subject area can react to the subject matter in the Package to assure activity and content validity.

A final element that must concern the principal is the protection of the innovation. Basic changes in the instructional system are extremely fragile and teachers attempting to individualize will many times become disheartened because of negative feedback they get from both students and peers. For example, when students are allowed to take the responsibility for their own learning, some of them seem unable to function effectively; they seem to have learned to conform to only that which the teacher directs them to do! Therefore, when given alternatives, they are unable to choose. At least two schools have clustered students with this learning characteristic into small "classes," so that they may learn to make choices in more traditional—and apparently more secure—surroundings.

As a teacher moves into an individualized system, the "learning noise" level tends to increase, mobility increases, and it is much more difficult to accurately assess individual learning without a different clerical system. These "differences" also cause comments from other staff members. While teachers quickly develop appropriate clerical systems to record conferences, papers and evaluation of each learner, the protection from the pressure of uninformed peers is a more complex problem. John Gardner has written that ". . . unfortunately the first restraining force for one who steps off the paths of custom and majority opinion is not lethal gunfire of opponents, but the clutching hands of intimates and colleagues."[3] In an attempt to neutralize this devastating and powerful pressure to conform, steering committees which include teachers, administrators, parents and students can be appointed. These steering committees can be made responsible for designing activities which will inform all concerned about the purposes and activities of the new program, and make suggestions to the teachers involved in the program as to how they might use feedback to make it more effective. In addition, a few well-written articles in the local newspapers or in professional journals have been a major source of encouragement for those teachers who have dared to move off the traditional path.

**Effects on Other Systems**

The development of a package system in a school will quickly affect all other systems within the school. That is, a package system is a method to increase the effect of the impact between the learner and his learning. As this is a most central activity in a school, any change made in this system can have significant consequences in many of the less central activities. The move from a teacher-directed, group-paced program into an individual-directed, performance-paced program will cause reactions in all other aspects of the educational system, including the utilization of personnel resources, facility resources, money resources, etc.

The following represents the many subsystems in an educational system affected by change:

Clearly, if the school has been operating with a group-paced and teacher-directed program, all of the subsystems noted above would be organized to service that program. Standard-sized room arrangements, standard-length class periods, large sets of the same textbooks, single-teacher control, the absence of aides, and highly controlled students would be typical.

Once the goals are changed, and an individualized Instructional Package program is inserted, many changes in these

THE EDUCATIONAL SYSTEM

| Clarification of Philosophy, Goals and Objectives | | |
|---|---|---|
| Instructional Development System | Curriculum Development Program | Staff Development Program |
| Materials and Media Utilization | Time Usage | Facility Usage |
| Community Orientation Program | Student Orientation Program | Organizational Management Program |
| Planning System | | |

Sub-Systems

sub-systems are either necessary or desirable. For example:

*Curriculum Development.* Now the true interdisciplinary plans can be developed. Students can be moving across subject matter lines with ease, as they concern themselves with problem-solving. A Package on "ecology," for example, might take the student into science, sociology, history, math, home economics, economics, etc., and what is more logical? This type of planning can be most effective if inter-departmental teams are organized.

*Materials and Media.* The class set of textbooks can be replaced by a multi-media center. Most schools starting the Package program convert library space into listening centers, viewing areas, discussion centers and equipment storage areas, as well as reading centers. What is needed is the widest variety of materials and media possible, organized into learning centers with maximum accessibility to all students.

*Time and Space Usage.* As programs are developed, the need for *larger* blocks of time and space become apparent. Sixty-minute modules, with ample opportunity for each learner to adjust to his own schedule within that block, become a most viable alternative.

Likewise, a "carpeted warehouse" would likely be the most appropriate space. Individualizing means that each will have the opportunity to learn in a particularistic way and rate. Time and space should therefore be adapted to the needs of the learner as much as possible.

*Community Inclusion.* While the community needs great doses of orientation to an insurgent Package program, it also needs a maximum amount of inclusion. The use of community aides in the school on a daily, regular basis is new to many faculties. These aides have been found to be exceptionally valuable as tour guides, testing center monitors and material organizers. The presence of parents on campus will not only inform the parents, but significantly aid the program.

*Staff Orientation.* The role of the teacher changes to a true learning guide. While the preparation of the packages takes many hours, the contact hours with students at school can be used primarily to help individuals or small groups of students. A major responsibility of the principal is to help the teachers become effective in small groups, in diagnostic practices, in learning to *listen* and in prescribing wide varieties of learning activities.

*Student Orientation.* Students also have new roles to play. What does one do when asked to choose learning activities? Really *choose?* Some students take to such decision-making easily and quickly; some must be urged and even pushed, while others can best be helped in a "remedial-decision-making" laboratory. Most schools have found it most satisfactory to start with a well-organized but rather tightly controlled plan and gradually increase the choice making as individual students demonstrate they can handle it with success. To suddenly change the rules for all students is unfair; to move too slowly is self-defeating.

The major purpose of this article was to identify and discuss several factors related to the development of an Instructional Package Program. The Package vehicle has opened many new avenues to the educational system, and only a few have been discussed here. The idea of students planning their own packages, pre-vocational and pre-occupational clusters, and the complete restructuring of age groups within the school, are examples of these other topics.

## Notes

1. See, for example, Howard James. *Children in Trouble: A National Scandal.* New York: David McKay Co., Inc., 1969.

2. Given by the author for teachers in the Fresno (California) City Schools, during the spring, 1970.

3. John W. Gardner. *Self-Renewal: The Individual and the Innovative Society.* New York: Harper Colophon Books, 1964, p. 73.

# 8

## Classroom Strategies for Success with Packages

Roger Tunks

Regardless of how carefully learning packages are planned and prepared, other considerations must be made to insure their success with students. Frequently teachers rush into the classroom with a few learning packages, expecting great improvements in student learning and motivation. Unfortunately, in too many cases the result is failure. Teachers make such comments as "Learning Packages don't work," and "Students are not motivated." Upon closer examination the trouble is often found not to be the instructional materials but the management of the program and the approach that is used by the teacher. To maximize the individualization that learning packages can provide for students, the following areas should be explored with emphasis on meeting the needs of students commensurate with their ability, interest and motivation.

### Schedule and Teacher Requirements

Teachers and administrators who are beginning a program utilizing learning packages are usually concerned with student scheduling. Frequently the question is asked, "What kind of a schedule is needed?" or "How long should the period or module be?" The schedule is not the single determining factor for program success. A learning package program can operate quite successfully with a seven-period or a twenty-one module day. Granted a

Reprinted from *Journal of Secondary Education*, Vol. 46, No. 5, May 1971, pp. 210-216, by permission of author and publisher.

schedule that is less restricting on student time would be an advantage but not an absolute requirement.

Far more important than the schedule is what goes on in the classroom within the available time. Will the teacher be an authoritarian, omnipotent source of knowledge, or an instructional manager available to assist students in their learning? Many teachers feel threatened when asked to experiment with the role of instructional manager. Changing the curriculum to learning packages is not necessarily going to cause an improvement in the instructional process. The learning package is merely a form of providing instructions, and nothing more. If a teacher is not willing to assume another media or person to offer these instructions, the frustrations that result can be overwhelming and in most cases will spell defeat for an individualized program. Flexibility, both in planning and in implementation, is essential to insure the success of any individualized program.

## Classroom Success of
## Learning Activities

The learning styles of students should be of major concern as identified in the learning activities of a package. A first or second grade student's learning style includes all of his senses, or more simply, he learns any way he can. Conversely, the primary learning style of a college graduate is "reading." It is like a giant pyramid, the base being the first grade level with many different styles and methods of learning. As the educational process moves up, the pyramid becomes narrower, until it is primarily limited to reading at the top. It should be the goal of any instructional program, individualized or otherwise, to broaden this pyramid and to keep it as wide as possible, for as long as possible. It should allow students to learn by using many different methods and by encouraging a curiosity for learning and creative thinking. Limited learning styles (activities) available to students in the classroom have considerable negative effect on the motivational success of the program. If the majority of learning activities in a learning package is reading and discussion, in all probability the students will become bored, and motivation for continuing will be lost. The initial interest may be from the Hawthorne effect, but as this wears off, motivation will decline until apathy or discipline problems occur. Diversified learning activities must be available to allow students to operate in whatever learning style best suits their needs.

### Record Keeping

Simplicity is of primary importance in designing and implementing a record keeping system. The students must be able to understand and interpret the data recorded. The system used may range from a computer centered CRT Readout to a simple wall chart or file card system. Regardless of the form used, it must be flexible enough to allow students to enter the program and exit at any time without a complete reorganization. Two systems which require a minimum amount of maintenance and financial backing are the simple wall charts which can be found in most 2nd and 3rd grade classrooms, and a 3-ring notebook, using a separate sheet for each student. Notebooks and wall charts have the advantage of being readily accessible and the flexibility of adding or removing students as movement occurs. For example, on a wall chart the students' names may be listed alphabetically on the left side with titles of the packages across the top. As a student completes a package, his square is simply stamped or marked indicating that it has been completed. Many systems start out working very effectively, but because of their complex nature prove to be ineffective.

Usually teachers starting a Learning Package program refer to them by number. The only problem with numbering packages is that this suggests completion of the packages in a sequence. In most cases, this is not necessarily true. A program which consists of 30 packages may have only 4 or 5 packages which must be completed in sequence, while others may be completed at random. This is true of English, social studies and many other areas of the curriculum, depending upon the nature and content of the course, and the design of the learning package. There are some packages that must be completed in sequence but the majority may occur in any order.

**Consumed or Exchanged Packages**

In a refined and thoroughly field-tested program it is not necessary to have individual packages prepared and available to every student in the class; e.g., if there are 30 students in a course, it is not necessary to have 30 of each package on the shelf for the students to select. There may be only 10 packages available for each idea being taught. As a student completes a package he returns it to the shelf and another is selected. This also reinforces the premise that packages may be selected at random, and not necessarily completed in sequence. Selection can be made under the direction and supervision of the teacher or teacher aide.

Another question to consider is whether a learning package is a consumed item or should be returned. In most cases, the first and second time a package is field-tested, it can be considered a consumed item. As the students progress through the program, the teacher will find new ways to present materials and the students will identify problems within the packages which have to be corrected. This will encourage, and in some cases, force the teacher to revise and improve the packages. After a series of packages has been adequately field-tested, the teacher may reach a point where the quality is acceptable and may then be used on a more permanent exchange basis.

**Student Appeal**

The format and organization of the learning package has considerable effect on its success in the classroom. The package must be organized in such a way that the students will be able to locate its major ingredients quickly and without confusion. It should be a provider of instructions and directions and not a learning experience in and of itself. Whatever organization and format is used within the school should be consistent with every department and program. If a student has several classes operating with learning packages, he should not have to operate under a different system in each class. In agreeing on a building-wide format, specifications should be identified as to what the package should contain and also its organizational arrangement. With the competition of television and graphic advertising it is important that every effort be made to produce a learning package which is attractive and interesting to students.

Some general guidelines to be considered in developing a program which has student-appeal are:

1. To use colored paper with a variety of colors whenever possible.

2. To keep the *maximum* size of the package to about eight pages. If necessary, use both sides of the paper. Cartoons, graphs, charts, pictures should also be used whenever possible.

3. To have objectives easily identified and readily accessible, and not hidden within the package.

4. To reflect pride on the part of the teacher with clearly stated instructions and ideas that are easily read. It should contain neither poor printing nor vocabulary beyond the level of the student's ability to understand.

To meet the needs of students that have limited reading skills the package can be recorded on other media. It may be on a cassette, cards for a language master, flip charts, cartoons, film strips, etc. The imagination of the teacher or the author is the only limitation.

The size and design of the package is determined by the maturity level of the students involved. If the students are young and are not able to grasp ideas that may require two or three weeks of involvement, it may be necessary to have a learning package that would be limited to one page with only one objective. More mature students may be able to grasp more complex ideas and work for a week or two, perhaps even a month, on a single package. It is not uncommon, however, for a learning package, at any level, to be of the single page variety. Also, students may be working on more than one package at a time, e.g., in a biology class there may be an activity dealing with propagation of plants in which a student is to perform several experiments. The outcome or conclusion of the experiments may require several weeks. In the meantime, the student would work on another package while awaiting the results of the experiment. The average amount of time a student should spend working on a single learning package is about one week. A full year's course would consist of approximately 30 to 35 learning packages. This is merely a guide, since the total number of packages in a course would be determined by the maturity level of the student and by the length of the course and the difficulty of the material.

### Student Evaluation

With the current emphasis on accountability, it becomes increasingly important for accurate and complete evaluation and testing. In a program which has open entry and open exit, information must be collected about a student's abilities to assist in determining the next step in the instructional program.

In most cases an individual program requires two types of testing. There should be some diagnostic and prescriptive testing to assess a student's ability and knowledge upon entry into the program. With the concepts and objectives for a traditional two-year high school algebra program placed on a continuum, with the simplest at the bottom and the most difficult at the top, a carefully prepared testing program becomes increasingly important. For accurate placement a standardized test such as the California Test of Basic Skills or the Iowa Test may be used. Based on the results of the standardized test and a conference with the student, an instructional program could be planned. It would be determined at which point he would enter this continuum and begin the program of learning packages. Every effort should be made to test the student at his ability level and not to give him a generalized test in mathematics which covers many grade levels. In most cases, there are test results available from previous years that can give a general idea of a student's ability. If a student is operating at a sixth grade level, he should be tested at that ability level. This kind of testing will be more accurate in determining student potential.

A second purpose of a testing program would be to determine student-mastery of individual packages within the continuum. There are many opposing ideas as to the kind of testing which should occur in a classroom using learning packages. Some people maintain that students should be given a *pretest* for each package, a *selftest* to monitor his progress through the package, and a *posttest* at the end for the instructor to determine the mastery of the objectives. There are several problems with this kind of testing program. Most high school teachers work with 125 or more students per day. With a course of 30 packages, at the end of the school year the students would have completed over 3700 learning packages, and if each package contains three tests, the students would have taken more than 11,000 tests by the end of the school year. This figure can become overwhelming from the administrative standpoint as well as from a student's point of shuffling papers and tests back and forth in order to finish the program.

Many classroom teachers are saying, "Let's do away with the pretest, give the student the learning package, and let him start working through it." Under this system, when he feels he can master the objectives as indicated, the student is allowed to take the test at his request without questioning whether he has the necessary knowledge and skills. At this point the posttest and the pretest are combined. In observing teachers who are using this system, it is interesting to note that at the beginning of a program students may not complete the first test at an acceptable level and it becomes necessary for the student to take a second test which is similar and hopefully with equal validity. It is significant that in completing the first few packages, students often have to take the second test, but after they have completed 3 or 4 packages, the second test becomes unnecessary. One of two things has occurred: either the student has learned to use the learning package and the activities identified with it, or he is becoming more honest with himself when he looks at an objective. He identifies accurately those objectives which he can and cannot do. Being honest with themselves is an important trait that students should be learning.

In a learning package program, it is interesting to observe student reaction to the testing program. The teacher is no longer considered the evaluator as in most group paced classes. The role of the teacher is enhanced considerably and is perceived as a helper or aide to assist the student in mastering the information and tests. The objectives clearly outline what is expected and the test is merely confirmation that the student has mastered the items that are identified.

A solution to the classroom testing program is to remove it to a testing center. This would be a center similar to a resource center in its operation. The students would be free to enter and leave the center at any time with a clerk, or an aide, available to manage the center. Several file cabinets with locks on them would be used to store the tests for several programs within the school. Larger departments may have an entire cabinet while a smaller department would use one drawer in a cabinet. A student would enter, request a particular test, show the package title and course. The aide would select the proper test from a file cabinet and hand it to the student. The student would complete the test and return it to the aide. At this point it is very important that the aide correct the test and give the student immediate feedback on the results. In the classroom it is hard for the teacher to correct a test immediately and to give results to the students because of the other activities involved. However, in a test center it would be the only responsibility of the aide to administer and give immediate feedback to students. If the student has the results of the test immediately after taking it, he is more likely to go back and review the work that may be needed or to go on to the next package.

Many criticisms are leveled against a testing center. It does, however, enhance the teacher's role of becoming an assistant or aide in helping the student with his learning and decrease negative student attitude toward the teacher as an evaluator. This is an important role-shift that a teacher should encourage. Concern over dehumanizing the instructional program and having a sterile room for testing is not necessarily a valid criticism. It depends a great deal on the personality and attitude of the aide assigned to that particular room. The room should be comfortable, attractive, and a low-risk area for students to enter into. Depending on the skills and competency of the aide, simple manipulative performance tests may also be administered in the testing center.

**Classroom Atmosphere**

To an outsider observing a classroom using learning packages, there may appear to be some confusion and disorder in the management of the room. However, after a closer inspection of each student's activities, meaningful learning experiences can usually be found. Classrooms using learning packages will have multiple activities going on; there may be a corner divided off with bookcases for quiet reading; listening posts attached to cassette recorders or records, and other audiovisual equipment; a section set up for small group discussion; a section for independent study or another for manipulative types of activities, such as lab experiments. The room will have a wide variety of activities with student movement about the room. Unfortunately, many people see a parallel between student learning and noise level. Individualized classrooms will have a noise level greater than most traditional classrooms.

The teacher may go several days or weeks before the entire class is called together and a lecture or demonstration is presented. Again this is a role-shift for the teacher to work with smaller groups and not to be as concerned with large groups. If a student asks the teacher for assistance the teacher should sit at the student's learning station. Before working with the student it is important for the teacher to ask quietly if any others are having problems with that particular objective or learning activity. Invariably 3 or 4 students will gather around and the teacher would have a small group discussion or demonstration for the students. Fifteen minutes after the instruction has been given another student may ask for the same help. The teacher may be a little concerned that the student did not participate when the instruction was given a few minutes earlier. At this point the teacher has at least two options available. Repeat the instruction again, or ask a student who had received the previous instruction to assist the student. The benefit here is that there is reinforcement with one student helping another. The notion of "kids teaching kids" is a very important idea that should be encouraged in all classrooms. If one student is helping another student, this does not necessarily mean that the teacher goes off and leaves that activity. Assistance may be given to another student while eavesdropping on the conversation that is going on to insure that it is not the blind leading the blind.

## 100 Percent Packages or Part Time

The question is always asked, "Does the program have to be 100 percent learning packages or can you start with a few and ease into a full program?" Unless a program has very interesting and motivating learning experiences for the student, a 100 percent packaged program can have motivational problems. In most cases it is important that there be some parallel activity to a learning package program within the classroom. For example, in the foreign language program the writing, reading and speaking of the language could be the individualized portion with learning packages. Concurrently, paralleling this activity would be a group program dealing with the culture of the country. It could be in the form of movies, field trips, group discussions, etc. In a social studies program the concepts that are being dealt with could be on an individualized program and paralleling that activity could be current events or social problems which are discussed by the students. Looking at it from a time standpoint, perhaps a student would be working with learning packages 2, 3, or 4 days a week and having parallel activities 1 or 2 days a week.

## Summary

Teachers should be cautious about experimenting with their new-found idea of learning packages without carefully planning their implementation strategy. A few students having a poor experience with learning packages can convince others that packages are ineffective. The widespread use of learning packages in a school can be destroyed by a teacher rushing about experimenting with various forms of learning packages. Ideas and attitudes are formed very quickly by students and members of the faculty. It takes only a few students giving negative comments for other students and faculty members to make their own value judgments against the program.

# BIBLIOGRAPHY

## The Transition from Group to Individualized Instruction

Abbott, M. "Teacher Aide Training Program, Grand Forks, North Dakota, 1970," Office of Education, 1970, 107 pp., ERIC No. ED045587.

Adamson, Elizabeth C. "Individualizing Instruction Through Grouping," *Utah Educational Review*, Vol. 62, No. 3, January-February 1969, pp. 14-15.

Allen, Dwight W. "How You Can Individualize Instruction, Right Now," *Nation's Schools*, Vol. 81, No. 4, April 1968, pp. 43-46 and 51.

Bannister, Richard. "Writing and Illustrating Multi-Media Lessons," *Educational Media*, Vol. 1, No. 4, July-August 1969, pp. 19-22.

Barone, F. "Communication Arts: Individualization Through Curriculum Content and the Small Group," *California English Journal*, October 1969, 4 pp., ERIC No. ED042747.

Becker, James W. "Incorporating the Products of Educational Development Into Practice," *Journal of Research and Development in Education*, Vol. 3, No. 2, Winter 1970.

Bicknell, John E. and others. "Summer Workshop in Individualization of Instruction, 1970. Selected Papers," State University of New York, Fredonia, 1970, 101 pp., ERIC No. ED049163.

Bolvin, J.O. and Glaser, Robert. "Developmental Aspects of Individually Prescribed Instruction," *Audiovisual Instruction*, Vol. 13, October 1968, pp. 828-831.

Bumstead, Richard. "Individualized Instruction," *Educate*, Vol. 2, January 1969, pp. 17-23.

Carrier, Robert. "Individualizing in One Room," *The Instructor*, August-September 1970, p. 70.

Dauw, E.G. "Individualized Instruction for Potential Dropouts," *National Association of Secondary School Principals Bulletin*, Vol. 54, September 1970, pp. 9-21.

Davies, Don. "Come Out from Under the Ivy," *American Education*, Vol. 6, No. 2, March 1970, pp. 28-31.

Deep, Donald. "The Teacher's Changing Role," *Elementary School Journal*,

Vol. 69, No. 2, November 1968, pp. 84-88.

Douglas, P. "Theory, Practice, and Perils of Independent Education," *Improving College and University Teaching,* Vol. 16, Autumn 1968, pp. 273-276.

Drumheller, Sidney, Jr. "Developing Individualized Instruction Program: A Transitional Support System for the 1970's," *Educational Technology,* Vol. 11, No. 10, October 1971, p. 34.

Dugger, Chester W. "A Teacher Discovers Individualized Instruction," *The Elementary School Journal,* Vol. 71, No. 7, April 1971, pp. 357-360.

Dunn, James A. "The Development of Procedures for the Individualization of Educational Programs." Paper presented at the American Psychological Association Convention, Miami, Florida, September 1970, 17 pp., ERIC No. ED043700.

Dunn, Rita S. "Individualized Instruction: Teaming Teachers and Media Specialists to Meet Individual Needs," *Audiovisual Instruction,* Vol. 16, No. 5, May 1971, pp. 27-28.

Dunn, Rita S. and Dunn, Kenneth. "Practical Questions Teachers Ask About Individualizing Instruction—And Some of the Answers," *Audiovisual Instruction,* Vol. 17, No. 1, January 1972, pp. 47-50.

Edling, Jack V. *Individualizing Instruction, Teaching Research,* Continuing Education Publishers, 1969.

Edling, Jack V. "Individualized Instruction The Way It Is—'70," *Audiovisual Instruction,* Vol. 15, No. 2, February 1970, pp. 13-16.

*Educational Leadership,* Vol. 27, No. 8, May 1970, see entire issue entitled "Projects, Packages, Programs," 110 pp.

Empey, D. "What is Individualized Study all About?," *Journal of Secondary Education,* Vol. 43, No. 3, March 1968, pp. 104-108.

English, Fenwick. "Questions and Answers of Differentiated Staffing," *Today's Education,* March 1969.

Esbensen, Thorwald. "Individualized Instruction and Self-Directed Learning," Washington, D.C.: National Science Teachers Association, 1970.

Flanagan, John C. "How Instructional Systems Will Manage Learning," *Nation's Schools,* Vol. 86, No. 4, October 1970, pp. 65-69 and 120.

Flanagan, John C. "Individualizing Education," *Education,* Vol. 90, No. 3, February-March 1970, pp. 191-206.

Foshay, Arthur W. "Curriculum for the '70s: Agenda for Invention," Center for the Study of Instruction, NEA, Washington, D.C., 1970, 77 pp., ERIC No. ED053075.

Frantz, Nevin R., Jr. and McConeghy, Gary L. "Individualized Instructional Systems for Industrial Education," *Audiovisual Instruction,* Vol. 17, No. 2, 1972, pp. 19-23.

Frazier, Alexander. "Individualized Instruction," *Educational Leadership,* Vol. 25, No. 7, April 1968, pp. 616-624.

French, Russell L. "Individualizing Classroom Communication," *Educational*

*Leadership,* Vol. 28, No. 2, November 1970, pp. 193-196.

Gard, Robert R. "Group Instruction with the Individual Touch," *The Clearing House,* Vol. 46, No. 2, October 1971, pp. 73-77.

Garvey, T.F. "Possible Over-Emphasis on Large-Group Instruction," *Education,* Vol. 89, February 1969, pp. 213-214.

Gehret, Kenneth G. "Richland's Teachers Prescribe Instruction the Way Doctors Prescribe Pills," *The American School Board Journal,* August 1969.

Green, Phyllis. "The P.E.P. Approach to Learning Diagnosis," *P.E.P. Capsules,* Vol. 2, No. 1, July 1968.

Grimsley, Edith E. "Before I Look Inside," *Educational Leadership,* Vol. 27, No. 8, May 1970, pp. 772-774.

Grobman, Hulda. "Educational Packages—Panaceas," *Educational Leadership,* Vol. 27, No. 8, May 1970, pp. 781-783.

Harmon, Katharine. "Getting Ready to Individualize," *Instructor,* June-July 1970, pp. 78-79.

Hawk, R.L. "Individualized Instruction in the School Setting," *Education Horizons,* Vol. 49, Spring 1971, pp. 73-80.

Heathers, Glen. "A Definition of Individualized Education," paper presented at AERA Annual Meeting, New York, 1971, 5 pp., ERIC No. ED050012.

Henderson, George L. "Individualized Instruction: Sweet in Theory, Sour in Practice," *Arithmetic Teacher,* Vol. 19, January 1972, pp. 17-22.

Holland, James A. "The Misplaced Adaptation to Individual Differences," paper presented at the American Psychological Association Convention, 1969.

Howes, Virgil M. *Individualizing Instruction in Reading and Social Studies: Selected Readings on Programs and Practices,* Macmillan, 1970.

Howes, Virgil M. *Individualizing Instruction in Science and Mathematics: Selected Readings on Programs, Practices and Uses of Technology,* Macmillan, 1970.

Hunter, Madeline. "Tailor Your Teaching to II," *Instructor,* Vol. 79, No. 7, March 1970, pp. 53-63.

Jahorik, J.A. "Individual Instruction and Group Instruction: A Case Study," *Journal of Educational Research,* Vol. 62, July 1969, pp. 453-455.

Jasek, Marilyn. "Breaking Barriers By Individualizing," *Childhood Education,* October 1968.

*Journal of Secondary Education,* Vol. 46, No. 5, May 1971. See entire issue entitled "Learning Packages: Management, Instructional and Learning Strategies," 45 pp.

Kapfer, Philip G. "An Instructional Management Strategy for Individualizing Instruction," *Phi Delta Kappan,* Vol. 49, January 1968, pp. 260-263.

Kapfer, Philip G. "Practical Approaches to Individualizing Instruction," *Educational Screen and Audiovisual Guide,* Vol. 47, May 1968, pp.

14-16.

Klausmeier, Herbert J., Sorenson, Juanita S. and Ghatala, Elizabeth Schwenn. "Individually Guided Motivation: Developing Self-Direction and Pro-social Behaviors," *The Elementary School Journal*, Vol. 71, No. 6, March 1971, pp. 339-350.

Klingstedt, Joe Lars. "Developing Instructional Modules for Individualized Learning," *Educational Technology*, Vol. 11, No. 10, October 1971, pp. 73-74.

LaPlante, William A. "Real Reforms Still Needed on Individualization," *Nation's Schools*, Vol. 87, No. 2, February 1971, p. 64.

Lee, Dorris M. "Do we Group in an Individualized Program," *Childhood Education*, Vol. 45, No. 4, December 1968, pp. 197-199.

Lieberman, Marcus. "Individualized Instruction," *Illinois Education*, Vol. 58, No. 9, May 1970, pp. 389-392.

Lynch, William W. and Ames, Carole. "Factors Related to Individual Training," Indiana University, Bloomington, 1971, 27 pp., ERIC No. ED049156.

McKeegan, Hugh. "What Individualized Instruction Means to the Curriculum Director," *Audiovisual Instruction*, Vol. 13, No. 3, March 1968, pp. 232-239.

McQueen, Mildred. "Individualized Instruction: Many Names, Many Sponsorships, But One Common Element," *Education Digest*, Vol. 36, No. 8, April 1971, pp. 25-28.

Melching, William H. "Behavioral Objectives and Individualization of Instruction." Paper presented at the Annual Meeting of the Southwestern Psychological Association, Austin, Texas, April 1969, 13 pp., ERIC No. ED048821.

Miller, Jack W. and Miller, Haroldine G. "Individualizing Instruction Through Diagnosis and Evaluation," *Childhood Education*, Vol. 46, No. 8, May 1970, pp. 517-521.

Morley, Franklin P. "The Commercial Package and the Local Supervisor," *Educational Leadership*, Vol. 27, No. 8, May 1970, pp. 792-795.

Neufeld, K. Allen. "Individualized Curriculum in Instruction." Proceedings of International Conference on Elementary Education, Banff, Alberta, October 1969, 220 pp., ERIC No. ED046122.

Nichols, Eugene D. "Is Individualization the Answer?," *Educational Technology*, Vol. 12, No. 3, March 1972, pp. 52-57.

Nunney, Derek N. and Hill, Joseph E. "Personalized Educational Programs," *Audiovisual Instruction*, Vol. 17, No. 2, February 1972, pp. 16-18.

O'Donnel, Patrick A. and Lavaroni, Charles W. "Elements of Individualized Instruction," *Education Digest*, Vol. 36, No. 1, September 1970, pp. 17-19.

Peck, Robert F. "Personalized Education: An Attainable Goal in the Seventies," Office of Education (DHEW) Bureau of Research, January

1970, pp. 1-18, ERIC No. ED0510137.

Powell, William. "The Nature of Individual Differences," in *Organizing for Individual Differences*, Newark, Delaware: International Reading Association, 1968.

Read, Edwin A. "Educational Practice and the Theory of Continuous Pupil Progress," *Audiovisual Instruction*, Vol. 15, No. 2, February 1970, pp. 38-40.

Reeves, Harriet Ramsey. "Individual Conferences—Diagnostic Tools," *The Reading Teacher*, Vol. 24, February 1971, pp. 411-415.

Rhetts, J.E. "The Impact of Student Learning Style on Curriculum Assignment and Performance in the PLAN Program of Individualized Instruction," *Education*, Vol. 90, No. 3, February-March 1970, pp. 248-251.

Ringis, R. Herbert. "What Is an Instructional Package?," *Journal of Secondary Education*, Vol. 46, No. 5, May 1971, pp. 201-205.

Saratain, H.W. "What Are the Advantages and Disadvantages of Individualized Instruction?," *International Reading Association Conference Proceedings*, No. 13, Part 2, 1969, pp. 328-356.

Scanlon, Robert A. "The Expansion of an Innovation," *Audiovisual Instruction*, Vol. 13, November 1968, pp. 946-948.

Scanlon, Robert A. and Brown, Mary V. "Inservice Education for Individualized Instruction," *Educational Technology*, Vol. 10, No. 2, February 1970, pp. 62-64.

Scanlon, Robert and Moshy, Claire. "Teacher Education for Individualized Instruction," *Teacher Education and Individualized Instruction*, mimeographed paper, Philadelphia: Research for Better Schools, Inc., May 1968, 10 pp.

Shavelson, R.J. and Munger, M.R. "Individualized Instruction: A Systems Approach," *Journal of Educational Research*, Vol. 63, February 1970, pp. 263-268.

Singh, J.M. "Investigation of the Effect of Individualized Enrichment Homework Upon the Academic Achievement of Children in the Fourth, Fifth and Sixth Grades," International Reading Association, May 1970, 5 pp., ERIC No. ED042585.

Stanhope, C.L. "Independent Study Option: Timberlane Regional High School," *Journal of Health, Physical Education, Recreation*, Plaistow, New Hampshire, Vol. 42, September 1971, 24 pp.

Starr, Robert J. "A Suggestion for Individualizing Instruction Within a Traditional School Organization," *Audiovisual Instruction*, Vol. 16, No. 8, October 1971, pp. 68-70.

Stodghill, Ronald. "New Goals for Individualization," *Educational Leadership*, Vol. 29, No. 4, pp. 295-300.

Tanzman, Jack. "Individualized Instruction Requires Media Training," *School Management*, Vol. 15, March 1971, p. 28.

Taylor, Gary R. "The Lone Learner," *Audiovisual Instruction*, Vol. 16, No. 4, April 1971, pp. 54-55.

Thompson, M.M. "A Survey of Independent Study Practices at the University Level," *Educational Record*, Vol. 51, Fall 1970, pp. 392-395.

Tramel, M.E. "Use Norwalk Ideas and Most of Your Teenagers will Learn at Their Own Pace: Learning Packages," *American School Board Journal*, Vol. 155, March 1971, pp. 40-47.

Ubben, Gerald. "A Look at Nongradedness and Self-Paced Learning," *Audiovisual Instruction*, Vol. 15, No. 2, February 1970, pp. 31-33.

Unruh, Glenys. "Can I be Replaced by a Package?," *Educational Leadership*, Vol. 27, No. 8, May 1970, pp. 763-766.

Weisse, E.B. "Curriculum Restructuring," *Wisconsin Journal of Education*, Vol. 100, January 1968, pp. 11-12.

Wiener, Wik and others. "Reorganizing the Schools for IPI: Jamesville DeWitt Central Schools, New York," *National Association Secondary School Principals Bulletin*, Vol. 55, March 1971, pp. 59-67.

White, Beverly L. "The Package and the Supervisor," *Educational Leadership*, Vol. 27, No. 8, May 1970, pp. 788-791.

Wolfe, Elaine. "Individual Instruction" in *Organizing for Individual Differences*, Newark, Delaware: International Reading Association, 1968, pp. 47-68.

# PART 2

## ESTABLISHED
## INDIVIDUALIZED INSTRUCTION FORMATS

# PART 2

## Established Individualized Instruction Formats

The selections in Part 2 review the program characteristics of several of the more successful and widely utilized individualized instruction formats.

The first format is the system of Individually Prescribed Instruction, known as IPI, which was initiated by the Learning Research and Development Center at the University of Pittsburgh and the Oakleaf Elementary School of Pittsburgh. The project has grown tremendously and presently includes over a hundred different schools scattered throughout the country. Research for Better Schools, Inc., of Philadelphia, has taken over the responsibility of disseminating, evaluating and redesigning materials to effectively meet the individual needs of each learner in the IPI system.

The second format is entitled Project PLAN, or Program for Learning in Accordance with Needs. The PLAN system was developed by the American Institutes for Research and the Westinghouse Learning Corporation in Palo Alto. These two organizations, working with a select group of schools in various parts of the country, developed an individualized learning system for grades 1 through 12 in the areas of language arts, science, social studies and math. The PLAN system has been expanded and is in use on a self-supporting basis in schools all over the country.

The third format is the LAP, or Learning Activity Package, system, which was originally developed by the Nova School System of Fort Lauderdale in an attempt to upgrade their curriculum by providing materials designed to compensate for the individual differences among learners.

The fourth approach is the UNIPAC concept, which began as a Kettering Foundation project designed to establish a "bank" of individualized instruction materials which could be drawn upon by any teacher who joined the system. The UNIPAC system is now being disseminated by the UNIPAC Teachers Exchange in Salt Lake City, Utah.

Several aspects of each of these formats are presented in order to provide the reader with a general overview of each system. The bibliography at the end of the section contains information related to a large number of programs designed to implement individualized instruction programs in particular schools or subject areas.

In the first article, Robert Scanlon presents an overview of the IPI approach to individualized instruction. Scanlon lists six aspects of instruction as they relate to individuals as his main plea for IPI. He also goes through a few historical aspects and provides rationale for IPI expansion on a carefully controlled basis. The author includes a diagram of an IPI system and a diagram that depicts the special characteristics of IPI.

Hosticka goes on to further explain IPI, by presenting examples of the IPI elementary math program. The article reveals how the math curriculum is broken down into content areas and describes how a learner is diagnosed and placed on the IPI system.

The next article deals with the PLAN approach to individualized instruction. John Flanagan, the director and father of Project PLAN, designates the three main functions of any educational program and describes how these functions are achieved in the PLAN program. He goes on to break down the major components of the design and implementation of PLAN and provides comments on the program's significance and possible future development.

The next two articles discuss interpretations of the Learning Activity Package system. The first article, by Arena, is a brief introduction to LAPs, including a description of the LAP format. Arena discusses the applicability of LAPs to all schools and provides a list of suggestions for schools contemplating individualizing their programs.

In the second article on LAPs, Sally Cardarelli provides an in-depth description of the individual components that comprise a Learning Activity Package. She lists the four basic philosophies of the LAP program and touches upon several further considerations, from student responsibility to teacher orientation. Also included in the article are student suggested problems and group solutions to demonstrate the effectiveness of classroom management.

The next article explains the UNIPAC concept of individualized instruction. Kapfer and Swenson review the operations of the UNIPAC system. Also included is a complete description of the components of a UNIPAC and a working plan for implementing a continous progress individualized curriculum utilizing UNIPACs.

The last article in this section discusses the similarities between the various individualized instruction packages. It breaks down the package structure into seven basic components and elaborates on each one. The purpose of this article is to describe the common components of an individualized instruction package in order that they may be used as a guide for evaluating the various package designs discussed in this section. Included in this article is an evaluation guide which may be used to evaluate the strengths and weaknesses of the basic components of an individualized instruction package.

# 9

## Individually Prescribed Instruction:
## A System of Individualized Instruction

Robert G. Scanlon

Individually Prescribed Instruction (IPI) is an instructional system based on a specific set of educational objectives, and has correlated to these objectives diagnostic instruments, teaching materials and methods.

Since IPI curriculum is based on a carefully sequenced and detailed specification of educational objectives, these objectives are used in planning most other aspects of the instructional system. Lesson materials, teaching methods, instructional settings and diagnostic tests, as well as the monitoring systems, are geared to the instructional objectives, thereby permitting pupils to proceed quite independently.

A basic aspect of IPI is a rather detailed provision for diagnosis of pupil skills and abilities and continuous monitoring of pupil progress. Detailed diagnosis is made of the initial state of a learner coming into a particular instructional situation. Four types of assessment instruments are used in IPI. They include a placement instrument, used in locating students on the learning continuum; a pretest of each unit of work used to measure the specific objectives within a unit; a posttest of each unit to determine mastery; and curriculum-embedded tests measuring progress toward an objective.

A unique feature of IPI is its requirement that each pupil's work be guided by a written Prescription prepared to meet his

Reprinted from *Educational Technology*, Vol. 10, No. 12, December 1970, pp. 44-46, by permission of author and publisher.

individual needs and interests. The Prescription is an important two-way communication link between the student and the teacher. The teacher communicates to the student the choices made in different materials and different settings to achieve an objective. Information about student progress is communicated to the teacher through the Prescription. For the initial Prescription the teacher will generally consider the following factors: (1) the ability level of the child, (2) the general maturity of the child, (3) the type of learner and (4) the student's reaction in various instructional settings.

The student generally begins work independently on the prescribed materials. Most of the students can proceed through the prescribed materials with a minimum of teacher direction and instruction. When assistance requiring extended explanations or instruction is required, the teacher gives such assistance. In order to free the teacher for instructional decision-making, tutoring and evaluation of student progress, the scoring of materials and tests and the tabulation of the student data are done by teacher aides or in some cases by the children themselves.

Inherent in the design of the IPI system is its capability for improvement. An essential aspect of individualized instruction is the provision for charting the progress of each student as he moves through the curriculum and the availability of these reports for teacher use. This information is necessary for individual Prescriptions and classroom organization. The data to be used for Prescription writing should include: (1) general ability level in the given subject, (2) the degree of mastery or lack of mastery in each skill in the particular unit assigned to the student, (3) information related to the child's progress in previous units directly related to the skills in the present unit, (4) detailed information related to the pupil's progress as he moves through the various tasks related to the particular skill or objective assigned and (5) general learning characteristics of the pupil as they relate to the assigned task.

Information needed by the teacher for day-to-day classroom organization must include: (1) level, unit and skill of each pupil in the class, (2) the approximate length of time (days) the student has been working on a given skill and (3) the next immediate skill for each pupil in the class. With this information the teachers can organize the classes for small and large group instruction, peer group discussions or individualized tutoring. The availability, accuracy and the format of these reports are crucial to the success of IPI.

Furthermore, these data are used for continual evaluation and strengthening of the curriculum and instructional procedures, permitting the developers constantly to improve the system.

The mode, as developed, considers the following aspects of instruction as they relate to the individual: (1) detailed specification of educational objectives, (2) organization of methods and materials to attain these objectives, including a variety of paths for attainment of mastery of any given objective, (3) a procedure and process for the diagnosis of student achievement in terms of the educational objectives, (4) individual daily evaluation and guidance of each pupil, including a system for individually prescribing the learning task that the student is ready to undertake, (5) provision for frequent monitoring of student performance in order to inform both the pupil and the teacher of progress toward an objective and (6) continual evaluation and strengthening of curriculum and instructional procedures.

Figure 1 displays the system of Individually Prescribed Instruction.

Special characteristics of Individually Prescribed Instruction are depicted in Figure 2.

## Historical Aspects

The Learning Research and Development Center at the University of Pittsburgh is the creator of Individually Prescribed Instruction and specializes in the research and basic design of new educational technology.

Individually Prescribed Instruction was developed by Drs. Glaser, Bolvin and Lindvall with the cooperation of the University of Pittsburgh and the Baldwin-Whitehall Public Schools of suburban Pittsburgh.

During the school year of 1963-64, the Learning Research

# Figure 1

## The System of Individually Prescribed Instruction

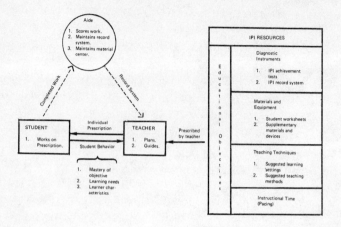

# Figure 2

## Special Characteristics of IPI

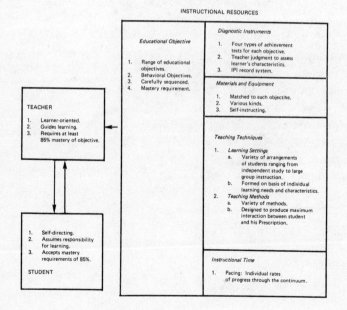

and Development Center and the Baldwin-Whitehall Public Schools initiated an experimental project to investigate the feasibility of a system of individualized instruction in an entire K-6 school. This came about as a result of a series of prior exploratory studies, begun in 1961-62, designed to test preliminary notions on a smaller scale in single classrooms. The work started with the use of programmed instruction in an intact classroom—"intact classroom" being defined as a classroom unit in which the teaching practices were oriented toward the conventional grade-by-grade progression of learning.

As work proceeded, it soon became apparent that the significant individualization feature of programmed instruction could not be manifested unless the intact classroom changed its organization to permit a more flexible progression.

As a result, a second set of studies was instituted, using programmed instruction and other materials in a more flexible context. Out of this experience grew the Individually Prescribed Instruction project currently in progress, in which various combinations of instructional materials—including programmed materials, special workbook and test procedures—and teacher practices are being used for the purpose of adapting them to individual student requirements.

Research for Better Schools, a Title IV Regional Educational Laboratory, has the major responsibility for the field development, field testing and dissemination of Individually Prescribed Instruction. Included in this responsibility is the study of problems encountered in a variety of institutional settings. It also includes the investigation of the strategies that are necessary for widespread dissemination of IPI. This activity is of major proportion, since the task of implementing this type of instruction in a variety of ongoing school programs is quite different from that of implementing IPI in the Oakleaf School.

## Summary and Comments

The model, as developed, considers the following aspects of instruction as they relate to the individual: (1) detailed specifications of educational objectives, (2) organization of methods and materials to attain these objectives, (3) careful determination of each pupil's present competence in a given subject, (4) daily evaluation and guidance of each pupil on an individual basis, (5) frequent monitoring of student performance and (6) continual evaluation in order to inform both the pupil and teacher of progress toward an objective as well as to strengthen the curriculum and instructional procedures. It appears that the specific model for the development of Individually Prescribed Instruction has generalizable aspects for the development of instructional systems that permit a high degree of individualization.

Historically, the Learning Research and Development Center and its work in the Oakleaf School as well as the efforts of Research for Better Schools in establishing demonstration projects and *expanding IPI on a carefully controlled* basis has long-term payoff. Blending of resources has hastened the development and refinement of the IPI project. The critical mass of talent and resources is a unique experience in American education. Certainly the identification of specific problems related to an innovation and progress toward their solution have been accelerated.

Specifying criteria for readiness to accept IPI as a school program has been highly relevant. School administrators need precise information to communicate effectively about the introduction of IPI into their schools. The variety of audiences that must be satisfied—teachers, students, parents and school boards— have the right to know what the adoption of such an innovation means, in terms of both philosophy and finances.

Training of administrators and teachers is absolutely essential for effective implementation of IPI. New roles are served by both groups, and retraining is necessary. Most elementary school principals are not familiar with the need for developing flexible scheduling, in order to provide children with both professional and non-professional services when they need them. Since IPI depends on the administrator of the school to be the instructional leader, to have the ability to meet with his staff, and to help his teachers refine the system and solve problems, communication skills are a necessity. Analysis of data is another critical area in retraining of administrators. The principal needs new skills in looking at the flow of information that is passing over his desk concerning both the teachers and students in his school. Knowing what to look for in this wealth of data, and how to analyze it in terms of refining the project, become critical. Teacher education efforts have been concentrated on the development of a training program that would enable the school to work on its own training program.

IPI is one innovation based on research which uses current information to improve its techniques, procedures and materials. The strategy for expansion is a unique step in American education. The success generated has provided significant insight into the age-old problem of providing an individual plan for each youngster based on his needs and characteristics.

# 10

## IPI: A Program for Individualizing Elementary Mathematics Instruction

Alice Hosticka

Individualization of a curriculum requires that the curriculum make provisions for each person's strengths, his weaknesses and his present level of knowledge in the content area which is being individualized. There are some common misinterpretations concerning individualization that many people make, due to the fact that these features appear in many programs that are presently individualized: 1) Individualization requires that a person work alone. This is not true. Individualization allows for several people who share the same needs and who are at the same point to work together on that need (all such groupings should be extremely fluid). 2) Individualization means working at one's own rate. This statement is not completely accurate. Rate or speed of work is certainly one factor necessary for individualization, but style of learning, interest in subject matter, strengths and weaknesses in communication skills, and ability to work in the abstract are also important factors to be included in an individualized program. 3) An individualized program uses a programmed text. An individualized curriculum may include programmed texts; but if the curriculum is completely individualized, it must also provide other types of lessons to attempt to provide for different learning styles.

While many efforts have been made to individualize classrooms and curricula, perhaps the most far-reaching non-commercial effort is being carried out jointly by the Learning Research

Reprinted from *Educational Technology*, Vol. 12, No. 3, March 1972, pp. 20-23, by permission of author and publisher.

and Development Center at the University of Pittsburgh and Research for Better Schools in Philadelphia. This program is Individually Prescribed Instruction (IPI). IPI is presently working in three main content areas: math, science and reading. The Math Curriculum is the IPI program discussed in this article.

Before one can effectively teach a student a concept, it is important to be able to state: 1) exactly what it is you want the student to learn, 2) how you will know when the student has learned it, 3) what the student already knows about the subject to be learned and 4) what more the student needs to know. The more one knows about each learner's style of learning, the easier it is to facilitate the learning of the specified content.

In order to know what you want the learner to learn, one must know the structure of the content. It is necessary to analyze and sequence the steps and skills in the content area being taught. In IPI Math, the total curriculum is broken down into ten content areas: Numeration/Place Value, Addition/Subtraction, Multiplication, Division, Fractions, Money, Time, Systems of Measurement, Geometry and Applications.[1] Each content area is broken down into levels of difficulty. When put into a matrix format, each cell represents a unit. This matrix is presented in Figure 1.

Each unit is composed of a series of objectives stated in behavioral terms. These objectives are ordered with prerequisite objectives defined in the unit, so that it is not necessary to proceed from the first objective in a unit to the last in an ordinal sequence. In Level C, Addition and Subtraction, for example, there are eight objectives which can be structured as follows:

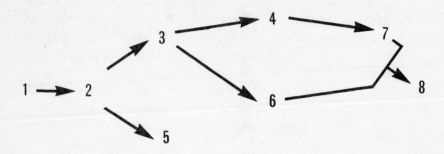

*Figure 1*

*Diagram of Units*

|  | A | B | C | D | E | F | G |
|---|---|---|---|---|---|---|---|
| Numeration/<br>Place Value | X | X | X | X | X | X | X |
| Addition/<br>Subtraction | X | X | X | X | X | X | X |
| Multiplication |  | X | X | X | X | X | X |
| Division |  | X | X | X | X | X | X |
| Fractions | X | X | X | X | X | X | X |
| Money | X | X | X | X |  |  |  |
| Time | X | X | X | X | X |  |  |
| Systems of<br>Measurement |  | X | X | X | X | X | X |
| Geometry |  | X | X | X | X | X | X |
| Applications |  | X | X | X | X | X | X |

X= Units with objectives.

This means, upon mastery of objective 1, the student in this unit must proceed to objective 2. Mastery of objective 2 implies readiness for either objective 3 or 5, and so on. Some possible sequences through this unit are:

1, 2, 5, 3, 4, 6, 7, 8
1, 2, 3, 4, 7, 6, 8, 5
1, 2, 5, 3, 4, 7, 6, 8
etc.

Once the content has been defined and sequences for a curriculum established, the problem of defining the correct placement of the child within the content and sequence is necessary. In IPI this is done by a series of criterion-referenced tests.[2] The child must have 85 percent of each test correct in order to be considered to have mastery of the items on the test. To be placed in the curriculum, the student takes a placement test at a level selected by the tester. The test is subdivided into units and selected skills. For each section (or unit) at the level of the placement test in which the student receives 85 percent or better, he is tested at the next higher level in that area; for each sub-test score of 20 percent or under, the student is tested at the next lower level in the area for all scores greater than 20 percent and less than 85 percent (20 percent $<$ X $<$ 85 percent) the student places in the unit tested. For example, if a student's placement test (profile) looks like the one in Figure 2, it means the student was first tested at Level C. This can be determined by noting that every unit in Level C shows a placement test score.

Column C shows his scores on this placement test. Based on this set of scores, the following actions would be taken: (1) the student placed at Level C in the areas of Numeration/Place Value (50 percent), Multiplication (80 percent), Division (60 percent), Systems of Measurement (48 percent) and Applications (84 percent). (2) For the units in Fractions (20 percent) and Time (13 percent), the student would take a placement test at Level B. (3) For the areas of Addition/Subtraction (90 percent), Money (85 percent) and Geometry (100 percent), the student takes placement tests for Level D. (4) This process is repeated until the student has a score between 20 percent and 85 percent in a unit for each area. (There are two exceptions to this; they are: (1) when a student scores lower than 20 percent on the first unit in an area, he starts in the first unit; and (2) when he scores greater than 85 percent in the last unit in the area, he is finished with the area.) The student with a placement profile as in Figure 2 is working at Level A in Time; Level B in Fractions; Level C in Numeration/ Place Value, Multiplication, Division, Systems of Measurements and Applications; Level D in Addition/Subtraction and Level E in

Geometry. Although he has a score of 85 percent in money at Level D, this is the last unit in Money (refer to Figure 1); and, therefore, the student has completed the money area.

*Figure 2*

|        | A   | B   | C    | D   | E   | F | G |
|--------|-----|-----|------|-----|-----|---|---|
| Num/PV |     |     | 50%  |     |     |   |   |
| Add/Sub |    |     | 90%  | 83% |     |   |   |
| Mult   |     |     | 80%  |     |     |   |   |
| Div    |     |     | 60%  |     |     |   |   |
| Frac   |     | 60% | 20%  |     |     |   |   |
| Mon    |     |     | 85%  | 85% |     |   |   |
| Time   | 80% | 20% | 13%  |     |     |   |   |
| SOM    |     |     | 48%  |     |     |   |   |
| Geom   |     |     | 100% | 90% | 40% |   |   |
| App    |     |     | 84%  |     |     |   |   |

A student with this type of placement profile theoretically has many places to go. The teacher may choose to place the student in Level B Fractions, pick up Level A Time, then go on to Level C Place Value, and work the Level C units, followed by Level D, etc. (skipping those units which the student has mastered). Or, the teacher may choose to begin in Level A Time. The option is always open for the teacher to administer a pretest on any or all units a student has placed out of. This pretest then acts as an extra safety measure to ensure that the student passed the placement test because of knowledge of the subject area and not because of some fluke. Most of the units require some skills from units preceding them in a given level, as well as skills from units in still other preceding levels.

When a student starts work in a unit, he is first pretested on every skill within the unit. For example, if the student whose placement profile is shown in Figure 2 begins in B Fractions, he will be given a pretest which tests all four skills in that unit. At this point a score of 85 percent or better will allow the student to pretest out of the unit. If the student's pretest score showed that he needs work on skills 2 and 4, but had mastery in skills 1 and 3, he would be given work only on those skills he did not master. This skill lesson plan for each student is called his *prescription*.

The materials for each skill are varied. The constant set of materials is the *Standard Teaching Sequence Booklet*. This booklet is set up in a quasi-program format. This is done with as little reading as possible in the booklets and an attempt to make them self-instructional. Some skills, especially at the lower levels, include lessons that are on taped discs or cassettes, for those students with reading limitations. Lessons that use concrete materials are now being developed for the beginning lessons.

The prescription for each student tells the order in which he will proceed through the objectives in the unit and what work he will do for each objective. If a teacher judges from test information that a student knows most of the information and only needs some quick review to master the objective, the prescription may only consist of two or three pages in the *Standard Teaching Sequence Booklet*. If, on the other hand, the teacher feels that the student needs a great deal of concept development in an objective, the teacher may assign work with concrete materials, arrange to have a small group seminar, use taped materials, work on all pages in the *Standard Teaching Sequence Booklet*, or work with a combination of any of these materials.

As a child proceeds through a lesson, he is again tested to see if he has reached mastery. These tests are embedded in the teaching materials and are called Curriculum Embedded Tests

(CETs). When a student receives mastery on a CET, he proceeds to the next skill to be mastered in the unit. If he receives a score of 85 percent on the posttest, he proceeds to the next unit. If not, he goes back and continues work on the skills in which he is weak within the unit.

All tests used in the curriculum are parallel tests. The items are designed to be of equal difficulty on each test and to cover the domain of the objective.

To this point, the focus of this article has been the explanation of the hardware of the model: (1) behavioral objectives to define the content, (2) levels and area of study to define sequence and (3) testing instruments to place the child in the curriculum and to monitor his progress through the curriculum.

A program which claims to be individualized cannot meet this claim without a mode for interaction between the student in the program and the program itself. In IPI this most important mode of interaction is the classroom teacher. When the classroom focus shifts from the needs and abilities of the norm to the needs and abilities of the individual, the role of the teacher must also change. The teacher needs to spend less time preparing materials, lectures and activities to be used by the entire class at one time and more of her energies thinking about tutoring situations and self-instructional materials. The teacher needs to know more about the subject-matter, since she comes into closer contact with more students who are having trouble and who need her to identify what their problems are and how to remedy them. She needs to know how to build upon the child's own self-initiation and control to help accomplish academic ends and spend less energy teaching him to conform to a group expectancy. The evaluation process becomes more of a diagnostic process in which the teacher has to be able to identify what a child needs in order to accomplish the given objective.

IPI has given teachers instruments for evaluation of the individual and the beginning set of materials to use. It has not, however (as many critics fear), led the teacher's role away from student contact and concern, and toward that of a technician. In an IPI model, the teacher actually has more contact with his students. The teacher must work closely with the student in a one-to-one situation when the *Standard Teaching Sequence Booklet* is not meeting the student's needs, and must also plan small seminars and tutorial lessons. The evaluation required of a teacher is more rigorous than norm group evaluations. The teacher is given data on each student from an objective instrument and is asked to make decisions about the student's mastery and needs, based on the data. If errors are judged by the teacher to be due to other than lack of knowledge on the student's part (carelessness, unclear questions, etc.), the 85 percent mastery can be waived. IPI, instead of replacing a teacher, requires the teacher to possess more knowledge of the student and to make more decisions that affect the child's education than in a norm-referenced classroom. The teacher becomes the essential (diagnostic and teaching) factor necessary to make an individualized program feasible.

## Notes

1.   All examples and specifics for the IPI Math Curriculum are based on the 1970 Research for Better Schools Continuum.

2.   Here, a criterion-referenced test refers to a test that the child masters when he meets a criterion level. In IPI this level is set at 85 percent of all given problems. Group norms are not used in the IPI testing situation. A score less than 85 percent is not considered a failure, but, rather, an indication that the student needs more work in the area to obtain mastery.

# 11

## Project PLAN: Basic Assumptions, Implementation and Significance

John C. Flanagan

The findings from the national survey of education conducted for the United States Office of Education in 1960 emphasized certain important deficiencies in American education. Two deficiencies appeared central to the failure of local school programs. The first of these was the inadequate adjustment of the educational program to meet the needs of students having wide variations in their interests, backgrounds and current level of development. The importance of individualizing instruction has been loudly proclaimed for more than 50 years. However, the Project TALENT survey made it very clear that the homogeneous grouping, tracking, differentiated assignments and other efforts were not meeting the needs of students. The most striking evidence of the failure to adjust instruction for individual differences is provided by the low levels of reading ability found and the evidence of the assignment of inappropriate material for study by the students. This latter point is suggested by the finding that about 34 percent of both the boys and the girls in the twelfth grade stated that about half the time or more frequently, "I read material over and over again without really understanding what I have read."

The second important deficiency in education found in Project TALENT related to the guidance programs in the schools. It was found, for example, that only 19 percent of the boys who indicated in the tenth grade they were planning one of 30

Reprinted from *Journal of Secondary Education*, Vol. 46, No. 4, April 1971, pp. 173-178, by permission of author and publisher.

occupations as a career reported they had the same plans three years later. Clearly it is not possible to develop an effective individualized educational program for students who do not have relatively stable and realistic goals.

The basic functions of American education have been changing during the past 50 years, but the curriculum and methods have not kept pace with these new responsibilities. There is considerable agreement at the present time that the three main functions of the educational program should be: (1) the preparation of the student for an occupational role; (2) the preparation of the student for leisure time, avocational and cultural activities; and (3) the preparation of the student to assume personal, social and citizenship responsibilities. Thus, the schools, rather than being merely responsible for providing basic skills in reading, writing and arithmetic and preparing a small portion of the young people for advanced education in colleges and universities, are responsible for a much broader development. This would include such areas as how to think, learning how to learn, acquiring an understanding of opportunities in terms of roles and activities for which the students might prepare, and a meaningful understanding of the degree to which they have developed basic skills and abilities.

The approach and general considerations which provide the basis for the design of a Program for Learning in Accordance with Needs (PLAN) include the following ten points. These do not provide the basis for a new course of study or a new methodology for education, but rather a structured system within which an effective program of individualized education can be carried out.

1. The student must be the center of the educational program. In his new role the student will be assisted to formulate his educational goals, to plan a program for achieving them, to take responsibility for this educational program and to manage both the strategy and tactics for achieving his educational goals.

2. The teacher will play an important new role in this educational system. In this role the teacher will work with the students as individuals rather than as a class. The teacher needs to become better acquainted with each student both as a learner and

as a person. The teacher's functions will be primarily those of a diagnostician, tutor and special resource to the student.

3. The educational program of the student will be clearly stated in terms of both long and short range performance objectives. The progress of the student with respect to all of these objectives will be evaluated at periodic intervals. Schools using this system should be able to achieve a rather precise degree of accountability for their programs. They will also have the information required for the types of formative evaluation which will enable continuous improvement of the effectiveness of the program.

4. Programs will be developed using available published instructional materials, including audiovisual aids. The general principle underlying the design of these programs will be their efficiency in assisting the student to achieve the performance objectives in his program of studies.

5. To assist the teacher in the new role outlined above, the support of a computer is provided to perform numerous clerical tasks including test scoring, record keeping, matching the interests and abilities of the students with the available learning materials and assisting with the student's long range planning.

6. To insure optimal utilization of both the findings and procedures of research and development in education and related fields, the design and development staff includes behavioral scientists with experiences in both classroom teaching and educational technology. Many of the failures of innovative educational programs can be directly traced to the lack of sophistication of the development staff in this field.

7. The central importance of selecting the most appropriate topics and objectives from the various disciplines makes it essential that curriculum experts and scholars along with related specialists be used in deciding on both the content and objectives to be offered the students at various levels in the disciplines included in the program.

8. To utilize the experience and judgment of classroom teachers with respect to the interests and learning habits of students, the development and design of the teaching-learning

units for student use should be done by teachers. It is also important to try out the completed units in the classroom to obtain further insights with respect to the effectiveness of various types of instructional materials.

9. The wide variation in the needs and situations in local school districts makes it important that active school administrators assist in the design and adaptation of this type of educational system to meet local needs and local problems.

10. A major consideration in the development and design of a new educational system is that the costs of adding this system be kept within the range of existing school budgets. This indicates that it is essential that the benefits to be achieved by special expenditures for this program be defined and evaluated as accurately as possible.

## The Design and Implementation of PLAN

The initial design and development of PLAN was begun in 1966. In September 1971 it is anticipated that approximately 25,000 students in grades 1-12 will be participating in PLAN. During the academic year 1966-67 an instructional program for grades 1, 5 and 9 was developed. The tryout of this instructional program began in September 1967 in 12 cooperating school districts,* using about 2,000 students. Each year since then the American Institutes for Research and teachers from the cooperating school districts with support and assistance from the Westinghouse Learning Corporation have developed the instructional program for three additional grades. The design and present status of the five principal components of the system are as follows:

*Bethel Park School District, Bethel Park, Pennsylvania; Hicksville Public School District, Hicksville, New York; Pittsburgh Public Schools, Pittsburgh, Pennsylvania; Quincy Public Schools, Quincy, Massachusetts; Wood County Schools, Parkersburg, West Virginia; Penn-Trafford School District, Harrison City, Pennsylvania; Archdiocese of San Francisco, San Francisco, California; Fremont Unified School District, Fremont, California; San Carlos Elementary School District, San Carlos, California; San Jose Unified School District, San Jose, California; Santa Clara Unified School District, Santa Clara, California; Union Elementary School District, San Jose, California.

1. *Educational Objectives.* With the aid of four national advisory panels composed of scholars and curriculum experts in the fields of language arts, social studies, mathematics and science, the topics, objectives and general scope and sequence of the instructional materials have been developed for PLAN. These are primarily based on the reports of various committees which have been studying the curriculum in connection with new government-sponsored developmental programs. They are also somewhat limited by the availability of materials to meet all the instructional objectives the experts consider desirable.

There are approximately 1,500 specific objectives listed in each of the four fields. It is not expected that any one student would achieve all of these objectives. With the assistance of the records of his past achievements, his interests and his long range goals, the student would be aided in selecting for inclusion in his educational program those objectives most directly related to his anticipated goals.

2. *Learning Methods and Materials.* In structuring the learning program, about five objectives are grouped together in a module. Each of the objectives is intended to require two to three hours to achieve. Thus, the module is intended as approximately a two-week segment of instruction. To provide the necessary flexibility for individualizing education, more than one teaching-learning unit is usually provided for each module. A teaching-learning unit is a four-to eight-page guide which lists each objective along with materials to be used by the student in attaining this objective.

It has been possible to evaluate the effectiveness of the various instructional methods and materials by analyzing the results on tests taken by the students who have used various teaching-learning units. The modules make it possible to develop a program of studies for each student, using the information as to his present mastery of the objectives in the various modules and the indication of his needs in terms of his long range goals.

3. *Evaluation.* The progress of the student with respect to various objectives is accomplished with two types of assessment materials. The first type includes specific test questions focused on

the achievement of the objectives in a particular module. They are included in the module test taken after the student has completed his study of a particular module. Alternate forms of these questions are also included in achievement tests to check retention. They are scored in terms of specific objectives to indicate whether the student has mastered the objective or needs further study.

The second type of assessment procedure is designed to measure a long term objective. An example of one of the most important objectives of this type is reading comprehension. Other objectives of this type would include attitudes, appreciations, originality and other important skills and abilities which require more than two weeks to develop.

Procedures other than paper and pencil tests are used particularly to assess some of the long term objectives of the program.

4. *Guidance and Individual Planning.* The guidance and individual planning program of PLAN represents a major developmental effort in this educational system. The four main aspects of this program are briefly summarized.

(a) It is believed essential that all students be familiar with the variety of opportunities, roles and activities in the world of work, in cultural, recreational and other leisure time pursuits, and in personal, social and civic relations. This information includes the educational requirements for various occupations, the competencies in terms of developed abilities required for admission and success in these occupations, and the conditions and importance of each of the various roles. Similiar types of information will be provided with respect to the other types of adult activities for which the student might wish to prepare himself.

(b) It is essential that each individual be acquainted with the status of his development with respect to abilities, interests, physical and social characteristics, and values in the areas of education, vocations, social behaviors, citizenship and the use of leisure time. This program should include developing an understanding of individual differences during childhood, adolescence and maturity and the basic principles of learning.

(c) Each student is assisted to formulate his long term goals and to take the responsibility for and plan a developmental program to achieve these goals. Each individual will be assisted in relating his personal potentials for developing abilities, his interests and his values with opportunities likely to be available to him. The program would include substantial training in decision-making and problem-solving. In providing practice for the student in making decisions and plans, it is proposed that extensive use be made of the Project TALENT data. After the individual has shown considerable competence in making plans for students with specified characteristics, interests and values, he would be asked to make decisions having to do with his own development.

(d) It is believed important that the student learn to manage his own development. This development would be defined in terms of his goals and plans. It is anticipated that at least some students will learn to carry out a program of reinforcement of desirable behaviors which will correct and improve their behavioral patterns so as to enable them to carry out their developmental plans.

5. *Teacher Development.* There are four phases to the present teacher development program in PLAN. The first phase is an orientation phase in which the teacher visits PLAN classes being conducted by experienced teachers and participates in a program of directed observation and orientation. This is ordinarily conducted in the spring of the year prior to the teacher's participation in the PLAN system. This observation period is followed by a reading period extending over the summer. The reading materials include discussions of the basic concepts and philosophy underlying PLAN and individualized education in general. The third phase of the teacher development program consists of a three- or four-day individualized program, usually conducted in late August, which uses modules, teaching-learning units, objectives and tests designed to acquaint the teacher with the basic information and skills essential for conducting a class in the PLAN system. In this phase use is made of motion pictures and videotapes.

The last phase consists of the in-service training program. A PLAN consultant observes the teacher at frequent intervals during the early days of participation in PLAN and checks to see whether the teacher has achieved mastery of the procedures and skills important to the effective functioning of PLAN in the classroom. During this phase there is additional use of modeling and practice techniques, using motion pictures and videotapes, to develop effective behavior patterns with respect to advanced skills and tutoring and other aspects of individualized instruction.

### Significance, Implications, Present Status and Future Plans

On the basis of nearly three years' experience with the system in the classroom, it is clear that PLAN does, in fact, make possible the individualization of the educational program for the student. The curriculum and instructional programs offered in PLAN are judged by most observers to be somewhat better than those now available in most schools. There are plans for the continued revision of the instructional programs in the present four subject-matter areas and the extension of these to other fields included in the educational offerings of most schools. There is also need for further development to meet the needs of specific students and to improve both efficiency of learning and retention for all students. The specific and systematically planned program of studies developed by each student with aid from teachers, parents and the computer is much more systematically and comprehensively planned to meet the student's needs than in any other current educational system. One of the principal purposes of PLAN is to encourage the student to take more responsibility for his own educational development. It is clearly seen that especially students in the early school years are taking much more responsibility when given the opportunity in PLAN.

To meet the needs of students in the later school years, a comprehensive guidance program using Project TALENT findings is being developed. Only very limited implementation of this program was possible in the first two years, but in the spring of 1970 a fairly sophisticated prototype was developed for PLAN students in grades 9, 10 and 11. This program will assist the student to formulate long range goals and plan a program for achieving them. It is expected to be a valuable aid in assisting the secondary school students to take the same type of responsibility for their educational development now shown by PLAN students in earlier grades.

Some progress has been made, but much work remains to be done in the development and evaluation of a program for personal and social development.

The present program indicates that good progress has been made toward the development of a truly accountable system for education. Better means for assessing many of the important long-range goals are still needed.

Many of the available published instructional materials, both printed and audiovisual, have been given a preliminary evaluation in use in PLAN. Here again, more specific and systematic testing is needed to provide definitive evaluation data and to establish principles for defining effective instructional materials and methods.

Finally, the teachers are adapting easily and well to their new roles. The new training procedures are enabling them to work with each student as an individual and to make effective use of the computer as a clerical aid and resource for them and their students. For the teachers, adaptation to this type of an individualized system may take a few weeks. For the students, it seems to require only a few minutes.

# 12

## An Instrument for
## Individualizing Instruction

John E. Arena

Many persons believe that there is great demand for an educational system that can meet the needs of students at all ability levels. They hold that this goal can only be achieved through some form of individualized instruction. Proponents of "status quo" will argue that in theory individualized instruction is good but that in practice it will not work. This is an absurd contradiction. If one accepts the validity of the theory, then he must accept the idea that it can be successfully applied—the problem is to determine *how*.

Educators who have recognized the need for individualization of instruction have hesitated to undertake the task because of the lack of an effective instrument for implementation. *An instrument now exists.* It has proven its effectiveness and is readily available to you through the IMS project.

### The IMS Project

Since July 1, 1968, a staff of eight educators, funded by a U.S. Office of Education Title III grant, has been working on the Interrelated Mathematics Science project. The project is based at Nova High School, which is the educational research and development center for the Broward County Board of Public Instruction, Broward County, Florida. The *major objectives* of the project are:

Reprinted from *Educational Leadership*, Vol. 27, No. 8, May 1970, pp. 784-787, by permission of author and publisher.

1.  To design a conceptually based program of instruction in the fields of mathematics and science, grades 9-12, in which the subjects are interrelated, yet retain the basic source structure vital to continuity in each discipline.
2.  To individualize the instructional program according to the individual aptitudes, attitudes and interests of each student.
3.  To devise and evaluate a systems approach to individualized instruction, utilizing multimedia and multi-mode techniques, in order to provide the necessary alternate paths to learning.

### The Learning Activity Package

Specially designed booklets called Learning Activity Packages (LAPs) are being written in both mathematics and science. This learning instrument was conceived and developed at Nova High School about six years ago. Because of its proven effectiveness and increasing employment by educators throughout the nation, the LAP system was adopted by the IMS project.

The primary function of the LAP is to guide the student through a highly structured program of learning materials. Each contains a brief rationale as well as a statement of the performance objectives written in behavioral terms. Pretests and posttests provide one means for evaluating student progress. In any LAP, several paths to reach a particular objective are possible. The path a student takes is determined by the individual's abilities, needs and interests.

The *format* for the learning packages, which evolved after considerable trial and error, is as follows:

1.  Rationale
2.  Performance Objectives
3.  Pretest
4.  Pretest analysis
5.  Basic references
6.  Program for learning
7.  Self-evaluation test

8. Self-evaluation test analysis
9. Appendix—references, problems and applications, supplementary information, glossary, etc.

## How a Student Uses the LAP

Each student receives a Learning Activity Package. The first thing he will do is read the rationale. This is a short introduction to the unit which explains why the content of the LAP is important to him. It also makes evident the continuity between LAPS and the need to progress from one to the other in an orderly fashion. All students are required to read the rationale.

A list of the behavioral objectives for the entire unit follows the rationale. By reading the objectives the student gets a clear verbal picture of what he is expected to accomplish.

After reading the objectives the student takes the pretest. This test is keyed to the behavioral objectives. Upon completing the pretest, the student has a conference with the teacher to determine a suitable program of instruction. The teacher advises on the possibility of exempting certain objectives and assists the student in the selection of texts, audiovisual aids, and other materials that the student will use to accomplish the goals.

He is now ready to go through the program of instruction. Working independently, or at times in a small group, he will do any combination of the following activities: read, view films, solve problems, attend a lecture, go on a field trip, write a research report, study transparencies, listen to audio tapes, perform experiments, etc., as detailed in the program of instruction. If at any time the student needs help or advice, the teacher is available for consultation.

When the student feels that he has successfully completed the program of instruction, he takes the posttest. This test is also keyed to the objectives so that the student can determine whether he has in fact mastered the objectives or has need to recycle certain ones.

If, on the basis of posttest results and teacher consultation, it is determined that the student has successfully completed the LAP, he is permitted to take the unit test to establish a grade and receive credit for the unit.

## Alternate Ways to Use a LAP

A school need not adopt a totally individualized instructional program in order to use the learning packages. The packages may be used in many different ways, a few of which are listed below:

1. In an independent study program involving only a portion of the school population.
2. As an alternate means of instruction, to be used periodically in conjunction with the conventional system.
3. As a mechanism for encouraging and implementing programs of study in subject areas not contained within the existing curriculum.
4. To provide in-depth studies for students of higher ability.
5. To provide remedial activities for students experiencing difficulty, either in the subject area or with prerequisites necessary to success in the subject area.

## Applicability to All Schools

At first, the staff was writing the program of instruction phase for all the LAPs. When the LAPs were used by several schools in Broward County, Florida and at Valhalla, New York, difficulties arose. The major roadblocks to success were the following:

1. Some of the schools did not have the prescribed texts or audiovisual materials.
2. In many cases teachers who had developed some of their own laboratory experiments, worksheets, etc., objected to not being able to incorporate these into the program of instruction.
3. Some of the texts used in the LAP were not on the list of state-adopted books or they were disliked by the teachers.

4. Even minor revisions to the scope and sequence were not possible due to the rigidity of the program of instruction.
5. Some schools lacked the physical facilities or resources to carry out the program of instruction.

On the positive side, most teachers thought the format was good and that the scope and sequence were compatible with what they had been doing. The performance objectives were clear and concise and the diagnostic pretest and posttest proved very valuable to both teachers and students.

One of the problems encountered in the evaluations was anticipated by the staff but it was decided deliberately to invoke the problem to determine its extent and effect on the program. This problem was the lack of teacher and student orientation to the methods employed in individualized instruction. Notes were made on the procedures used by teachers in implementing the program, as well as the nature and number of questions asked by the students.

As a result of all this feedback, certain very pertinent things were learned that effected some major changes and revisions. The most prominent change in procedure was concerned with the program of instruction. Instead of the IMS staff's prescribing the program of instruction, it was decided to outline a model program and provide blank spaces in the LAPs for individual schools to design and write their own program of instruction.

With this one simple expedient, most of the problems discussed earlier were eliminated. The LAPs could now be used by any school and could be adapted to fit almost any curriculum.

At present, different LAPs are being used employing this new idea and re-evaluation of them is in progress. Indications are that the materials will prove very successful and will be employed by many more schools in the near future.

Accompanying the new LAPs is an orientation booklet for students explaining how the LAP is to be used, what the student's responsibilities are, and the educational advantages of individualized instruction. Also accompanying the LAPs is an orientation booklet for teachers. This booklet familiarizes the teacher with the basic philosophy and mechanical procedures necessary to assure a successful program. It also familiarizes the teacher with: (a) the format of the learning packages, (b) the purposes of the different parts and (c) the role of the teacher in this unique method of instruction.

**How About Individualizing?**

Through the efforts of Nova High School and projects such as IMS, it is now possible for any school to achieve a successful program of individualized instruction, even on a limited scale, if so desired. The author offers the following suggestions to any administrators or teachers contemplating the individualization of instruction:

1. Carefully study the literature and project reports available on the subject.
2. Visit some schools now utilizing this method of learning.
3. Formulate a plan which will allow a slow but cautious and deliberate entrance into this endeavor.
4. Prepare for adequate in-service training of teachers.
5. Prepare for adequate orientation of students who will be participating.
6. It would probably be best to start with the higher ability students and work toward incorporating students at all ability levels as the project progresses.
7. Employ team teaching wherever possible—*after* full orientation of staff.
8. If economically feasible, make use of teacher aides to release the teacher from clerical chores.
9. Plan ahead for possible conversion of existing space to include resource centers, special media rooms and small group facilities.
10. By all means avoid a "crash program"—orientation is *essential.*

# 13

## The LAP—A Feasible Vehicle of Individualization

Sally M. Cardarelli

Individualized instruction has long been a goal of American education. Concern for the individual child and meeting his needs dates back to the one-room schoolhouse.

However, despite our convictions that the child is an individual—learns at his own rate, has a unique style or mode of learning, has different topics that interest and motivate him—teachers too often continue the traditional "class" approach to teaching. Their instruction aims at the mythical "average student," who is not even there. We always have great excuses: My class is too big! My preparation time is too short! My resources are too limited! Too big—too short—too limited! I always wanted to add: Too bad, for the individual child!

The Learning Activity Package is not a panacea for all our money, class size and time problems, but it does provide us with a vehicle that makes individualization feasible.

The LAP not only takes into account the rate of learning, style of learning and interest of the individual student, it actually is designed to provide for these basic variables of learning. The *uniqueness* of each student is preserved—he is no longer forced to fit into the mold of the mythical "average student." The LAP is the most exciting innovation on the educational scene today.

Reprinted from *Educational Technology*, Vol. 12, No. 3, pp. 23-29, March 1972, by permission of author and publisher.

## Why Change?

Each teacher as an individual has, during the course of his classroom experience, attempted to devise an approach to teaching with which he is comfortable. Admittedly, it may not solve all the problems of the typical classroom, but it is the way the individual teacher has determined to function in the face of present constraints. It is the feasible solution the teacher has decided to live with, even at the sacrifice of some high ideals which characterized his initial entry to the classroom. It is the teaching style which has become uniquely his own.

With reluctance will many such teachers give up the security of their tried and true methods in the traditional, teacher-centered classroom. After all, why should they? They have been teaching successfully for 10, 15 or more years. Students have learned in the past using their methods. What's so different about today's students?

Let us take a serious look at that student, at the society of today and at the society of the future in which he is going to have to survive. Population explosion is not the only explosion the society of the future has in store for this student. There is a knowledge explosion, too, as the accumulation of knowledge doubles every 7 years. Today's student is no longer a child we are trying to prepare for an exam. He is no longer the child whose need is simply to regurgitate facts, to operate on the knowledge or memory level.

This student's need is to be able to take basic knowledge and build with it: to translate it into a different form; to interpret and extrapolate, using it as his starting point; to apply this knowledge to new situations; to analyze and evaluate new situations in the light of learned principles and generalizations; to uniquely synthesize all this as he copes with the society of the future. In short, we are trying to produce a "new student" capable of creatively solving the problems of and forging a future in a "new society."

The traditional approach to teaching inhibits the very initiative, creativity, independence and ability to get along with others that society will demand of the student. There is an ever-increasing number of teachers who have become convinced that the Learning Activity Package is a tremendous tool in helping both teacher and student adopt a new role in preparing for this new society.

## My Route

Like thousands of other teachers, I have always been convinced that individualization is not just a nicety in the classroom, but is a necessity. During my 15 years of teaching, this conviction has led to many trial-and-error attempts to allow the child to learn at his own speed, in the way that suits him best, using the routes that most interest him. However, like educators everywhere, without sufficient materials, additional planning time and clerical help, these attempts left individualization more a dream than a reality.

The summer of 1969 was a turning point for me. After a month at UCLA developing mathematics behavioral objectives for IOX,* I returned to my school district to work on an Independent Study Project, developing a unit for use with seventh grade math students. The commercial programs surveyed in connection with this project were interesting, but costs were prohibitive for the typical teacher in the typical tight-budgeted school district. There had to be a feasible program that would allow a teacher to individualize, even if she were the only teacher in a traditional school pursuing this route.

It was at this point that I heard about LAPs. It was all so logical, so obvious! Why hadn't I thought of it before? Really, in a way, I guess I had when I gave students objective-directed activity sheets. However, the LAP went further: it blended together in a neatly structured package all the good parts of my numerous trial-and-error attempts at individualization. Then and there I determined that my math students were going to have LAPs—a determination that resulted in the most dynamic experience in my teaching career—as well as many nights burning the midnight oil.

---

*IOX (Instructional Objectives Exchange), Los Angeles, California.

**The Structure of the LAP**

The Learning Activity Package (LAP) had its conception at the Nova High School in Florida about six years ago. The number of in-service workshops presently conducted on this topic seems to indicate considerable interest in this teacher-developed strategy for individualization.

Basically, the LAP is a booklet on a given topic, containing objectives related to this topic, diverse activities to reach these objectives and evaluations to determine if the objectives have been met. The flexibility of the LAP program is well illustrated by the fact that each individual teacher, and each school district that adopts the LAP program, sets up a format that is somewhat unique, devised to meet specific needs. The interpretation presented here is one the author evolved originally for her own classroom and eventually for the math program in two adjoining school districts. It is the design the author has presented in teacher workshops conducted for numerous educator groups.

The components of the LAP are:

| | |
|---|---|
| Topic | Pretest |
| Subtopics | Activities and Self- |
| Rationale | Evaluations |
| Behavioral | Quiz(zes) |
| Objectives | Posttest |

*Topic and Subtopics*

The student's initial introduction to a LAP is the statement of the *topic* and *subtopics*. The extent of coverage of this topic depends on the individual teacher, the type of student utilizing this LAP and how long the child has been using LAPs. In the beginning it is wise to develop Mini-LAPs that cover a week's work at a maximum. As the child becomes accustomed to the LAP, the teacher may want to extend the LAP to cover as much as an entire unit. However, it is the experience of the author that it is far better to divide a unit into Mini-LAPs that the student will perceive as accomplishable than to overcome him with a LAP that is a 40-page booklet.

### Rationale

The topic and subtopics are followed ordinarily by the *rationale*. As the name indicates, the rationale is aimed at providing the student with a reason for studying this topic. This is the beginning of the romance stage of learning spoken of by Whitehead (1929), the wonderment stage through which we try to encourage the student to explore and experiment. This is the stage through which, hopefully, the student is motivated to become involved in a topic, to pursue the more sophisticated precision and generalization learning stages.

The rationale can take a variety of forms: a stimulating film, a large group presentation, a challenging experiment, an explorative study or a written rationale which enunciates the relevance of this topic within the framework of the total curriculum, the student's everyday life or his future life.

### Behavioral Objectives

After this brief introduction to the topic, the student reads the objectives for this particular LAP. All objectives are behaviorally stated, that is, expressed in terms of what the student will be able to do upon completion of the LAP. The completeness of these objectives should depend on the level of development of the student involved. In the LAP, the function of the objective is to communicate goals to the student, and thus should be written in his language. In the beginning, this may be simply a performance objective. However, most secondary students will profit by the direction provided through precise behavioral objectives, especially if the students are encouraged to establish their own minimal level of acceptable performance.

How often do students try to outguess teachers on exams simply because what they are expected to learn is kept a secret until testing time? The student has a right to know what is expected of him. He has the need for direction in his studies, not to the extent that the direction becomes a harness, but a springboard from which eventually he will be able to take off in pursuit of his own objectives with a perceived purpose, rather than a haphazard plunge.

Once the student has read his objectives, the decision-making, which is part and parcel of the LAP philosophy, comes to the fore. In the light of the given objectives, Johnny must decide if a *pretest* would be valuable.

### Pretest

For some LAPs the teacher may determine that the *pretest* is at the option of the student. In such a case, when the objectives unveil a topic or math concept with which the student is totally unfamiliar, his decision might well be to omit the pretest and immediately begin the LAP. One the other hand, as usually happens in math, there is built into each unit a review of a number of prerequisite skills, a review which can be a waste of time for many students. It is not unusual to have students attain a mark in the 90's on a pretest. It makes one wonder how often a traditional teacher-centered program has wasted 90 percent of such a student's time, to say nothing of the fact that it has "turned him off" to the many unexplored facets of math which could be exciting to him.

In many traditional classroom settings, the student is expected to fit into a predetermined mold. Failure to reach this class level of performance results in remedial work, which the student looks upon as punishment. The pretest, on the other hand, in diagnosing weaknesses ahead of time and directly routing the student to necessary activities, provides the student not with failure, but success, insuring a more positive, rewarding learning experience.

### Activities and Self-Evaluations

The *activities* of the LAP attempt to provide the student with a multimedia, multi-modal, multi-level road to reach the objectives of the LAP. The multimedia activities, in directing the student to readings, transparencies, tapes, filmstrips, demonstration models, etc., provide for the learning style of the individual child. The multi-modal activities include within the flexible program large group, small group and independent activities, thus developing student social skills in a variety of real-life situations. The multi-level activities, in providing the pupil with the opportunity to start at the base of his particular weakness, also provide him with a success story for his learning experiences, instead of failure followed by unwanted remediation.

These activities may allow varying amounts of directiveness in meeting various objectives. An objective aimed at fostering curiosity or interest in a topic might include a stimulating film in its activities, followed by the opportunity to pursue this interest. An objective directed toward an exploratory or discovery approach might take a form very similar to the assignment of task cards mentioned by Biggs and MacLean (1969). For example:

> Make a collection of multi-colored cubes on your desk. How many red cubes are there? What is the total number of cubes on your desk? If you placed the cubes in a box, closed your eyes and took one from the box, how often do you think the cube would be red? Half of the time? A quarter of the time? Make a guesstimate. Try it 100 times to see how close you come to your guesstimate. Make a table to record such data for each color cube. Discuss your findings with a partner. Can you formulate a rule, a generalization?

Such activities provoke stimulating teacher-pupil and pupil-pupil discussions and often lead students to the ultimate goal of education referred to by Whitehead, the Generalization of Learning.

A reinforcement objective to increase or insure accuracy might direct a child to a textbook activity with answers available for immediate feedback. More open-ended objectives are the emphasis of the quest activities which encourage the student to select a topic of his own interest and, where possible, outline his own objectives. Student-developed Quest Mini-LAPs and Assignment Cards provide a stimulating file of interesting topics which other students can profit by and build on.

These diversified activities, while providing for individual student needs and interest, also provide for teacher needs. In pulling together all available teaching aids for the activities of a LAP, the teacher is enabled to better analyze needs, so that purchasing of commercial materials is guided by more than haphazard selection.

### Quizzes

Built into the LAP is the philosophy that if anything is worth teaching, it is also worth knowing that it has been learned; this is coupled with the belief that a child has more effective learning experiences, if allowed to progress step by step at his own rate. Frequent quizzes give the student a frequent success record and insure immediate remediation by rerouting the child to activities for which further reinforcement is required. In this way, his learning is a progressive development which will prevent him from getting in over his head.

All quiz items are designed to test specific objectives and thus encourage the teacher to be fair with the student. The objectives at the beginning of the LAP outline for the student what is expected of him. It is on these objectives that he is tested, not some inferred idea in the back of the teacher's mind; this is in keeping with Taba's (1962) statement that the validity of evaluation instruments tends to improve in the measure in which they are consistent with objectives.

Thus, a student might have a quiz testing fulfillment of objectives 1 through 5, a second quiz on objectives 6 and 7, and a third quiz on objective 8. The number of objectives evaluated by a particular quiz depends on the importance and the extent of the objectives involved. The critical point is that the student may take a quiz when *he* is ready for it, not when the class is ready for it.

### Posttest

The *posttest* is comparable to the pretest in that it evaluates student fulfillment of all objectives of the LAP, at least the terminal objectives if not all subobjectives.

In the past, evaluation has been the end product of a unit summarized by that red mark recorded neatly in our little black marking book as we sailed on to the next topic. Our need is to make evaluation not an end, but a beginning—a beginning of searching for more appropriate activities, a beginning of analyzing and evaluating our methods of teaching—a beginning of a "success story" for each student. Through LAPs, evaluation assumes its full role, not only evaluating the student, but evaluating teacher and program effectiveness as well. The validation process, the test-revision cycle, applies not just to Johnny, but also to the teacher and the tools she uses in meeting Johnny's instructional needs.

*An Aid to Diagnosis and Prescription*

In the LAP model derived by the author, all number systems are coordinated for objectives, activities and testing, in order that evaluations become a diagnostic and prescriptive tool capable of being interpreted by both teacher and student. For example, if the pupil correctly answers all parts of questions 4 and 7 on a pretest, he has already met LAP objectives 4 and 7, and completion of questions 5 and 6 on a pretest would provide an immediate diagnosis of weaknesses on objectives 5 and 6 and a built-in prescription to complete the corresponding activities 5 and 6.

This seems like a very simple addition to the LAP structure, and it is, but do not let its simplicity cause you to underestimate its importance. The majority of teachers would agree that the biggest problem in any individualized program is an organizational one, particularly when this individualization is a single teacher endeavor deprived of the support of an entire department, school or district.

Any step the teacher can take to increase student responsibility, independence and initiative in this regard is a giant step toward freeing the teacher from the burdensome organizational problems that have thwarted and stifled many otherwise worthwhile programs.

The format of this LAP model fosters student analysis of his own weaknesses, and student determination of necessary remedial or reinforcement activities. Student participation in this diagnostic and prescriptive role enables him to grasp the significance of activities which otherwise might have been viewed as teacher-imposed busy work.

Now the teacher has time to completely analyze the more obscure problems of the slower student who has been relatively ignored until now, and can more adequately fulfill her role as diagnostician and prescriber.

## The Philosophy of the LAP Program

The structure of the LAP is only the shell—an empty shell—if implemented without the philosophy behind the LAP program. What is that philosophy? To my way of thinking, the LAP philosophy could be summarized by these guiding beliefs:

1. Each student is an individual who has a right to receive instruction geared to his needs, his interests and his capabilities.
2. The teacher's role is that of diagnostician, prescriber, motivator and facilitator of learning.
3. The student's role is that of an independent person capable of making decisions, accepting responsibility for his own education and getting along with others.
4. The atmosphere of the LAP program classroom or school must reflect an open structure where initiative, creativity, exploration, meaningful interaction and awareness of the needs of others can flourish.

In short, the LAP philosophy would have us take a realistic look at what will be expected of Timmy when he moves into this society of the future, and set up a classroom atmosphere where the qualities he will need as a fully functioning person, not merely as an intellectual, are going to be fostered.

The traditional approach to teaching does a great job of preparing students for a totalitarian state—every student on the same page at the same time; every student fumbling through the same homework; every student spoon-fed the knowledge the teacher wishes him to remember; every student infallibly guided by teacher decision-making. Johnny is not expected to *think* as much as he is expected to *do as he is told.* Let us hope that his is not the picture of the society of the future. Let us hope that we, as educators of today, can adjust our approach to teaching so as to produce the creative, spontaneous and innovative people of tomorrow—who will not only be able to cope with, but will be able to contribute to, the society of the future.

## Further Considerations
### Study in Isolation

Many lay people and educators alike view individualized instruction and independent study as relatively unguided study in isolation. Their mind's eye sees the teacher handing Billy his book and saying: "Here's your book, Billy. You can travel at your own pace. You're individualized now." And off trots Billy to his individual carrel, not to be seen or heard for the next three or four weeks.

In implementing an individualized program there is a need to keep a constant eye on the person of the student, not just the intellect. Perhaps, intellectually, there are a few students who can learn best via a virtual study in isolation; but it is not merely intellectual growth with which we are concerned. Our interest is in the growth and development of the whole person.

We want to develop a well-rounded human person who is able and willing to share with others, who can participate positively in group discussion, who can discuss problems with his peers with an open mind. Small-group and partner activities are essential to this growth. The individualized program that deteriorates into continual study in isolation has lost this vision of the individual as a person.

### Student Responsibility

Though it is true that individualized instruction aims at increasing a student's responsibility for his own education, Esbensen (1968) reminds us:

Children cannot suddenly be turned loose to direct their own schooling. The matter is not that simple. What we need to do is provide a variety of learning activities that (1) will be highly motivating, (2) will have enough self-instructional features to ease the problem of class-room management, (3) can accommodate a wide range of individual differences and (4) will encourage the accomplishment of worthy objectives.

The LAP program, properly implemented, will accomplish all of the above and much more, but we cannot expect student transformation overnight. The importance of gradual increase of responsibility cannot be overly stressed, particularly for the slower student with many years of spoon-feeding behind him. His need is a gentle release from the teacher-dominated classroom scene to the more open, experimental exploratory atmosphere of the student-centered approach.

First steps in responsibility development might include determining his own homework, setting reasonable deadlines for himself for a given segment of reinforcement activities, and participating in a group discussion on classroom management problems.

*Classroom Management*
The implementation of any new program is accompanied by problems of classroom management—problems both physical and philosophical in nature. The LAP program, with its increased emphasis on student responsibility, attempts to foster student involvement in solving these problems. A simple census or a classroom suggestion box allows the student to voice his opinion about issues he wishes brought up at the next class discussion. To prevent this from becoming a negative "critic's column" the student is encouraged to submit at least one possible positive solution for every problem he cites.

The problems then become the focus of the next group discussion as the teacher assumes the role of group leader, encouraging open-mindedness and decision-making in the students as they discuss a number of alternative solutions before they vote for the one to be used in their program. Below are some typical examples of student-suggested problems and group solutions.

*Student Problem 1:*

"I don't like having to decide what homework I need to do to reach an assigned deadline. I'd like the teacher to tell me my homework each day, so I won't end up staying up half the night the day before a deadline." (This group was a better math class with a district-prescribed curriculum. Hence, deadlines!)

*Group Solution:*

Ninety percent of the class favored the freedom of assigning their own homework. Thus, they could work ahead on nights when they were not busy and could omit math when overburdened with homework in other subject areas. Further, they pointed out that a student who didn't want this responsibility was probably one of the ones most in need of it.

*Student Problem 2:*

"Many times I can't find materials, because kids leave them at their desks even after they finished using them."

*Group Solution:*

1. Set aside a table for use of teacher copies so that students can both find and share them.
2. One student volunteered to ring a bell two minutes before class termination as a signal to return all materials to the appropriate place so the next class could find them readily. Students agreed that they should accept the responsibility of finding materials and should not expect the teacher to locate them.

*Teacher Comment:*

This student decision saved the teacher at least 20 frustrating questions per period.

*Student Problem 3:*

"It's great having access to Teacher Answer Keys during class time, but I wish we could have dittoed copies of answers to check extra work at home."

*Group Solution:*

Students volunteered to make Answer Key dittos for the entire class.

*Student Problem 4:*

"I'd like to have more tapes, filmstrips, etc., as LAP activities."

*Group Solution:*

"We can develop A-V learning tools: tapes, games, charts, transparencies and flashcards in Math Club or during a free period."

*Teacher Comment:*

It provided an excellent opportunity for creativity on the part of the students. It was decided to set aside one class period at the beginning of each LAP for this purpose. Fabulous teaching tools resulted and kids really became involved.

*Student Problem 5:*

"Many times when I try to get into a group for a group activity, kids tell me to go to another group. I think they should let any kids into their group."

*Group Solution:*

"Any student who wants acceptance into the group has to come ready for work. Nobody wants kids who just monkey around and waste everybody's time, but we should accept them into the group and try to help them."

*Teacher Comment:*

Needless to say, solutions from students' peers make a far greater impression than the best teacher rhetoric. These are just a few samples of the kinds of things that can "happen" when we begin to turn kids loose into a democratic, rather than totalitarian, classroom.

*Orientation Guidelines*

This segment is directed to administrators and curriculum specialists, since they are more likely to handle this aspect of the program than the classroom teacher. It is the conviction of the author that the success of a new program depends to a great extent on a successful orientation program.

Teacher training sessions can best be conducted by an experienced consultant who has, if possible, written LAPs and conducted a LAP program in the classroom—not just by someone who has read about LAPs. Problems can be most adequately and convincingly resolved by someone who has directly experienced them. One session with a good consultant would be far more worthwhile than three sessions with someone who has just heard or read about LAPs.

This consultant would be the one to help plot long-range plans, even before an initial presentation to teachers is made. An afternoon workshop with no follow-up and no expected involvement becomes no more than an interesting afternoon. An afternoon workshop keyed to involve teachers in an inservice course, followed by the opportunity to participate in a summer program developing LAPs, becomes an afternoon keyed to a commitment and an active involvement on the part of the teacher.

A worthwhile inservice course should include discussion and application of the following:

a. A systems approach applied to LAPs.
b. Behavioral objectives at all levels of the taxonomy.
c. Structure of the LAP.
d. Philosophy of the LAP program.
e. Implementation strategy.

Inservice training that emphasizes team development of LAPs increases awareness of the more diversified program that can be produced by absorbing into a single LAP the ideas of two or more teachers. The author has found this team approach usually continues long after the inservice course is completed.

Remuneration of teachers by salary increments for participating in such an inservice course and implementing its strategy in their classrooms lends administrative support and commitment to the importance of the endeavor, a point not to be underestimated.

**A Realistic Beginning**

Perhaps ideally the teacher or administrator would want a LAP program that would extend student decision-making to a choice of topics and a determination of the order in which LAPs will be completed. We envision LAPs developed for an entire year, with many Quest LAPs to spur student interest; we see a multimedia center with hundreds of teaching aids to assist an individualized program.

If we wait for all this to become a reality, we may never get started. Budgets are getting tighter, demands on teacher time are getting greater and the need for individualization cannot wait any longer. So let us talk about a realistic beginning.

Many limitations may have to be lived with or circumvented as the program gradually develops to its full stature. Beginnings will differ as teachers differ. One teacher may choose to individualize just one class. Another teacher may want the option of initiating the program with one of her more mature classes— with a group of students who are more flexible and willing to experiment as the program gets organized. Another may choose to develop one LAP for each of her classes at the outset.

The extent of teacher training, the availability of resource materials to which the child may be routed, together with the availability of another teacher who is interested in developing LAPs at the same level are three tremendous factors that will affect the initiating of a LAP program. District support in providing for summer workshops to further development of LAPs will strengthen these beginnings.

Earlier in this article we discussed the importance of gradual implementation for the sake of student adjustment. Here we speak of the even greater necessity of gradual implementation to facilitate teacher adjustment. This is a new role the teacher is assuming; he will try to erase the image of teacher as preacher and replace it by a facilitator and motivator of learning interested in the whole child, not just his intellect. His classroom, formerly teacher-dominated, will now assume a more open atmosphere in which the child is the central figure. His didactic approach is to be replaced by an exploratory, independent learning situation. He, like the student, needs time to adjust. He needs to choose his own route, to determine his own realistic beginning. The LAP interpretation presented here was the author's realistic beginning.

## References

Bernabei, R. and Leles, S. *Writing and Using Behavioral Objectives: A Learning Packet.* Tuscaloosa, Alabama: Drake and Son, 1964.

Biggs, Edith E. and MacLean, James R. *Freedom to Learn.* Ontario, Canada: Addison-Wesley, 1969.

Bloom, Benjamin S. *et al. Taxonomy of Educational Objectives—The Classification of Educational Goals, Handbook I: Cognitive Domain.* New York: David McKay, 1956.

Eiss, A.F. and Harbeck, M.B. *Behavioral Objectives in the Affective Domain.* Washington, D.C.: National Science Supervisors Association, 1969.

Esbensen, T. *Working with Individualized Instruction.* Palo Alto, California: Fearon, 1968.

Howes, Virgil M. *et al. Exploring Open Structure.* Los Angeles: Educational Inquiry, Inc., 1968.

Kibler, R.J., Barker, L.L. & Miles, D.T. *Behavioral Objectives and Instruction.* Boston: Allyn and Bacon, 1970.

Koran, J.J., Montague, E.J. and Hall, G.E. *How to Use Behavioral Objectives in Science Instruction.* Washington, D.C.: National Science Teachers Association, 1969.

Krathwohl, D.R. *et al. Taxonomy of Educational Objectives, Handbook II: The Affective Domain.* New York: David McKay, 1964.

Lindvall, C.M. (Ed.) *Defining Educational Objectives.* Pittsburgh: University of Pittsburgh Press, 1964.

Mager, R.F. *Preparing Instructional Objectives.* Palo Alto, California: Fearon, 1962.

Montague, E.J. and Butts, D.P. Behavioral Objectives. *Science Teacher,* Vol. 35, March 1968.

Sanders, Norris M. *Classroom Questions, What Kinds?* New York: Harper and Row, 1966.

Taba, Hilda. *Curriculum Development Theory and Practice.* New York: Harcourt Brace Jovanovich, 1962.

Whitehead, Alfred North. *The Aims of Education and Other Essays.* New York: Macmillan, 1929.

Wood, R. Objectives in the Teaching of Mathematics. *Educational Research,* Vol. 10, No. 2, February 1968.

# 14

## Individualizing Instruction for Self-Paced Learning

Philip G. Kapfer and Gardner A. Swenson

"Individualizing instruction," like "quality education," is a very difficult goal to tie down to definite referents in reality. Both terms are high level abstractions which sound good and contain "in-group" words but do not really commit one to a specific course of action. Many commitments to individualizing instruction can be found in the history of American education, but evidently no systematic structure for continuous progress has proven successful. How can such a laudable goal as individualized instruction be achieved, or, for that matter, even approached?

Some progress has been made in providing a setting for individualizing instruction. Architects are designing more flexible buildings. Administrators are involving teachers in decisions concerning the length of class periods and the sizes of class groups so that both can be appropriate to the educational purpose. Teachers are becoming more effective through the increased adaptability of team teaching. All of these increased flexibilities, however, are lost on inflexible and rigid curricula! The vast majority of instructional materials which presently are available were designed to make group-paced instruction workable, regardless of what is known about how children learn and about their individual learning styles.

In group-paced instruction, the teacher frequently is teaching for the "average" or "conforming" student. It is almost impossi-

Reprinted from *The Clearing House*, Vol. 42, No. 7, March 1968, pp. 405-410, by permission of authors and publisher.

ble, however, to provide for individual differences in a lesson plan that must aim for a mythical average with a single methodology and common media. Even though children learn in different ways and at astonishingly different rates, curricular materials designed for instructional strategies which effectively group-pace youngsters are the mainstay of published materials. For example, textbooks, however necessary and important, often are the greatest detractors from increased curricular flexibility. Even if success in teaching for the so-called average student could be assumed, both fast and slow learners still would lack stimulation and, in particular, slow learners time and again would find themselves academically in over their heads. The rigid instructional "slot" inhibits maximum learning for all learners.

Most teachers will agree that selective instruction based on individual learning ability and style should replace our presently used "batch" process. U.S. Commissioner of Education Harold Howe has provided a guideline in his statement that "we need more individualized instruction throughout the entire educational system—ideally, each student should have his own personal track."[1] Howe then goes on to talk about the use of computers and other of the newer educational media in the individualization process.

But what can be done about the problem *now* without sophisticated electronic devices in every school? How can teachers and curriculum specialists respond to the obvious need for individualized instruction while still saddled with the curricular materials which presently are available?

**A Center for Individualizing Instruction**

The Materials Dissemination Center, an activity of the Institute for the Development of Educational Activities (I/D/E/A), became effective on July 1, 1966. The Center is a curriculum bank which serves teachers participating in the I/D/E/A Demonstration Schools Project as well as other teachers throughout the country. Teachers deposit and withdraw materials from the curriculum bank which are specifically designed for individualization instruction.

The following assumptions are basic to the operations of the Materials Dissemination Center:

1. That the Center will collect, disseminate, house and evaluate curricular materials in the form of learning packages (UNIPACs).[2] In addition, the personnel and consultants of the Center will motivate and counsel teachers to produce such materials at workshops, conferences and at individual schools throughout the nation.

2. That teachers will produce continuous progress curriculum materials with the assistance and consultation of learning psychologists, subject-matter specialists, and curriculum programmers.

3. That teachers will be given the opportunity to demonstrate and evaluate these materials in their classroom.

4. That teachers will produce these materials specifically for self-instruction and independent study by students, thus facilitating continuous progress learning.

5. That the UNIPAC will have a system of quality control. This system will include field-testing by the Demonstration Schools and evaluation by consultants who are specialists in educational systems, educational psychology, subject-matter and educational writing. Consultants and teachers must approve the UNIPAC before the Materials Dissemination Center officially disseminates the material.

**Development of the UNIPAC Concept**

The concept of the UNIPAC was developed to include five seemingly essential ingredients for individualizing instruction.

1. *Concepts.* UNIPACs should be centered about learnable ideas or concepts and/or skills. Bruner has pointed out the importance of teaching specific topics and skills in relation to the "broader fundamental structure of a field of knowledge."[3] By relating what is learned to such a structure, learning becomes more economical, rewarding, useable and readily retained. Skills in

routine operations and knowledge of facts, rather than being ends in themselves, serve as the learner's entree to comprehension of concepts and ideas. By preparing UNIPACs which are concept-centered, such skills and facts can be organized into meaningful patterns. Specialized inquiry processes also can be related to general principles through UNIPACs.

2. *Behavioral Objectives.* Good teachers have always told their students what performance and achievement levels were expected of them at evaluation time, but often this has been accomplished orally and informally. In individualized instruction, students break out of the curricular lockstep and progress at their own best rates, working toward their behavioral objectives. Although student learning teams are formed, consisting of perhaps two to six students, the membership of such teams fluctuates. One student might be studying completely different materials, at a given point in time, than other students, and thus a learning team could not be formed. Therefore, in individualized instruction it is necessary for teachers to formalize behavioral objectives in writing, and to include these objectives in each UNIPAC.

3. *Multi-dimensional learning materials and activities.* Students do learn in different ways; each student has his own unique learning style. Riessman stated that "these styles may be categorized principally as visual (reading), aural (listening), or physical (doing things), although any one person may use more than one.[4] In order to provide for such variability, alternative materials and activities for achieving each behavioral objective should be suggested to the student in the UNIPAC. Provision should be made for student use of a wide variety of commercially prepared visual materials such as selections from textbooks and other books, programmed materials, filmstrips and 35mm slides; aural materials such as tapes and other recordings; physical activities such as model building, experiments and acting; and combinations such as audiovisual films, small group discussions, field studies and interviews. Teacher-prepared material also should be included. The more extensive the diversification of material and methodology of instruction in the UNIPAC, the greater will be the utility of the package.

4. *Pre-, self- and post-evaluation.* The combination of pre- and post-evaluation by the teacher serves to measure learning growth which cannot be measured by post-evaluation alone. In addition, pre-evaluation permits the teacher and student to determine which behavioral objectives might already have been achieved, so that the student is able to invest his time wisely in areas in which he is weak. Self-evaluation serves to help the student monitor his own progress; when he has achieved one objective, he can go on to the next one, and when the results of self-evaluation indicate to him that he is ready for teacher evaluation, he can request the post-evaluation. Directions to the student to contact the teacher for pre- and post-evaluation need to be built into the student's copy of the UNIPAC.

5. *Quest.* Although the UNIPAC provides structure for students' learning experiences, decisions inherent in using UNI-PACs encourage the development of self-initiative and self-direction. However, even greater self-initiating and self-directing experiences should be made available to every student. UNIPACs should include opportunities for quest—for enrichment study, whether in breadth or in depth. Problem statements might be included so that the student is stimulated to define a problem for quest study, carry out his research, and achieve some level of resolution of the problem which he has chosen.

The synthesis of the above five elements in the form of UNIPACs can serve as an important advancement in providing for self-paced learning through individualizing instruction. Of course, none of the five elements to be included in UNIPACs is individually new, at least to experienced curriculum workers. However, as Goodlad stated, "The well-designed learning package, like love, is not enough."[5] The role of the teacher must change if self-paced learning is to replace group-paced instruction; the teacher's role must become that of a manager of learning for individual students. The teacher will *monitor* each student's progress, *diagnose* learning problems, *prescribe* possible alternative learning materials and activities which will help to solve the problems, and *evaluate* each student's progress in achieving stated behavioral objectives. The time for such managing of learning can be found as teachers do less and less operating of instruction for groups of students. (When the teacher imparts knowledge as a lecturer to groups of students, for example, he is operating instruction instead of managing learning.) Some of this kind of instruction is valid and necessary, especially as a motivational technique, but, as progress is made in individualizing instruction, much less operating of instruction will occur than presently takes place in most classrooms.

A model[6] and a flow chart[7] have been designed to help teachers conceptualize their role as managers of learning. Both the model and the flow chart integrate the Large Group, Laboratory, Small Group and Independent Study phases of instruction with a strategy for individualizing instruction through the UNIPAC. Although the purpose of this article is not to present and describe an instructional model, the reader should be aware of the need for such a conceptualization if UNIPACs are to be used effectively.

*Initiating Individualized Instruction*
In any school in which individualization of instruction through UNIPACs is being initially attempted, a number of problems will appear. For example, the first UNIPAC which is prepared by a given teaching team is always the most difficult for that team. Time-consuming problems are encountered, some of which can be avoided through experienced leadership, and some of which are simply a part of the learning process for the teaching team.

In preparing UNIPACs, delimiting the area of study together with writing concept statements seem to be the most difficult tasks for many teachers. Their initial tendency is to prepare UNIPACs which would take the "average" student more than a week or two to complete, thus overburdening themselves with the task of preparing UNIPACs and overwhelming the student with too many concepts and behavioral objectives to use in a reasonable length of time. In order to resolve both of these problems, once a general area of study has been identified, it often proves to be more useful first to write behavioral objectives and then to return to the development of concept statements. Mager's *Preparing*

*Instructional Objectives*[8] is an excellent initial reference source for teachers working in this area. Bloom's *Taxonomies*[9] also are helpful, particularly when the teacher has mastered writing simple behavioral objectives of the type described by Mager.

A practical problem frequently arises in obtaining and using multi-dimensional learning materials designed to provide for individual differences in learning style. Identifying media, in addition to textbooks, which would be *readily* available to individual students and to small learning teams, is often a challenge for teachers. Examples of sources listing a wide variety of multi-media materials are the fourteen-volume *Educational Media Index*[10] and Hendershot's *Programmed Learning*.[11] Filmstrips, audio tapes, 8mm film loops, and the like are economically feasible and readily available commercially for citing in UNIPACs and for placing in resource centers for student use. Sixteen-millimeter films, however, often are housed in central district facilities or are obtained from rental agencies, and therefore are not as readily available or convenient for a continuous educational progress curriculum. When materials are not available commercially, teachers either may prepare them or may suggest to students the preparation of such materials as appropriate learning activities for achieving objectives stated in UNIPACs. Students are capable of preparing excellent audio and video tapes, 33mm slides, and 8mm movies.

As teachers become more sophisticated in writing behavioral objectives and evaluation questions, they are able to bring these two elements into balance. A behavioral objective, for example, that tells the student, "you will be able to discuss," should not be evaluated by multiple choice test items in which the student is required to "identify" rather than to "discuss." In addition, as teachers work in these areas they will begin to examine the objectives which they write to be sure that the requested types and levels of student performance relate to the conceptual orientation of the UNIPAC being prepared. Further, as teachers evaluate a partial or complete UNIPAC with students, they will find it useful to collect information to revise and improve the UNIPAC. Thus teachers, in an informal sense, become researchers.

**A Working Plan**

It is evident that considerable effort is expended by teachers involved in the initial phase of developing a continuous progress individualized curriculum through UNIPACs. Progress is slow when teachers must devote time during evenings, weekends and vacations, without remuneration or compensatory time, to developing UNIPACs. However, progress in individualizing instruction *can* be made within the limitations of time and inadequate funding. The entire faculty of a school can meet for a large group presentation on the concept of continuous educational progress based on UNIPACs. A simplified flow chart can be used to help the faculty conceptualize the manner in which UNIPACs can be used. Behavioral objectives can be explained in detail; they can be identified as a first step in individualizing instruction. To maintain consistency and reality, actual behavioral objectives for an initial large group faculty presentation on individualizing instruction can be given to the faculty at the time of the presentation, and might include the following:

(1)  Based on the information in the presentation on continuous educational progress, you will be able to name from memory, either orally or in writing, all five UNIPAC ingredients which are necessary for self-paced learning.

(2)  Based on the information in this presentation on continuous educational progress, you will be able to name from memory, either orally or in writing, all three elements of a behavioral objective.

The faculty then can be divided into small groups for the purpose of writing at least one behavioral objective. Following the small group discussions, a member of each group can present the group's behavioral objective to the entire faculty in a second large group meeting. Thus, the immediate goal, for at least an entire school year, can be to involve the total faculty in writing behavioral objectives and making these objectives available to students. At the same time, selected teams can be preparing UNIPACs. Each year's step toward the long-range goal of total faculty participation in preparing UNIPACs must, of course, be planned carefully with teacher and administrator involvement in the decision-making process.

## Summary

Flexible buildings, flexible schedules and flexible teachers are necessary ingredients for individualizing instruction and for quality education, but they are not sufficient ingredients. The real deterrent to progress in individualizing instruction is caused by the lack of flexible curricula. Perhaps the cart has been placed in front of the horse by innovators who have concentrated on buildings, schedules and team teaching. More than likely, changes in these areas are simply more readily and easily accomplished than are basic changes in the curriculum.

Individualizing instruction will increasingly cast the teacher in the role of a manager of learning for individual students. For such a role change to occur, teachers themselves must be involved in the change process. Involvement in the Materials Dissemination Center will facilitate such changes for improvement in the quality of the educational program through individualized instruction.

Questions regarding the functions, services and involvement in the Materials Dissemination Center and The Teachers UNIPAC Exchange should be directed to:

Gardner Swenson, Director
Teachers UNIPAC Exchange
1653 Forrest Hills Drive
Salt Lake City, Utah 84106

## Notes

1.  Harold Howe II, "On Libraries and Learning," *Library Journal,* XCII (February 15, 1967), pp. 841-844.

2.  The name "UNIPAC" is used to designate the units of instruction or learning packages developed and disseminated under the auspices of the Materials Dissemination Center.

3.  Jerome S. Bruner, *The Process of Education* (Cambridge, Massachusetts: Harvard University Press), 1963, p. 31.

4.   Frank Riessman, "Styles of Learning," *NEA Journal*, LV (March 1966), pp. 15-17.

5.   John I. Goodlad, "Directions of Curriculum Change," *NEA Journal*, LV (December 1966), pp. 33-37.

6.   Philip G. Kapfer, "An Instructional Management Strategy for Individualized Learning," *Phi Delta Kappan*, Volume XLIX (January 1968), pp. 260-263.

7.   Philip G. Kapfer and Glen F. Ovard, "Flow Chart of Continuous Educational Progress Based on Learning Packages" (Unpublished manuscript, 1966).

8.   Robert F. Mager, *Preparing Instructional Objectives* (Palo Alto, California: Fearon Publishers, 1962), 62pp.

9.   Benjamin S. Bloom (ed.), *Taxonomy of Educational Objectives, Handbook I: Cognitive Domain* (New York: David McKay Company, Inc.), 1956, 207pp.

     David R. Krathwohl, Benjamin S. Bloom, and Bertram B. Masia, *Taxonomy of Educational Objectives, Handbook II: Affective Domain* (New York: David McKay Company, Inc.), 1964, 196pp.

10.  *Educational Media Index* (New York: McGraw-Hill), 1964, 14 volumes with supplements.

11.  Carl H. Hendershot, *Programmed Learning* (Delta College, University Center, Michigan, 48710: By the author, 1964), 243 loose-leaf pp. with quarterly supplements.

# 15

## What's Contained in an Individualized Instruction Package

James E. Duane

The "package" is becoming an increasingly important method of organizing resources in an individualized instruction curriculum. A package may be defined as simply an appropriate set of learning materials which are organized to help a learner achieve specified objectives. Packages differ from other modes of instruction in that individualized instruction packages must allow the student to proceed at his own rate and in a manner consistent with his own learning styles.

In reading the literature, it appears that there are almost as many formats of packages as there are schools using them. Most schools or commercial concerns involved in developing packages tend to label their package with a unique title or acronym. Some of the better-known package titles include: the TLU, the LAP, the ISU, the ILP and the UNIPAC. Although most packages have unique titles, they all contain very similar elements. After several years of research and experimentation, an almost standardized format has been developed. This format has proven to be an effective method of organizing individualized instruction materials. Seven components form the basic structure of a package. These are:

1. Rationale
2. Content Description
3. Behavioral Objectives
4. Alternative Learning Activities
5. Optional Quest or Attitudinal Activities
6. Pre-evaluation, Self-evaluation and Post-evaluation Instruments
7. Teachers' Guide

It is the intent of this article to describe each package component and to explain its functional relationship to the package in general. The last part of the article outlines a guide for evaluating each package component.

### Rationale

The rationale describes the purpose of the package and its importance for the student's course of study. It establishes a continuity with the student's previous learning experiences and forms a framework for his subsequent experiences. The rationale should explain what is going to be learned and why it should be learned.

### Content Description

The content description indicates the level and complexity of the content and identifies the concepts, skills or values that the learner should be able to demonstrate after completing the package. The major content area should be specified along with any sub-content areas that are included. Most packages are designed to deal with a single or small number of concepts, skills or values.

### Behavioral Objectives

The entire individualized instruction package is designed to help a learner achieve specified terminal objectives or behaviors. These behavioral objectives are the foundation of an individualized instruction package, upon which the remainder of the package is based. The behavioral objectives translate the package concepts, skills or values into a form which provides direction to the learner in order that he may acquire and demonstrate proficiency after completing the package.

The behavioral objectives describe what the learner is to do, the conditions under which he is expected to do it, and the minimum level of acceptable performance. The student therefore knows exactly what is expected of him and exactly on what he will be tested at the conclusion of that particular package. Behavioral objectives also serve as planning guides for both the package developer and the learner. The package developer uses behavioral objectives to outline the appropriate activities to be included in the package. The learner uses behavioral objectives to plan his study and determine the appropriate instructional resources that he will need to help achieve the terminal behaviors. By specifying the package's behavioral objectives the learner, after reading the objectives, can determine which of the objectives he already possesses and concentrate his study on those unfamiliar areas, eliminating redundant study and wasted time.

### Alternative Learning Activities

Alternative learning activities must be made available in order to meet the varied and unique characteristics of each learner. An individualized instruction package is not truly *individualized* unless a choice of activities is presented to the learner so that the learner may choose activities best suited to his own particular learning style. Alternative activities should be organized in a manner that allows the learner to choose different methods of achieving the specified behavioral objectives. Activities may include writing, reading, viewing, listening, discussing, participating or any other exercise related to achieving the package objectives. To further help account for individual ability and comprehension levels, the alternative activities should be developed on differing levels of sophistication.

Within the alternative activities there must be a diversified variety of media and materials. In mastering an objective the learner should be able to work with resources such as books, films or filmstrips, audio or video tapes, slides, programmed instruction materials or kits and games. These diversified resources may be used singly or in various combinations in order to help the learner achieve certain objectives. As with the alternative activities, a diversity of resources should be provided to allow for variations in learning styles and rates. The individualized instruction package must try to provide learning activities and resources to fit the needs of each learner.

In addition to outlining the learning activities, detailed instructions must be provided so that the learner can independently complete the package. It is usually helpful to suggest at least a tentative sequence that the learner may follow in working with the resource materials. Some learners may follow the suggested sequential plan while others may pick and choose activities and resources to satisfy their own needs and interests. Providing a choice of learning activities allows the learner to decide how he will learn.

**Optional Quest or Attitudinal Activities**

Many individualized instruction packages include optional quest or attitudinal activities which provide the learner with the opportunity to search or study in depth beyond the limits of the structured learning activities. These activities can be either an extension of the concepts, skills or values studied in the package or a deeper exploration of related concepts, skills or values. The package author may suggest several activities which challenge the learner to engage in activities beyond the limits of the package or these activities may be left to the discretion of the learner and be entirely learner initiated. These optional quest activities allow the learner to express or develop attitudes, beliefs or feelings concerning the content of a package and to apply these values to real-life experiences. Quest activities enable the individualized instruction package to become a developmental and creative learning experience as well as a performance-oriented learning exercise.

**Pre-Evaluation, Self-Evaluation,
Post-Evaluation Instruments**

In order to monitor a learner's progress in achieving the terminal objectives, three types of evaluation instruments are included in an individualized instruction package. The first instrument is a *PRETEST*. The pretest serves as a guide to the learner by indicating what material or objectives he already knows and what materials he must learn. Using this assessment as a basis, the learner can choose the most appropriate resource materials to fulfill his particular needs, or he may test out of this package and proceed on to the next package.

A second evaluation instrument is a *SELF-TEST*. This test is a form of self-assessment used by the learner to monitor his own progress while completing the learning activities. The self-test may be a formal quiz or merely directions for the learner to periodically review the behavioral objectives in order to evaluate his progress in achieving each of the objectives.

The third evaluation instrument is a *POSTTEST*, which is utilized after the individualized instruction package is completed, to determine if the learner has attained the minimum competencies specified for that package. The posttest is usually administered when the learner feels that he is prepared to demonstrate that he has achieved the terminal objectives. If the learner does not successfully complete the posttest, he should be directed to go back and restudy the learning activities until he can successfully complete the package objectives.

All three evaluation instruments are similar in that each evaluates the learner's performance in terms of the initially stated behavioral objectives. The format of the evaluation instruments is usually some form of paper and pencil multiple choice test. However, the evaluation instruments may take other forms, such as oral or manipulative exams, or laboratory exercises or projects. The evaluation instruments may or may not include questions concerning the quest activities. Ordinarily, the three evaluation instruments are utilized before quest activities are begun.

## Teachers' Guide

A teachers' guide should be developed along with the individualized instruction package in order to provide supplementary information relating to the content and use of the package. This guide should include any explanatory information which will help another teacher effectively utilize the individualized instruction package, the answer keys for the evaluation instruments, a list of any special materials required, and a description of any necessary equipment or facilities that are used in conjunction with the package.

   Individualized instruction packages are the foundation of the individualized approach to instruction and are extremely powerful teaching and learning devices. To be effective, however, they must be carefully planned, sequenced and utilized in an environment which enhances their contribution to the learning process.

   The following pages contain a summary of the components in an individualized instruction package in the form of an evaluation guide. This guide may be used to evaluate completed packages or as a component reference that may be used while developing new packages.

### Individualized Instruction Package Evaluation Guide

*IIP Title* .................................................................................

*Producer* ................................... *Production Date* ...................

*Subject Area* .............................. *Grade or Age Level* ................

*Rationale*

                                 Yes   No

   Does the rationale explain the purpose of the package?    ........   ........

   Does the rationale indicate what is going to be learned and why it should be learned?    ........   ........

*Content Description*

   Is the subject area described?    ........   ........

   Are the package concepts, skills and values identified?    ........   ........

|  | Yes | No |
|---|---|---|

Is the level and complexity of the content described?  ........  ........

## Behavioral Objectives

Is the package content translated into behavioral terms?  ........  ........

Is there an objective to cover all concepts, skills or values identified in the content section?  ........  ........

Does each objective state what the learner is to do and how he is to do it?  ........  ........

Do the behavioral objectives tell the learner exactly what is expected of him?  ........  ........

## Alternative Learning Activities

Are there at least 2 or 3 alternative learning activities designed to achieve the objectives?  ........  ........

Are instructions for the activities clearly stated?  ........  ........

Are there a variety of activities on varying levels of sophistication?  ........  ........

Do the learning activities allow for individual differences in learning styles and abilities?  ........  ........

|  | Yes | No |
|---|---|---|

Do the activities contain diversified media either commercially available or locally produced?

Is the media utilized justified in terms of the type and level of the package?

### Optional Quest or Attitudinal Activities

Do the quest activities relate the package content to material or situations outside the package?

Do the quest activities provide the learner a chance to develop personal attitudes or values toward the subject matter?

Do the quest activities allow the learner to study in depth beyond the limits of the structured learning activities?

### Pre/Self/Post Test Evaluation Instruments

Are all three evaluation instruments included?

Do the evaluation instruments relate directly to the behavioral objectives?

Do all three evaluation instruments cover the same content?

Do the evaluation instruments effec-

|                                                                                    | Yes      | No       |
| ---------------------------------------------------------------------------------- | -------- | -------- |
| tively measure the package content?                                                | ........ | ........ |

*Teachers' Guide*

|                                                                                          | Yes      | No       |
| ---------------------------------------------------------------------------------------- | -------- | -------- |
| Does the Teachers' Guide explain procedures for utilizing the package?                   | ........ | ........ |
| Does the Teachers' Guide list any special materials required by the package?             | ........ | ........ |
| Does the Teachers' Guide describe any equipment or facilities necessary for utilizing the package? | ........ | ........ |
| Does the Teachers' Guide contain evaluation instrument answer keys?                      | ........ | ........ |

# BIBLIOGRAPHY

## Established Individualized Instruction Formats

"Administrative Training Program for IPI Mathematics." Unpublished Paper, Philadelphia: Research for Better Schools, Inc., 1969.

Adelmen, H.S. and Feshback, S. "Experimental Program of Personalized Classroom Instruction in Disadvantaged Areas Schools." *Psychology in the Schools*, Vol. 8, April 1971, pp. 114-120.

Anderson, D.E. "Using IPI in Math Makes Progress in Bethel Park," *Nations Schools*, Vol. 83, April 1969, p. 82.

"Aspects of Instructional Design in PLAN," Project PLAN, Palo Alto, California: Westinghouse Learning Corp.

Baley, John D. and Benesch, Mary D. "A System for Individualized Math Instruction in Secondary Schools," TRW Systems Group, Redendo Beach, California, July 1969, 9 pp., ERIC No. ED050555.

Barone, Frank. "Communication Arts: Individualization Through Curriculum Content and the Small Group," *California English Journal*, Vol. 5, No. 3, October 1969, pp. 27-30.

Beck, Isabel L. and Bolvin, John O. "A Model for Non-Gradedness: The Reading Program for Individually Prescribed Instruction, Part III of a Symposium: Language Arts in the Non-Graded Schools," *Elementary English*, Vol. 46, February 1969, p. 2.

Becker, James W. and Scanlon, Robert. "Applying Computers and Educational Technology to Individually Prescribed Instruction," Paper presented to Eastern Regional Conference on Science and Technology, Boston, April 1970.

Behrendt, David. "Away with Tradition," *American Education*, Vol. 6, No. 1, January-February 1970, pp. 18-20.

Beltz, G. and Kohn, D.A. "Independent Study in Five Missouri High Schools," *Clearing House*, Vol. 44, February 1970, pp. 334-337.

Berg, D.W. "Independent Study: Transfusion for Anemic English Programs," *English Journal*, Vol. 59, February 1970, pp. 354-358.

Bergeson, John B., Roettger, Charles and Sanders, William B. "Two Experiences in Individualizing," *Instructor*, Vol. 80, No. 6, February

1971, pp. 70-73.

Bolvin, John and Glaser, Robert. "Developmental Aspects of IPI," *Audiovisual Instruction*, Vol. 13, October 1968, pp. 828-831.

Bullough, Robert V. "Individualizing Instruction on a Shoestring," *Audiovisual Instruction*, Vol. 17, No. 2, February 1972, pp. 37-39.

Burkman, E. "ISCS: An Individualized Approach to Science Instruction," *Science Teacher*, Vol. 37, December 1970, pp. 27-30.

Bybee, R.W. "Effectiveness of an Individualized Approach to a General Education Earth Science Laboratory," *Science Education*, Vol. 54, April 1970, pp. 157-161.

Calvin, Allen D. "Student Centered Instruction," *Educational Media*, Vol. 2, No. 2, May 1970, pp. 13-15.

Campbell, V.N. and others. "PLAN Social Studies: The Match Between Long-Range Objectives and the 1970-71 Curriculum," American Institutes for Research, July 1970, 80 pp., ERIC No. ED045491.

Carmichael, Dennis and Kallenback, Wallen. "The California Teacher Development Project: An Individualized Approach to In-Service Education," *Journal of Secondary Education*, Vol. 46, No. 1, January 1970, pp. 16-20.

Carrier, Robert. "Individualizing in One Room," *Instructor*, Vol. 80, No. 1, August-September 1970, p. 79.

Cole, C. "Independent Study in Science," *School Science and Math*, Vol. 71, March 1971, pp. 236-244.

Daniel, A.W. "Example of Individual Instruction in Developmental Physical Education," *Journal of Health, Physical Education and Recreation*, Vol. 40, May 1969, p. 56.

Davis, F.W. and Lucas, J.S. "Experiment in Individualized Reading," *Reading Teacher*, Vol. 24, May 1971, pp. 737-743+.

Deep, Donald. "PLAN—Educational Automat," *Journal*, December 1969.

Denby, R.V. "Independent Study Programs NCTE/ERIC Report," *English Journal*, Vol. 53, December 1969, pp. 1376-1400.

DeRenzis, Joseph J. "A Summary List of Problems That Exist in the Standard Teaching Sequence Booklets Which Are Used in the IPI Math Curriculum, Including Suggested Changes." Unpublished paper, Philadelphia: Research for Better Schools, Inc., 1969.

DeRenzis, Joseph J. "An Investigation into the Attitude Patterns and Their Relationship to Prescription Writing Procedures of Teachers Using the IPI Instructional System in Elementary Math." Unpublished Doctoral Dissertation, Philadelphia: Temple University, 1970.

DeRenzis, Joseph J. "Individually Prescribed Instruction: Background Information and Research," Paper presented at the International Reading Assoc. Convention, Atlantic City, New Jersey, April 1971, 19 pp., ERIC No. ED051974.

Derose, J.V. "Independent Study in High School Chemistry," *Journal of*

*Chemical Education,* Vol. 47, August 1970, pp. 553-560.

Dover, N.B. "Individualized Instruction Offers Challenge," *Business Education Forum,* Vol. 25, December 1970, pp. 17-18.

Duffey, B.R. "Individualizing Mathematics; Tape Helps Each Student Do His Own Thing," *Audiovisual Instruction,* Vol. 14, February 1969, pp. 55-56.

Dunn, James A., "Project PLAN, Guidance Through the Instructional Process," *American Institutes for Research,* 1969.

Dunn, Rita Stafford. "Individualized Instruction Through Contracts—Does It Work With Very Young Children?" *Audiovisual Instruction,* Vol. 16, No. 3, March 1971, pp. 78-80.

Eastman, S.W. "Biology in an Individualized School," *American Biology Teacher,* Vol. 32, December 1970, pp. 533-536.

*Educational Technology,* Vol. 12. No. 3, March 1972, see entire issue entitled "Individualizing Mathematics Instruction," 59 pp.

Edwards, R.K. "At Lansing Community College: Audiovisual Tutorial Instruction in Business," *Junior College Journal,* Vol. 39, May 1969, p. 56+.

Elkins, F. Clark. "1971 Distinguished Achievement Award," *Excellence in Teacher Education,* Published by the American Association of Colleges for Teacher Education, p. 5.

Engel, D. and Jorgenson, K.J. "Individualized Science with Behavioral Objectives," *Science Teacher,* Vol. 37, November 1970, pp. 22-23.

Erhart, H.R. and Mellander, D.S. "Experiences with an Audio-Visual-Tutorial Laboratory," *Journal of Geography,* Vol. 68, February 1969, pp. 88-92.

Esbensen, Thorwald. "Student Learning Contracts: The Duluth Model," *Educational Screen and Audio-Visual Guide,* Vol. 48, January 1969, pp. 16-17.

Fagan, E.R. "Individualizing the Study of English," *English Journal,* Vol. 60, February 1971, pp. 236-241.

Fairman, Marvin. "Individualizing Instruction Through IPI," *Educational Leadership,* Vol. 28, No. 2, November 1970, pp. 133-136.

Fisher, R.L. "Physical Science Project; An Individualized Two-Year Chemistry and Physics Course," *Science Teacher,* Vol. 36, December 1969, p. 60+.

Fitzpatrick, Edmund W. "Model for Designing a System to Individualize Instruction and Guarantee Learning. Final Report," Sterling Institute, Washington, D.C., August 1970, 329 pp., ERIC No. ED043791.

Flanagan, John C. "Program for Learning in Accordance with Needs," *Psychology in the Schools,* Vol. 6, No. 2, April 1969, pp. 133-136.

Foster, Kenneth L. "Student Goal Centered Learning Program," *The Clearing House,* Vol. 45, No. 4, December 1970, pp. 212-215.

Fulton, H.F. "Individualized vs. Group Teaching of BSCS Biology," *American Biology Teacher,* Vol. 33, May 1971, pp. 277-279+.

Gibbs, W.E. "Individualizing Bookkeeping Instruction," *Business Education Forum*, Vol. 23, January 1969, pp. 21-22.

Glass, L.W. and Yager, R.E. "Individualized Instruction as a Spur to Understanding the Scientific Enterprise," *American Biology Teacher*, Vol. 32, September 1970, pp. 359-361.

Glines, Donald. "Wilson Campus School," *Automated Education Newsletter*, Vol. 5, No. 2, February 1970, pp. 3-8.

Gordon, W.M. and others. "ImPALLA: A New Approach to Secondary School Language Arts," *English Journal*, Vol. 59, April 1970, pp. 534-539.

Gougher, Ronald and Bockman, John, Eds. "Individualization of Foreign Language Learning in America, I," West Chester State College, Penn., December 1970, 9 pp., ERIC No. ED051684.

Haefele, Donald Z. "Self-Instruction and Teacher Education," *Audiovisual Instruction*, Vol. 14, No. 1, January 1969, pp. 63-64.

Harmon, Katharine. "Getting Ready to Individualize," *Instructor*, Vol. 79, No. 10, June-July 1970, pp. 87-89.

Herd, Arthur A. "Successful Practices in Individualized Instruction," *Education Digest*, Vol. 37, No. 7, March 1972, pp. 37-40.

Hinex, J.C. "School for Autonomy," *Instructor*, August-September 1970, pp. 44-46.

Holt, D. "Individualized Business Courses," *School and Community*, Vol. 55, April 1969, pp. 24+.

Hosier, R.J. "Individualized Learning in Business Subjects," *Business Education Forum*, Vol. 24, February 1970, p. 2.

Humphreys, D.A. "Individualized Audio-Visual Tutorial Methods in Undergraduate Chemistry," *Journal of Chemical Education*, Vol. 48, April 1971, pp. 277-278.

Hunt, L.C. "Six Steps to the Individualized Reading Program (IRP)," *Elementary English*, Vol. 48, January 1971, pp. 27-32.

Hunter, C. "Individualized Instruction in the Auto Shop," *School Shop*, Vol. 29, May 1970, pp. 38-40.

Husband, David D. "The Autotutorial System," *Audiovisual Instruction*, Vol. 15, No. 2, February 1970, pp. 34-35.

Jenness, L.S. and Benier, G.G. "Independent Study Seminar Approach to Afro-American History," *National Association of Secondary Schools Principals' Bulletin*, Vol. 54, April 1970, pp. 58-66.

Johnson, T.D. "Bibliography for Self-Directed Practice in Reading," *Journal of Reading*, Vol. 13, February 1970, pp. 370-378.

Kaplan, Abraham. "Individualization Without Nongradedness," *Instructor*, Vol. 79, No. 6, February 1970, pp. 66-67.

Klausmeier, Herbert J. and others. "Instructional Programming for the Individual Pupil in the Multiunit Elementary School," *The Elementary School Journal*, November 1971, pp. 88-100.

Krockover, G.H. "Individualizing Secondary School Chemistry Instruction," *School Science and Math,* Vol. 71, June 1971, pp. 518-524.

Kroenke, Richard G. "Individualizing Reading Instruction at the Junior High Level." Paper presented at the International Reading Assoc. Convention, Atlantic City, New Jersey, April 1971, 14 pp., ERIC No. ED051971.

Krynske, Elizabeth. "Individualizing Reading," *Instructor,* November 1971, p. 104.

Langstaff, Ann L. and Volkmor, Cara B. "A Method for Creating and Continuing Individualized Instruction," Paper presented at the conference of the Association for Children with Learning Disabilities, Fort Worth, Texas, March 1969, 14 pp., ERIC No. ED044320.

Lazerick, Beth. "We Individualize Math," *Instructor,* Vol. 79, No. 7, March 1970, p. 64.

Lipe, James Gary. "The Development and Implementation of a Model for the Design of Individualized Instruction at the University Level," Florida State University, Tallahassee, October 1970, 196 pp., ERIC No. ED046252.

Lipson, J. "Individualization of Instruction in Junior High School Mathematics," Published by N.C.T.M., November 1970, 29 pp., ERIC No. ED046742.

Lloyd, A.C. "Meeting Individual Needs of Office Clinical Students Through Individualized Programs of Instruction," *Business Education Forum,* Vol. 23, February 1969, pp. 12-14.

Long, Charles R. "Individualized Mediated Learning in Business and Office Education for the Disadvantaged," *Educational Technology,* Vol. 9, No. 3, March 1971, pp. 47-48.

Lum, Lillian A. "They Packaged Concept 9," *Audiovisual Instruction,* Vol. 16, No. 8, October 1971, pp. 39-41.

Marusek, J. "Program Providing Highly Individualized Instruction for Slow Learning Math and Science Students," *Science Education,* Vol. 53, April 1969, pp. 217-219.

McCurdy and Fisher, R.L. "A Program to Individualize Instruction in Chemistry and Physics," *School Science and Mathematics,* Vol. 71, June 1971, pp. 508-512.

McBurney, W.F. "Individualized Instruction: A Case for the Independent Student Investigation in Science," *School Science and Mathematics,* Vol. 69, December 1969, pp. 827-830.

McCurdy and Fisher, R.L. "A Program to Individualize Instruction in Chemistry and Physics," *School Science and Mathematics,* Vol. 71, June 1971, pp. 508-512.

McNeil, A. and Smith, James E. "The Multis at Nova," *Educational Screen and Audiovisual Guide,* Vol. 47, No. 1, January 1968, pp. 16-19 and 43.

Miller, W.H. "Organizing a First Grade Classroom for Individualized Reading Instruction," *Reading Teacher,* Vol. 24, May 1971, pp. 748-752.

"Model Programs: Childhood Education, Project PLAN," American Institutes for Research, Palo Alto, California, 1970, 22 pp., ERIC No. ED044751.

Morton, John. "Contract Learning in Texarkana," *Educational Screen and Audiovisual Guide*, Vol. 49, February 1970, pp. 12-13.

Myers, F.G. "Plan for All Seasons: Independent Study in an English Electives Program," *English Journal*, Vol. 59, February 1970, pp. 244-246+.

Odom, S.C. "Individualizing a Reading Program," *Reading Teacher*, Vol. 24, February 1971, pp. 403-410.

O'Donnel, Patrick and Lavaroin, Charles W. "What Are You Doing About the IQ Level in Your District?" *California Journal for Instructional Improvement*, Vol. 13, March 1970, pp. 26-37.

Ogston, T.J. "Individualized Instruction: Changing the Role of the Teacher," *Audiovisual Instruction*, Vol. 13, No. 3, March 1968, p. 243.

Olson, A.L. "Learning Management Model Designed to Individualize the Learning of Skills, Concepts, and Attitudes Inherent in the Clerical Sector of Learning," Seattle Public Schools, August 1970, 12 pp., ERIC No. ED042857.

O'Toole, R.J. "Review of Attempts to Individualize Elementary School Science," *School Science and Math*, Vol. 68, May 1968, pp. 385-390.

Pease, D.W. "Independent Study of a Foreign Language at Levels One and Two in High School," *Modern Language Journal*, Vol. 55, February 1971, pp. 88-92.

Perkin, R.I. "Structured Independent-Study Course in Chemistry," *Science Teacher*, Vol. 37, November 1970, pp. 19-20.

Piercnek, Florence T. "A Survey of Individualized Reading and Mathematics Programs," Calgary Separate Board, Alberta, 1969, 66 pp., ERIC No. ED047894.

"The PLAN Classroom. A Guide for Consultants," Westinghouse Learning Corporation, Palo Alto, California, 1969, 18 pp., ERIC No. ED045576.

Politzer, Robert, "Toward Individualization in Foreign Language Teaching," *Modern Language Journal*, Vol. 55, No. 4, April 1971, pp. 207-212.

Postlethwait, S. "Mediated Self Instruction," *American Annals of the Deaf*, Vol. 114, November 1969, pp. 874-879.

*Progress Report II: Individually Prescribed Instruction.* Philadelphia: Research for Better Schools, Inc., March 1971, 97 pp.

"Projects on Individualizing Instruction," *The Arithmetic Teacher*, Vol. 18, March 1971, pp. 161-163.

Quale, Therald P. "Individualized Science for the Slow Learner," *Today's Education*, March 1970.

Rachofsky, M. "Math with an Individual Twist," *School Science and Math*, Vol. 71, April 1971, pp. 325-326.

Rahmlow, Harold F. "Use of Student Performance Data for Improvement of Individualized Instructional Materials," American Psychological Assoc. Symposium, Washington, D.C., September 1969.

Richard, P.W. "Experimental Individualized BSCS Biology," *Science Teacher,* Vol. 36, February 1969, pp. 53-54.

Richard, P. and Sund, R.B. "Individualized Instruction in Biology," *American Biology Teacher,* Vol. 31, April 1969, pp. 252-256.

Richardson, R.J. "Information System for Individualized Instruction in an Elementary School," *Education and Psychological Measurement,* Vol. 29, Spring 1969, pp. 199-201.

Rockhill, Theron D. "The Development of an Individualized Instructional Program in Beginning College Mathematics Utilizing Computer Based Research Units. Final Report." State University of New York, Brockport, June 1971, 79 pp., ERIC No. ED053966.

Rudder, Cynthia. "How Do I Get Them To Go Home?" *The Education Digest,* Vol. 36, No. 7, March 1971, pp. 32-34.

Ryberg, Donald. "Student Involvement, Flexibility and Individualization," *Washington Foreign Language Program Newsletter,* February 15, 1971, 8 pp., ERIC No. ED048785.

Sato, J.J. "Flexible Scheduling and Independent Study in Advanced Clothing," *Journal of Home Economics,* Vol. 60, November 1968, pp. 733-735.

Schiavone, James. "Individually Prescribed Instruction (IPI) in Reading," *Education,* Vol. 90, No. 2, November-December 1969, pp. 164-166.

Schueller, Arthur W. "Reading, First Steps to Individualization," *Instructor,* Vol. 81, No. 5, January 1972, pp. 53-55.

Schueller, Arthur, W. "Setting up Reading Stations," *Instructor,* April 1972, pp. 57-59.

Shipp, Pauline. "Step to the Back of the Class: An Approach to Individualized Learning," *English Journal,* Vol. 61, No. 1, January 1972, pp. 87-91.

Short, S.H. "Development and Utilization of a Self Instruction Laboratory: College Level Foods Course," *Journal of Home Economics,* Vol. 61, January 1969, pp. 40-44.

Short, S. "Innovations in Nutrition Education," *Audiovisual Instruction,* Vol. 16, October 1971, pp. 19-21.

Simmons, J.R. and others. "Independent-Study Methods and the Gifted Biology Student," *American Biology Teacher,* Vol. 33, October 1971, pp. 416-418.

Sinks, Thomas A. "Individual Progress—A Study of Seventh Graders," *The Clearing House,* Vol. 44, No. 8, April 1970, pp. 457-460.

Smith, Kenneth J. *A LAP on Writing LAP's,* Fort Lauderdale, Florida: Broward County Board of Public Instruction, November 1969, 37 pp.

Spaulding, Robert L. "Personalized Education in Southside School," *Elementary School Journal,* Vol. 70, January 1970, pp. 180-189.

Sorensen, P. "Program for Learning in Accordance with Needs," *Phi Delta Kappan,* Vol. 52, November 1970, pp. 180-181.

Steffan, Don C. "The Multimedia Classroom," *American Education*, Vol. 7, August 1971, pp. 28-30.

Stein, J.U. "Adapted Physical Education: Individualized Instruction in Diversified Physical Activities," *Journal of Health, Physical Education, and Recreation*, Vol. 40, May 1969, pp. 45-60.

Stuckles, E.R. "Planning for Individualized Instruction of Deaf Students at NTID," *American Annals of the Deaf*, Vol. 114, November 1969, pp. 868-873.

Studer, Harold R. "Individualizing Mathematics in an Integrated School," *Pennsylvania School Journal*, December 1969.

Summerfeit, A.E. "Individualized Learning in Home Economics," *Journal of Secondary Education*, Vol. 45, April 1970, pp. 185-187.

Sund, Robert B. and Richard, Paul. "Individualized Instruction in Biology," *American Biology Teacher*, Vol. 31, No. 4, April 1969, pp. 252-256.

Swenson, Gardner, "A Unipac on How to Make A Unipac," *Journal of Secondary Education*, Vol. 46, No. 5, May 1971, pp. 231-236.

Syrockl, B.J. "Audio-Video Tutorial Program," *American Biology Teacher*, Vol. 31, February 1969, pp. 91-96.

Tanner, L.N. and Tanner, D. "News Notes—Prescribing Instruction," *Educational Leadership*, Vol. 28, No. 6, March 1971, p. 685.

Tanzman, Jack. "Do It Yourself Mediated Packages for Your District," *School Management*, Vol. 15, No. 10, October 1971, p. 38.

Trusty, K. "Principles of Learning and Individualized Reading," *Reading Teacher*, Vol. 24, May 1971, pp. 730-739.

Tuckman, Bruce W. "The Student-Centered Curriculum: A Concept in Curriculum Innovation," *Educational Technology*, Vol. 9, No. 10, October 1969, pp. 26-29.

Turner, W.E. "Individualizing Spelling with 600 Students," *Instructor*, Vol. 80, August 1970, p. 142.

Ullery, J. William. "Individualized Instructional Systems for Vocational Education," *Educational Technology*, Vol. 9, No. 3, March 1971, pp. 22-25.

Van Dyk, H. and Beltrame, I. "Hillsdale Plan: Solution and Salvation," *Journal of Reading*, Vol. 12, December 1969, pp. 224-228.

Van Vlack, Milton. "Curriculum Materials Feature Learning Activity Packages," *Educational Screen and Audio Visual Guide*, Vol. 48, No. 10, October 1969, pp. 12-13 and 28.

Vars, Gordon F. "Student Evaluation: A Design for the Middle School," *The Clearing House*, Vol. 45, No. 1, September 1970, pp. 18-21.

Weisgerber, Robert A. and Rahmlow, Harold F. "Individually Managed Learning," *Audiovisual Instruction*, Vol. 13, No. 8, October 1968, pp. 835-839.

Wermer, M. "Computer-Assisted Planning and Scheduling of Individualized Programs of Study in Science and Mathematics at the Secondary Level,"

*Journal of Educational Research,* Vol. 64, November 1970, pp. 127-132.

Wheless, B.F. "Independent Study at Sollins," *Junior College Journal,* Vol. 41, October 1970, pp. 27-31.

Wiener, W.K. and others. "Reorganizing the Schools for IPI; Jamesville DeWitt Central Schools, New York." *National Association of Secondary School Principals Bulletin,* Vol. 55, May 1971, pp. 59-67.

Williams, William W. "An Experimental Investigation of Individualized Instruction in the Teaching of Quantitative Physical Science," Duke University, Durham, North Carolina, 1969, 101 pp. ERIC No. ED052015.

Wing, R. Cliff and Mack, Patricia H. "Wide Open for Learning," *American Education,* Vol. 6, No. 9, November 1970, pp. 13-16.

Wolfe, James E. "At Nova, Education Comes in Small Packages," *Nations Schools,* Vol. 81, No. 6, June 1968, pp. 48-59 and 90.

Wright, Calvin E. "Project PLAN Progress Report," *Education,* Vol. 90, No. 3, February-March 1970, pp. 261-273.

# PART 3

# MEDIA IN INDIVIDUALIZED INSTRUCTION

# PART 3

## Media in Individualized Instruction

The roles that media play in an individualized instruction program are considerably different from their roles in traditional group oriented instruction. In an individualized instruction program media are handled directly by the learner and are integral parts of the curriculum. Media become vehicles utilized to compensate for individual differences in learning styles and to provide alternative means of achieving objectives. The articles in this section discuss the changing role of media and describe several methods of effectively integrating media into the instructional program.

Torkelson approaches the utilization of media by first defining the rationale for media and stressing that the use of instructional media is neither a panacea nor a substitute that may be used in the place of well-organized instruction. Torkelson goes on to define precisely what media are and what media are not. He refers to a medium as anything that links the learner and his environment. He warns of misuse of terms, ineffective media presentations and technology used solely for its novelty.

Kemp sets forth guidelines for the selection of various media for instructional purposes. Selection is simplified with the inclusion of three media-decision diagrams. The diagrams break down large group presentation, small group interaction, and independent study into several types of experiences and suggest media which would help create the desired experiences.

In the next article the editor of this volume outlines the various types of commonly used instructional media in terms of their use in individualized instruction. A list is provided which summarizes the characteristics of both the media and the equipment required for viewing or listening to each medium. The article concludes with a chart which may be used as a handy reference for evaluating potential media selections.

Looking at the total school environment, Burr, an architect, succinctly summarizes many of the present trends concerning individualized instruction, and he translates these trends into future school building requirements. His design parameters center on individualized learning, with emphasis on the changing roles of the student, the teacher and the physical environment.

In the next article, Melcher emphasizes that the book is still one of the most abundant and potentially useful media available. He warns against automatically discarding the book in preference to newer media. He enumerates the advantages of books in comparison to other media, emphasizing the vast flexibility and cost differences. Though he agrees that textbooks have been greatly misused, he argues that books are still the mainstay of the learning process.

Weisgerber describes the various applications of technology as incorporated by Project PLAN, with its wide range of support services inside and outside of the classroom. The author discusses the requirements of facility design and the considerations that must be given to equipment selection. Weisgerber concludes with several suggestions for making media accessible to the learner, while maintaining an efficient control system. Weisgerber points out that systems for media control are an integral part of a mediated individualized instruction program.

The next two articles in this section concentrate on the development and use of learning centers. In the first article, Daniels emphasizes that learning centers are not merely hardware or independent study carrels. Daniels suggests several advantages of a learning center, but he also warns against media becoming the program, instead of a means to implement the program.

In the second article, North supports the argument that a building's form must follow its function, especially when following the educational philosophy of individualized instruction. He diagrams the functional relationships in a module and provides the actual floorplan.

In the final article in this section, Hooper looks at the future of education and discusses those current educational trends that seem likely to shape future development. He redefines the teacher's role in light of individualized instruction and the open school. With heavy emphasis on media, he evaluates educational opportunities and educational demands of today and as seen for the future.

equal option to say that since the school has nothing to offer, the student must look elsewhere for his education. So-called "free" schools are an attempt to provide unrestricted options.

A more moderate approach is one more widely used. Here the student selects optional paths and time units for accomplishing certain goals, even some he may suggest as radical departures from accepted school routine. Instead of an arbitrary division of the day into traditional units, the learner proceeds toward his goals at his own pace and with a distribution of time more suited to his needs. In high school, for example, a learner may decide to spend a week or two working solely on a science project. The fundamental understanding in this arrangement is that the learner will demonstrate competency in all the subjects demanded by the legal educational agency, although in some places even the arbitrariness of legal agencies is being questioned. The student's job is to plan his own activities to meet requirements.

The most conservative level of individualization provides optional ways for individuals to learn a prescribed curriculum. Flexibility may be provided in the time a learner spends on a given task, but the nature of the content and the deadlines to be met are fairly circumscribed. Individualization may mean simply preparing materials for independent study, with goals and activities prescribed, with standard materials used by each student.

In this setting when fundamental functions of schools are being questioned and where new patterns of instruction are emerging, what are contributions of the new technology?

## The New Technology

The first point to be made is that expecting the "new technology" to be a panacea for solving educational problems is apt to be misleading. Most educators would associate such things as television, video tape recorders, computer assisted instruction, remote access information retrieval, 8mm film loops, cassette tapes and information miniaturization as typical of the "new technology." While these materials and devices are part of the new technology, focusing upon them outside the perspective of teaching-learning processes may lead to unwarranted expectations about their capacities.

One of the problems that has arisen in individualized instruction has been the expectation that almost any of the new devices are applicable. Closed circuit television, for example, has had its greatest use in reaching a large, dispersed audience simultaneously and in demonstration magnification. Less attention has been paid to making the "distributed" television a way for individualizing instruction.

Closed circuit television is primarily a group instruction system which, in a sense, averages the individual's capabilities according to some assumed group norms. This in no way can be true individualization of instruction. One needs only to record the variance in abilities and motivations among members of a group organized on some "homogeneous" criterion to determine this fact. Realistically, closed circuit television must be recognized as instruction of groups, and individualization of instruction in only the grossest sense. On the other hand, where stored television images are made available to individuals via some retrieval system, we may begin to approach the application of television to the needs of individuals, assuming that the retrieval of the visual image is subject to each learner's personal request for visualization.

The potentials of the new technology for the individualization of instruction are realizable only out of an adequate perception of what is really meant by the new technology and upon a system of instruction which consciously organizes to determine the uniqueness of all means of *media* of instruction for different kinds of learners and for different kinds of instructional purposes. All forms of media are capable of helping learners to comprehend concepts, to acquire skills and to shape feelings.

Much research regarding the contributions of media to learning has tended to be non-additive in the sense that discrete research under isolated circumstances is not usually based on some broad theoretical conception of learning. This lack of clear evidence about media and the "new technology" is due also in part to the lack of precision in analyzing their place in the educational setting.

## Potentials of Technology

A case in point is the glib use of the term "instructional technology," popular jargon, but ofttimes not completely understood. To some, this term refers to the uses of equipment for teaching, as though technology refers to the mechanization of instruction. In actuality, technology is derived from the Greek word "technologia," which means "systematic treatment," or the process of analyzing a problem and then deriving a system of logistics and support, both material and personnel, to solve that problem. Given this context, *media* as traditionally known are only part of the total array of resources available for solving instructional problems. Also, media as a term is not confined to the new machines and the "software" they require.

It is more precise to say that *media* refers to mediators between the learner and his environment, interpreting "environment" in the broadest sense. One of a teacher's primary responsibilities is to select and prepare *media* or *surrogates* to represent the "reality" of the world. Most of what is provided in schools is a substitute for reality, most often of a symbolic and abstract nature. When the teacher uses words and gestures to give "reality" to some concept, the teacher is acting as a medium, one of an array of media available for representing reality. Thus, the teacher's biases, perceptions of reality, knowledge level and skill in communication color the message to which the learner must react. The teacher, therefore, must be regarded as a message system and scrutinized as carefully as a motion picture, a filmstrip, or a graphic device for the *uniqueness* each has to offer. Understanding this concept of *media* and *mediation processes* allows the teacher to analyze more objectively which *medium* or combination of *mediums* will provide the best learning situation for each learner.

The potentials for individualizing instruction for masses of students are greater today because of some of the newer instructional devices that can tirelessly present instruction on demand, can maintain records of student performance, and can print out each learner's progress. Where information, concepts and skills to be learned are amenable to the expository process and can be organized into retrievable forms, whether in a complex remote retrieval system, a multi-media system, or simply in the traditional textbook, the teacher can be relieved of activities he formerly had to perform because of the lack of substitute forms.

Given well-prepared materials, independent of continuous teacher direction, the potential for the teacher to begin to exercise more uniqueness as counselor, guide, confidant, synthesizer, provocateur, evaluator, creator of unique materials grows in proportion to the availability of those well-prepared materials. Please note that the teacher is not being replaced by machines, nor is the process of individualization inherently dehumanizing. Just the opposite is the real possibility. Group instruction should be used only when proved to be the best form for the occasion. Humaneness will come when personal attention is given each learner, adjusting for his unique abilities and assisting in the decision-making which he must engage in if there is to be compatibility between the purposes and processes of individualized instruction.

The reality of "new technology" applications to individualized instruction is much less than could be realized. This is due to several conditions. One is minimal understanding and commitment to the notion of individualization. It is naive for educators to expect that individualized instruction is going to blossom behind the facade of traditional programs which are being exercised in new forms, such as team teaching and modular scheduling.

Individualized instruction requires ample lead time to convert traditional instruction to the individualized format. It requires almost inordinate amounts of time for staff planning. It requires budgets which realistically face the problems of supplying adequate quantities of well-designed and validated materials. It demands logistics to uncomplicate the flow of people and materials. It demands an evaluation system which systematically gathers data about successes and failures. It requires a hard look at the viability of grades. It takes the time-consuming task of the actual production of materials out of the hands of teachers and allows them to concentrate upon the content and structure of these materials.

Individualized instruction requires a philosophical and professional commitment to the notion of allowing students and others to have a say in the content and form of instruction. It requires a fresh look at media and mediation processes, even to the point where part of the teacher's responsibility is to supply alternatives among mediation forms from which the learner chooses to suit his learning style, abilities and goals.

Individualization of instruction is consistent with the basic American dream of helping each learner to achieve his potentials. The obligation of the educational setting is to provide the best forms for learning about the essentials of one's society and a climate which allows one to accept the consequences of his own decisions. "New technology," "newer media," *all* media are central to this dream. How to provide the best *mediation* circumstance for each learner in a complex educational system needs a great deal of study.

# 17

## Which Medium?

Jerrold E. Kemp

On all levels of education we are giving increased attention to more exacting methods for designing instructional programs. Whether our method is called an "instructional system" approach or a "curriculum design" plan, the important elements include specifying objectives, deciding on instructional methods and learning activities, and then measuring and evaluating learning outcomes.

An essential part of this procedure is the selection of appropriate communications media as support for learning activities in terms of the requirements of objectives and subject content. How are media selected? On what basis is one medium chosen over another one?

Deciding on answers to these questions should be the responsibility of the instructional designer or the media specialist in cooperation with the teacher or instructional planning team. We are often very glib when telling others to " . . . now choose the *best* or *most appropriate* medium to serve an instructional need." How do you decide which is the *best* or *most appropriate* medium?

Often there is no real decision. An instructional resource, like a textbook or a 16mm film, may be conveniently available and this is what is used. Or, the choice may be entirely subjective, as when one kind of material is repetitively selected in preference to

Reprinted from *Audiovisual Instruction*, Vol. 16, No. 10, December 1971, pp. 32-36, by permission of author and publisher.

others which may be available. An example here is the teacher who always uses a filmstrip in each unit because it is the medium with which she is most comfortable or familiar. On the other hand, the availability of certain equipment, like newly acquired 8mm projectors, may be the determining factor. Also, novelty, as we may see with the use of education games, can influence the selection of a medium or technique.

These methods of casually deciding on resources for use are inappropriate and obviously are not the way to proceed when designing a systematic instructional program. They rarely give consideration to the objectives of instruction or to the kinds of stimuli students may require for effective learning.

Are there ways to make more objective decisions for selecting appropriate media to communicate content and to provide learning experiences in terms of objectives?

Answers to this and similar questions have been examined by some educational researchers. Robert Gagné, a psychologist, has been particularly interested in studying the conditions that facilitate learning. In the first edition of his book, he summarized the potential contributions of a variety of audiovisual and related media to such instructional functions as presenting feedback, and so on.[1] But in the accompanying descriptions for his tabulations one cannot find justification or a clear rationale for the recommendations made. To an experienced media specialist, some choices would seem plausible, others questionable. In the second edition of his book (1970), Gagné has dropped this table.

Another compilation of instructional media, relating to learning objectives categorized as factual information, visual identifications, principles, performing skills, attitudes and so on, was developed by William H. Allen.[2] He is a respected member of the research community in the media field and has been examining and summarizing research findings for many years. Again, while at first glance this summary seems of value, like Gagné's, it is difficult to translate the generalizations into practical guides for selecting media.

## Recent Experimental Approaches

Other researchers have attempted to deal directly with this relationship between instructional needs and media selection by setting up procedural models. Van Mondfrans and Houser suggest using a three-dimensional paradigm which matches concepts to be taught to stimulus characteristics of available media and to cognitive, perceptual and personality characteristics of the student group.[3]

Lavin developed a Media Potential Rating Scale that identifies media characteristics and learner characteristics, which, for a particular situation, are subjectively rated on a scale. This rating leads to a numerical value and selection of a medium or combination of media to serve the instructional task being considered.[4]

A matrix developed by Wilshusen and Stowe is reported in a book on design of instruction by Briggs.[5] They relate the factors of learner characteristics (instructional group size, individualization, etc.); task requirements (motion, sequencing, etc.); materials (reusable, time to obtain, cost, etc.); and transmission (equipment availability, instructor control, etc.) to a list of thirteen media. Those elements in the three categories that are generally applicable to each medium are indicated.

These approaches all seem to have similar patterns as they strive to correlate media selection with various instructional elements. Those who have developed them may understand the meaning of the descriptive terms they have selected, but like the Gagné and Allen tables, we find it difficult to apply the generalizations of these models to practical objective-based situations.

Briggs, who has been examining the matter of instructional development for many years, succinctly states the reaction of many practitioners of these models:

Unfortunately, it is not possible to make optimum media selections by simply following a chart, or table, or "cookbook," which would say essentially, "For this competency identify the type of learning listed in a column, find its intersection with type of learner listed

in a row and use the medium named at the intersection." Nor is it possible to make such mechanical
rules based on the instructional event to be supplied or
on the basis of the subject matter involved.[5]

Those of us struggling with ways to make concrete media decisions
also should heed this observation by Gagné:

> Most media of communications can readily perform
> most instructional functions. They can be performed by
> pictures, by printed language, by auditory language, or
> by a combination of media. So far as learning is
> concerned, the medium is not the message. No single
> medium possesses properties which are uniquely adapt-
> ed to perform one or a combination of instructional
> functions. Instead they all perform some of these
> functions well, and some not so well.[6]

This conclusion is substantiated by Hoban:

> When we say that each medium should be used for what
> it does best, we are begging the question. We don't
> really know, except on an armchair basis, either what
> each medium does best or how to maximize what each
> does best, if and when we clearly identify the unique
> functions of each medium.[7]

**Recent Empirical Approaches**

We cannot leave the matter of media selection to those who
make casual choices, nor can we wait patiently for the future
results from researchers. We do need some basis today for making,
if only logical, educated guesses that can lead to practical media
decisions. If we do not, then a severe weakness will continue to
exist in the systematic method of designing instruction. Furthermore, our services as professional media specialists and instructional designers will be seriously questioned.

There is at least one objective way to approach the selection
of media now—with reasonable probability of successful results.
This means that the designer can make logical decisions and then

other persons, handling the same or similar situations, would reach comparable media conclusions.

This method is based on developing a flow diagram or sequence chart with headings consisting of questions directed to point the way to specific media. Each question requires a "yes" or "no" answer, thus leading one through the levels of the diagram, terminating in a particular medium or group of related media.

Bretz, at the Rand Corporation, developed such a set of outline charts.[8] In each diagram there are a number of decision-point questions, such as:

- Is visual recognition an objective?
- Is there a significant instructional advantage in hearing narration while looking at the subject, rather than reading the narration either before or after looking?
- Is the manner of movement of a subject an important characteristic for recognition or description of the subject?
- and so on . . .

At the box for each question, branching paths are indicated and according to the "yes" or "no" answer, the user moves, as on a game board, to a more definitive question, and so on, until he ends at a point which indicates an appropriate media class for the instructional task or lesson segment. This seems a very practical and reasonable approach that could successfully be applied to arrive at most media decisions.

If you have a serious interest in this area, obtain a copy of the Bretz report and study it carefully.

Here at San Jose State College, as part of our instructional development work with faculty, we have developed an approach to instructional planning and the selection of media, employing media-decision diagrams similar to those described by Bretz. First, however, we raise general questions to indicate broad direction for instructional methods.

1. Which teaching/learning pattern (*presentation* to regular or large class, small group *interaction,* or *independent study*) or combination is selected or is most appropriate for the objective and the nature of the student group?

2. Which category of learning experiences (direct, realistic, experience, verbal or printed abstractions, or vicarious sensory experience) is most suitable for the objective and instructional activity in terms of the teaching/learning pattern?

3. According to the verb and content referent of the behavioral objective, what kind of teaching or learning activity is indicated?

After considering these questions, the media specialist or instructional designer, with in-depth knowledge of media characteristics, physical requirements, advantages, limitations and use features, refers to a media-decision diagram. (See figures at end of article.) Each diagram is a sequence chart under a teaching/learning pattern heading—presentation to groups, small group interaction or independent study.

Questions at various levels lead to media choices. Simplified versions of these diagrams accompany this article.

Often the decision leads to a group of related media, such as the need for still pictures (photographs, slides, or filmstrips). The final decision of the most practical form to use should be an empirical one based on any of a number of factors that need consideration. These are outlined in the author's recent book[9] on instructional design.

This criterion-questions/flow diagram method of media selection is in its early stages of development. It is proving to be a feasible one for use but requires refinement and possibly extension. Explore it for yourself as you move into instructional design activities.

### Notes

1.  Robert Gagne. *The Conditions of Learning.* Holt, Rinehart and Winston, Inc., 1965.

2.  William H. Allen. "Media Stimulus and Types of Learning." *Audiovisual Instruction,* January 1967, pp. 27-31.

3.  Adrian P. Van Mondfrans and Ronald L. Houser. *Toward a Paradigm for*

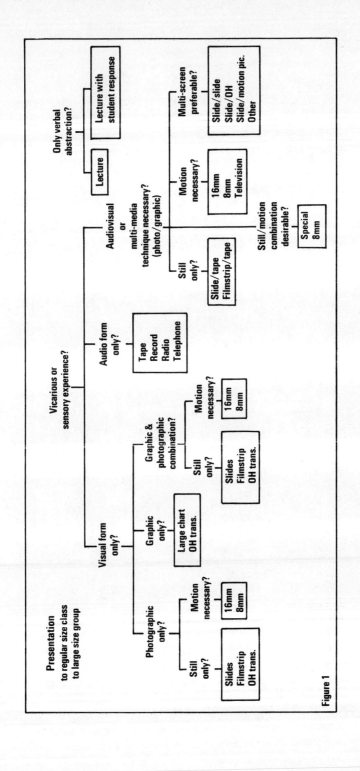

Figure 1

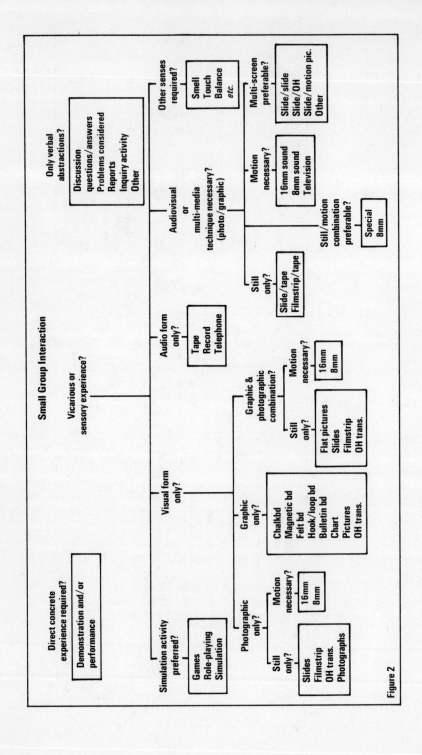

**Direct concrete experience required?**

Demonstration and/or performance

**Small Group Interaction**

Discussion
questions/answers
Problems considered
Reports
Inquiry activity
Other

**Only verbal abstractions?**

Vicarious or sensory experience?

**Other senses required?**

Smell
Touch
Balance
etc.

Audiovisual or multi-media technique necessary? (photo/graphic)

**Multi-screen preferable?**

Slide/slide
Slide/OH
Slide/motion pic.
Other

Motion necessary?

16mm sound
8mm sound
Television

Still/motion combination preferable?

Special
8mm

Still only?

Slide/tape
Filmstrip/tape

Audio form only?

Tape
Record
Telephone

Graphic & photographic combination?

Motion necessary?

16mm
8mm

Still only?

Flat pictures
Slides
Filmstrip
OH trans.

Visual form only?

Graphic only?

Chalkbd
Magnetic bd
Felt bd
Hook/loop bd
Bulletin bd
Chart
Pictures
OH trans.

Simulation activity preferred?

Games
Role-playing
Simulation

Photographic only?

Motion necessary?

16mm
8mm

Still only?

Slides
Filmstrip
OH trans.
Photographs

Figure 2

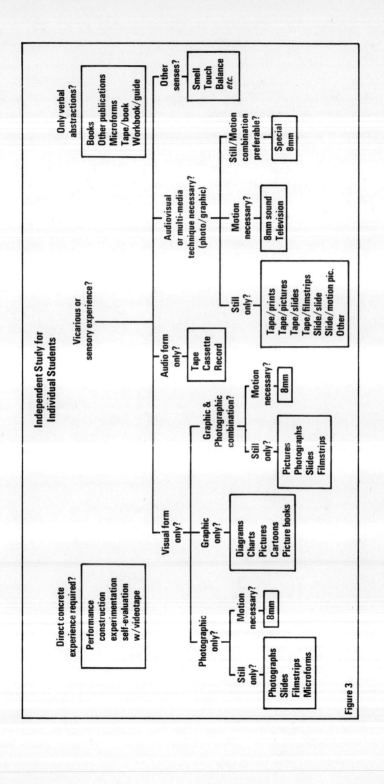

Figure 3

*Selecting Media to Present Basic Concepts.* Paper presented at the annual meeting of the American Educational Research Association, Minneapolis, Minnesota, March 1970.

4.  Marvin Lavin. *Media Potential Rating Scale.* College of Education, University of Iowa, 1970; unpublished.

5.  Leslie J. Briggs. *Handbook of Procedures for the Design of Instruction.* American Institutes for Research, Pittsburgh, Pennsylvania, 1970.

6.  Robert Gagne. "Learning Theory, Educational Media and Individualized Instruction." *Educational Broadcasting Review,* June 1970, pp. 47-64 (quote p. 60).

7.  Charles F. Hoban. "Communication in Education in a Revolutionary Age." *AV Communication Review,* Winter 1970, pp. 363-378.

8.  Rudy Bretz. *The Selection of Appropriate Communication Media for Instruction: A Guide for Designers of Air Force Technical Training Programs;* R601-PR. Communications Department, Rand Corporation, Santa Monica, California, 1971.

9.  Jerold E. Kemp. *Instructional Design: A Plan for Unit and Course Development.* Fearon Publishers, Belmont, California, 1971.

# 18

## Media and Individualized Instruction

James E. Duane

Individualized instruction has brought about new demands on media and media utilization techniques. In an individualized instruction environment each learner deals directly with learning materials and media resources. Because individualized instruction, by definition, considers individual differences in learning styles and abilities, a wide diversity of media must be available to compensate for these differences. Also, media in an individualized instruction environment must be readily available to the learner when and where the learner can most effectively utilize them.

These new requirements for media are forcing schools to shift from traditional, and expensive, group oriented media to newer forms of less expensive and more diversified media. Less use is being made of group media such as 16mm films, since 16mm films are extremely expensive, require expensive projection equipment and, due to our film library system, are usually only available for a few days at a time. It is simply not economically feasible for schools to purchase large numbers of films and film projectors.

Because of the need for diversity and availability, the present emphasis in individualized instruction is toward more versatile and less expensive media such as filmstrips, slides, audio cassettes and 8mm films. A number of these media and their required viewing or listening devices can be purchased for the price of a single 16mm film. Video cassettes, now being introduced, may prove to be the most useful medium of all for individualized instruction.

Most sources describing the characteristics of educational media describe media in terms of the traditional large group of

*213*

thirty or more students. Media which are efficient for a large group instruction may be inefficient and unrealistic for individualized instruction. The following list of characteristics surveys the most widely used media (at present) in terms of effectiveness in individualized instruction environments.

**Characteristics of Filmstrips and
Filmstrip Projection Equipment**

1. Filmstrips are compact, easily handled and always in proper sequence.

2. Filmstrips can be classified as having flexible pacing but fixed sequence.

3. Filmstrips are useful for group or individualized study and can be projected at a rate controlled by the user.

4. Filmstrips may be projected in small, lightweight and inexpensive viewers or on simple-to-operate projectors designed for group presentation.

5. Filmstrips may be projected in a lighted room when utilized with rear screen projection devices.

6. Filmstrips are available in three formats: (a) visual only, (b) visual with supplemental captions, (c) visual only with accompanying narration on record or cassette tape. (When a filmstrip is accompanied by a tape or record, the flexibility is reduced, due to the fixed pace of the recorded narration.)

7. Filmstrips are easily and inexpensively duplicated when a large number of copies are required.

8. Filmstrips are commercially available on a wide variety of subjects and grade levels.

9. Filmstrip cost—approximately $7.00 to $10.00 for commercially available filmstrips or approximately 30 cents per frame for locally produced filmstrips. Filmstrip projector cost—approximately $5.00 to $50.00 for filmstrip viewers, approximately $70.00 to $150.00 for large group filmstrip projectors and approximately $100.00 to $500.00 for sound filmstrip viewers and projectors.

## Characteristics of Slides and
## Slide Projection Equipment

1. Slides are compact, individual visual reproductions.

2. Slides can be classified as having both flexible sequencing and flexible pacing.

3. Slides may be projected in small, lightweight viewers or in simple-to-operate projectors designed for group presentation.

4. Slides may be projected in a lighted room when utilized with rear screen projection devices.

5. Slides are useful for group or individualized study and can be sequenced and projected at a rate controlled by the user.

6. Slides are an efficient format for developing materials since slide programs can be easily revised and updated.

7. Slides (both live shots and copy work) can be produced using inexpensive Instamatic cameras.

8. Slide cost—approximately 35 cents per slide. Slide projector cost—approximately $5.00 to $50.00 for slide viewers, approximately $50.00 to $100.00 for single slide projectors and approximately $100.00 to $150.00 for automatic slide projectors.

## Characteristics of the 16mm Film and
## 16mm Projection Equipment

1. 16mm film and projection equipment is primarily designed for group viewing.

2. 16mm film can be classified as having both fixed sequence and fixed pacing.

3. Most 16mm films are sound films.

4. Both 16mm film and 16mm projectors are relatively expensive. Projectors are complicated to set up, require considerable space and necessitate room darkening for large group viewing.

5. 16mm film may be projected onto a rear screen unit and may utilize headphones for individual or small group viewing.

6. A very large number of titles in all subject areas are commercially available on 16mm film.

7. Film cost—approximately $50.00 to $500.00 for commercially produced films. Film projector cost—approximately $600.00 per projector.

**Characteristics of 8mm Film and**
**8mm Projection Equipment**

1. 8mm films are less expensive, smaller in size and produce a lower quality image than 16mm films.

2. Like 16mm, 8mm film can be classified as having both fixed sequence and fixed pacing.

3. 8mm film and projection equipment is designed primarily for small group and individual use.

4. 8mm projectors are less expensive, smaller in size and easier to set up and operate than 16mm projectors.

5. Most 8mm films are silent and correspondingly most 8mm projection equipment is silent.

6. 8mm films may be purchased in two non-compatible formats: standard 8mm and Super 8mm.

7. Very few 8mm films are commercially available.

8. Commercially produced 8mm films are sold in a variety of non-standard continuous loop formats (see section on 8mm film loops) and reel formats.

9. 8mm films may be locally produced with inexpensive amateur equipment.

10. Film cost—approximately $20.00 to $30.00 for one- to five-minute commercially produced films and approximately $5.00 for three-and-one-half-minute locally produced films. Film projector cost—approximately $100.00 to $200.00 for silent projectors and approximately $200.00 to $600.00 for sound projectors.

**Characteristics of 8mm Film Loops and**
**Film Loop Projection Equipment**

1. Film loops are completely self-contained and do not require projector threading or take-up reels.

2. Film loops can be classified as having both fixed sequence and fixed pacing.

3. Loop projectors are lightweight, compact and self-threading, and are easy to set up and operate.

4. Short film loops are designed primarily for individual viewing with the loop format providing easily repeated viewings.

5. Film loops are more effective than still projection formats when motion is inherently part of the material presented.

6. Film loops may be projected in a lighted room when utilized with rear screen projection.

7. Film loops and loop projectors lack standardization or interchangeability between film loops or between projectors manufactured by different companies.

8. Film loops tend to have fair to poor quality image resolution and are susceptible to scratching and wear since the film rubs against itself in the continuous loop cartridge.

9. Film cost—approximately $20.00 to $30.00 for a single concept loop. Film loop projector cost—approximately $100.00 to $200.00 for silent loop projectors.

## Characteristics of Overhead Transparencies and Overhead Projection Equipment

1. Overhead projection is designed to enlarge visual materials for group presentation.

2. Overhead transparencies can be classified as having both flexible sequence and flexible pacing.

3. Overhead projection uses the simple-to-operate projector with presentation rate controlled by the user.

4. The overhead projector is not designed for self-instructional use since the original image used for projection is large enough for individual viewing by itself.

5. Overhead transparencies can be prepared by a variety of simple inexpensive methods.

6. Overhead transparency cost—approximately $1.00 to $3.00 for commercially available overhead transparencies and approximately 30 cents to 60 cents for locally produced overhead transparencies. Overhead projector costs—approximately $100.00.

## Characteristics of Audio Recordings and Audio Recording Equipment

1. Tape recording equipment is readily available, inexpensive, portable and simple to operate.

2. Tape recordings can be classified as having fixed sequence

and fixed pacing.

3. Tape recorders provide playback of commercially available prerecorded tapes or locally produced tapes.

4. Tape recordings are readily adaptable to either individualized instruction or large group instruction.

5. Cassette recorders are becoming the most widely used format since they are standardized in terms of tape size and speed, are light weight, are battery or A.C. operated and are self-threading.

6. Tape recorders are easily adapted to individualized listening by using headphones.

7. Tape recordings provide high quality reproduction even after being played a large number of times.

8. Tape recordings can be easily made from records, other tapes, film sound tracks, or television program sound tracks.

9. Tape can be erased and reused several times.

10. Multiple tape copies are easily made by connecting two or more tape recorders together.

11. Tape cost—approximately $1.00 to $3.00 for blank cassette tape and approximately $2.00 to $10.00 for pre-recorded cassette tapes. Tape recorder cost—cassette recorders approximately $20.00 to $120.00; reel-to-reel recorders, approximately $125.00 to $300.00

**Characteristics of Video Tape and**
**Video Tape Record/Playback Equipment**

1. Video tape record/playback equipment allows for the recording and immediate playback of locally produced programming and for delayed playback of commercially available programming.

2. Video tape recordings can be classified as having both fixed sequence and fixed pacing.

3. Video tape equipment is available in self-contained battery operated units.

4. Video tape equipment provides a system for recording and storing all forms of live and recorded audio-visual information.

5. Video tape recorders can provide distribution of a program

to various locations simultaneously.

6. Cassette video tape units are now available which are standardized in terms of tape size and speed and are self-threading.

7. Video tape equipment produces a poorer quality image than film projection equipment.

8. Video tape cost—approximately $20.00 to $40.00 for a blank 30-minute tape. Video tape recorder cost—approximately $800.00 to $5,000.00.

## Characteristics of Books and Printed Material

1. Books allow complete random access to both print and visual information.

2. Books allow students to progress at their own rate, and can be classified as having both flexible pacing and flexible sequencing.

3. Books do not require external projection or viewing equipment and therefore can be used anywhere at any time.

4. A book's content is easily located and identified using a table of contents or index.

5. Cost—approximately 50 cents to $10.00 for paperback editions and approximately $5.00 to $15.00 for hard cover editions.

## Characteristics of Programmed Instruction Materials

1. Programmed instruction materials are designed to be teacher independent and self-pacing.

2. Programmed instruction materials are available in two formats: (a) Linear, which can be classified as having fixed sequence and flexible pacing; (b) Branching, which can be classified as having both flexible sequence and flexible pacing.

3. Programmed instruction materials are readily adaptable to self-paced individualized instruction.

4. Programmed instruction materials are commercially available on a wide variety of subjects and grade levels.

5. Most programmed instruction materials do not require external projection or listening equipment.

6. Cost—approximately $1.00 to $20.00 depending on the length, type and sophistication of the program.

The following chart summarizes some of the more important media characteristics and presents them in a form which allows superficial comparison among the various media formats (see following page).

*Generalized Summary of Media Characteristics*

| | Cost (Hi, Med, Lo) | Pacing (Fixed, Flexible) | Sequencing (Fixed, Flexible) | Group Size (Lg, Sm, Ind) | Visual (Yes, No) | Motion (Yes, No) | Audio (Yes, No) | No. of Titles Commercially Available (Lg, Med, Sm) | Locally Without Special Equipment (Yes, No) | Requires Presentation Device (Yes, No) |
|---|---|---|---|---|---|---|---|---|---|---|
| Printed Materials | Lo to Med | Flex | Flex | Lg/Sm/Ind | Yes | No | No | Lg | Yes | No |
| Filmstrips | Lo | Flex | Fix | Lg/Sm/Ind | Yes | No | No | Med | No | Yes |
| Slides | Lo | Flex | Flex | Lg/Sm/Ind | Yes | No | No | Sm | Yes | Yes |
| 16mm Films | Hi | Fix | Fix | Lg | Yes | Yes | Yes | Lg | No | Yes |
| 8mm Films | Med | Fix | Fix | Sm/Ind | Yes | Yes | No | Sm | No | Yes |
| 8mm Film Loops | Med | Fix | Fix | Sm/Ind | Yes | Yes | No | Sm | No | Yes |
| Overhead Transparencies | Lo | Flex | Flex | Lg | Yes | No | No | Sm | Yes | Yes |
| Audio Recordings | Lo to Med | Fix | Fix | Lg/Sm/Ind | No | No | Yes | Sm | Yes | Yes |
| Video Recordings | Hi | Fix | Fix | Lg/Sm | Yes | Yes | Yes | Sm | No | Yes |

# 19

## The Schoolhouse of 1980

Donald F. Burr

My task is pleasant because it requires me to attempt a look at education in 1980. For me this is very exciting because I see forms of education and dreams that educators have had for centuries coming true. I am well aware that my topic involves an attempt to portray the physical facilities that will house the educational process in 1980; but to do this, it is mandatory that I first concern myself with education and develop what seems to be the form of the learning process for the 80s. Buildings to house the educational process, if they are to be great ones, must reflect the process they contain. Certainly you realize that buildings are not education. In the final analysis, they are big, cost a lot and show a lot, but, in the real sense, they are simply another of the educational tools like curriculum, a piece of chalk or a book.

Perhaps education is almost life itself. Certainly it is learning how to learn, and learning is a lifelong process. *As an architect, many would assume that my first concern is the building. This is not the case. My concern is the form and purpose of life that the building is meant to house.*

It is not difficult to paint a rather grim picture concerning much of education in America. It is clearly evident that there is considerable dissatisfaction with our present educational system—that there is a cry for change.

It seems to me, however, that in today's education there is

Reprinted with permission of the author who is a member of the American Institute of Architects' Committee on Architecture for Education.

much good. At the same time we acknowledge weaknesses, more and more we see schools doing things unthought of a decade ago. Many children in our schools are bright, alert, interested in life, excited about learning, eager to explore. We have teachers and parents willing to fight for better education.

Education is deeply involved in many of the social needs confronting our country today. There seems little question that the next ten years will see massive adjustment in education to accommodate various social needs. These adjustments will probably find education becoming almost the community itself. For as long as most of us can remember, education has worked essentially in an atmosphere of isolation. It happened at a particular place and a particular time. We believed we went to the schoolhouse and there we would learn; and when we left, we did something else. This is no longer the case, and educators can't even pretend that it is true anymore because communities will not permit it.

This is a logical time to discuss the rate of change factor. To me, the most powerful characteristic of our society today is the speed of change. *Change is the central fact of the world we live in, and it is literally impossible to overstate the significance of this fact.* There are no examples in earlier history that remotely resemble the pace at which change is taking place today. We have modified our environment so radically, and I use the word environment in the broadest terms to include education, that now we must modify ourselves and our systems in order to exist in this new environment. It simply is not possible to continue living in the old one. To be so naive as to assume that education is not involved is almost a criminal act when we consider the profound effect it can have upon the lives of our young people. We find ourselves bewildered, feeling lost, groping for answers to many questions, unable to understand much of what is happening; and we are only in the very beginning of this world of rapid change. *Our children are going to spend one-half of their lives in the 21st century, so how can any reasonable human being not question the irrelevancy, the isolation and the redundancy that exists in the majority of American schools.*

Amidst this dilemma, as one looks at the whole of education

throughout our country, there is a bright side, for we find exciting new forms of education, exciting new methods of teaching and exciting new tools for education. These discoveries are much like a jigsaw puzzle, and, currently, pieces are widely scattered and seldom, if ever, assembled in enough of a group to create totally new educational systems. We do appear, however, to be passing over the threshold in our knowledge of planning processes that enable us to put together many of these exciting segments, and thus begin to create the format that provides some insight on education 1980.

We were able to reach the moon because we developed outstanding planning processes, searched the country for all the pieces of information available, established pipelines to gather the information and fed it into central planning systems to focus on defined goals. The result was a dramatic landing on the moon. We have the full capability in America to make a moon landing in education anytime we make a reasonable assembly of the pieces available to us after following good planning processes.

Let us attempt to unravel the school of tomorrow. As I have stated previously, we will discuss educational concepts first because a school facility itself, the building, is only the result of an educational philosophy. To discuss the building, you must first discuss the educational program upon which its design is based. Although I am going to outline various educational concepts that seem clearly predictable for the design of the school facility of 1980, I must make it clear that no one can give you an absolutely accurate road map. None of the trends, the concepts or predictions I will discuss are mine alone. They are based upon extensive study of education and upon predictable technology. The trends to be discussed today are those that are most meaningful to me, as an architect, in carrying out my assignments to design new school facilities. There are other changes in the offing that perhaps are purely educational. In developing the statements on these trends, in many cases, I will be using facts derived from actual experience in designing facilities for education of the future. Most of the projects in our office utilize one or all of these concepts. Perhaps this would indicate that my discussion today is not about 1980, but, rather, the immediate future. This is probably true in that examples of facilities that I will describe, in some cases, are in existence today or in a design state. It is felt these are forerunners and indicate or give us a long distance view of education 1980 and the facilities that will house the educational system.

Consideration of individual students, differing in educational needs, capabilities and emotions will become paramount in the school of tomorrow. Perhaps the major difference educationally between the school of 1980 and that of today will be emphasis on *Individualized Learning.* Certainly, individualized learning is not a new goal for education. In fact, if you study the history of the learning process, you will find that as far back as you can go it seemed to be the prime goal of the educator. The significant factor at this point in time is that we now have the tools available to make this dream a reality. As an architect, individualized instruction obviously has additional meaning beyond simply changing the learning process. Considering this point, to me it is far more significant to understand what the educators are talking about and, from this, interpret the functions into bricks and mortar.

The vocabulary in our office does not include the word "classroom." It is not that we are opposed to classrooms, but that the word implies, visually and mentally, a box. Classrooms are an educational condition and a portion of an educational facility that has, for too many years, become the standard measurement in design of school buildings and judgment as to the quality of the educational system. The box approach places 25 to 30 students— each a unique human being with different abilities, different backgrounds, different emotions, different visual appearance and different desires—in a space called a classroom. The word classroom also implies a teacher who basically has been given or decides what facts constitute the learning that is to take place. This teacher presents facts verbally to the class. By most standards, the highest percentage of students reached by such a method would be in the neighborhood of 20 percent. The rest of the class is either ahead of the teacher, behind the teacher, or simply isn't inspired or motivated. The redundancy in such a situation is excessive. The sense of failure among students because of grading procedures is deplorable. Outstanding teachers attempt to cope with this situation by many methods. In the final end, the most ingenious and capable teacher is only able to moderately correct the tragedy of this cage-like approach to the learning process.

There seems little doubt that the majority of educators today feel that greater attention to the individual differences of students is absolutely mandatory. It will be a foundation of educational systems of 1980. There will be a variety of approaches to presenting an educational system that recognizes these unique differences in young people. But, regardless of these variations, there are profound implications not only in the educational system, but in the school buildings themselves.

Learning for students in the schools of tomorrow will be based primarily upon their individual abilities, motivations and interests. Integrated instructional materials will be developed in functional lesson units rather than large courses or curricula now existing. These lesson units will range from a few minutes to more than an hour and will provide concepts and related information which the student can transform into knowledge and judgment concerning the topic. The lesson unit approach to instruction will enable the student and the educational system to lessen the degree of redundancy in instruction and, at the same time, increase efficiency by permitting intensive learning to take place at the student's own pace. Schedules in a school facility of 1980 will be immensely flexible, and, in many cases, will be intimate, ad hoc arrangements between an individual student and a teacher. There will be no classes, per se, as we envision them today.

The condition of failure will be drastically curtailed because each student will be making regular achievements. The degree of achievement will, of course, vary from student to student but, still, the student will be achieving because he will be in competition with himself instead of the system. There are those who envision individualized learning as a very free situation where a student simply does as he chooses each day. This is not the case, and although students will be moving on individual schedules, they will, each day, have commitments regarding what they are going to do and what their activities will consist of. Planning will be done in close consultation with a teacher and it will be, essentially, a schedule that lists these activities the same as is done for students in school today. The heart of the difference is, of course, the tailoring of the learning process to the individual student and the building of his learning experiences around him.

There will be much technology supporting this individual learning. At some time in the future, perhaps by 1980, computer-assisted instruction will play a significant role. In the next ten years, there will be a vast array of new media available, designed with packages of learning for an individualized course of education. It is imperative that the full details of the meaning of individualized learning be understood by all of those involved in any phase of education.

Another clear trend is *The Changing Role of the Teacher.* The discussion on individualized learning provides a glimpse at a massive change in the educational process, and is a key to unlocking other trends. Perhaps the first door to change that is unlocked is the function and the role of the teacher. It is a startling fact that 70 to 80 percent of what a teacher does in most schools today will not be done in 1980. This alters the entire "game of education" and affects everyone involved. In 1980, the teacher's primary role will be to manage the learning process and educational program and also provide counseling and motiva-tional-inspirational support for his or her students. No longer the verbal source of facts, the teacher will spend time exploring concepts and ideas. In my discussions, I will use the term *manager of the learning process* because this term is common in education today. In my opinion, the word *manager* does not adequately describe the challenging, dramatic and exciting role of the decade ahead.

After accepting the premise that individualized learning will become the heart and core of future education, I found myself personally confused for a considerable length of time as to how these new systems were going to work. My most frequent request of educators, as an architect, was "Please describe as exactly as you can what a teacher will do each day and each week. Also, describe in detail what a student will do each day and each week." If you can gain an insight into these two areas, you will have the beginning of a solid concept of the school system and school facilities of 1980.

In attempting to outline this new role of the teacher, you must realize that the description is general in nature. A basic condition of education in America is that it reflects the needs and desires of each individual community where it exists and, thus, it has many subtle variations as you examine it from school district to school district. I do feel, however, there are basic principles involved that are very necessary for you to understand in order to comprehend the next decade in education.

I assume that you now realize education is not going to take place in a classroom with a teacher lecturing to a group. To present my viewpoint of the teacher's role, I will break it into six broad classifications. The functions are not extremely precise and variations will most certainly occur, but it does seem reasonable that a broad understanding of what teachers will do can be found among these six basic areas.

The teacher will become *A manager of the education program and learning process for a group of students.* The size of the group could vary, but indications are that it will range from 35 to 50 students. This initially indicates fewer certified teachers in the schools of tomorrow. Let me hasten to warn you that at the same time the number of certified teachers appears to be subject to reduction, there will be an addition of many teacher aides, professionals, interns, consultants and other personnel which will increase the number of adults in the schools. In the capacity of manager, the teacher is administering the learning process for each student, based upon individual needs. You will remember that curriculum materials will be in individual lesson units rather than larger pieces, and, also, that technology will be available to convey this knowledge to the individual student. Schedules will be immensely flexible, capable of change daily, if necessary, and based upon the learning needs of individual students. Teachers will function cooperatively as they seek guidance and knowledge from each other in order to devise and plan the learning needs for each student. Perhaps one-half of the teacher's time will be involved in this management role. Obviously, this implies a setting where learning is taking place in group sizes different than is found in today's normal classroom situation. Many educators and lay persons have a serious misunderstanding of the meaning of individualized learning and the teacher's role as a manager. They seem to envision it as a totally free situation in which a student literally picks and chooses what he desires to do each day. This simply is not the case. Most assuredly, there will be schedules which create commitments on the part of the student. It should be added that these schedules will be quite different from the computerized modular scheduling which we hear much about today, because today's scheduling creates an extremely undesirable, fixed situation. Scheduling is one of the keys for unlocking the possibility of this new educational system. Unless a completely different utilization of time is made in the school, conditions will be locked and goals will not be achieved.

Perhaps the second major role of a teacher will be to *provide counseling and motivational support for students.* The role of counselors appears to be on a threshold of great change. Today, in a typical high school, you will frequently find one counselor for approximately 250 students. In the next decade, this will probably change and we will find the teacher, in her management role, providing the majority of the day-to-day, week-to-week counseling and motivational support for students assigned to her group. The very nature of her task—to build learning experiences around the needs and interests of each individual student—will require her to have intimate knowledge of the background and emotional characteristics of each student. There probably will be professional counselors in the schools, but these counselors will primarily counsel the teachers rather than the students. They will act as professional advisors to the teachers.

An interesting logistical problem occurs as this function is carefully analyzed. How do we control and store the student's records? Because much of the information stored is of a confidential nature, in some cases it would be damaging if it became public knowledge. Traditionally, such records have been stored in locked vaults, usually near the front office of the school where there is constant observation and control when such a vault is unlocked. We do find cases now where these records have been placed on microfilm to conserve space, but the same locked situation occurs. This fails to work in this new form of education if for no other reason than pure logistics. If you have gained an insight into the role of the teacher, you now realize these teachers are widely dispersed throughout facilities and certainly cannot all be placed near one central storage point. It is simply impossible to place one set of records in a locked storage area at a point in the building that would be convenient to all the teachers. In fact, it would be a most aggravating problem of movement and probably would cause substantial failure in administrating these records. There is an easy way out, and, again, the computer provides the answer. By placing all student records in a central computer storage area and then providing terminals for the teachers, the whole problem can be solved. Dispersal of computer terminals will bring knowledge to where the teacher is working most of the time. Also, the confidential nature of the records is protected because there is no access to them unless you have the code to release the information from the computer. Further, with a computer, it makes it an easy task to either insert new information concerning a student or to correct or remove information from computer storage. It might be added, this change in definition of counseling functions along with other implications greatly changes the function and physical aspects of what we now consider the front office area of a school. When this is fully analyzed, you will find, essentially, that the typical front office suite does not exist.

Another function of the teacher will be to *develop and manage instructional materials in a particular subject area.* Teachers will still be, to some degree, specialists because they will still be primarily trained in such areas as English, science, history or other disciplines. As a specialist in a particular area, the teacher will probably find herself with the responsibility for the curriculum material in that school which is related to her particular subject area. Obtaining curriculum material and preparation of it within the school itself, based upon individualized learning units, will be managed, to a large extent, by the teachers. The fact-giving methods and techniques of curriculum development could involve learning activity packages, computer terminals, various audiovisual devices, or a variety of other means technology will be providing.

The teacher will *listen to small group discussions.* The teacher will spend part of her time listening. Please note I said "listen," not "lecture." The teacher in the schools of the next decade will not be a verbal source of facts. Since information will be delivered to the student on an individual basis by a variety of methods, she will not be required to talk, talk, talk. As a listener in small groups, this obviously indicates that not all learning happens as a single student is involved with a single learning device or piece of curriculum. Different size groups will begin to emerge.

It appears that another role of the teacher will be to *seek out and organize learning experiences in the community.* The school of 1980 will become, to a large extent, a home base or center of operations for the learning process. It will extend itself outward from this home base to encompass the entire community around it. A vast variety of learning experiences extremely valuable to development of individual students can be found outside the school. Schedules are immensely flexible. Movement is flexible. And the teacher is not tied to classroom lecturing. Thus, when the individual needs of the student will be bettered by utilizing a learning experience of some type in the community, such experience will be developed and utilized. It appears that the teacher will have a major role in this, due to her management position.

Lastly, the teacher will *manage interns, aides and secretarial help.* The new role of the teacher is obviously a very demanding one and will require the very finest of professional ability. The school of 1980 will not waste the valuable time of teachers doing an assortment of administrative chores. They will be given support in the form of a variety of people to do many of the household chores and functions that can be delegated. Their role in this situation will be simply the management of these services.

The implications for facilities to accommodate the new role

of the teacher can only be described as fantastic. It behooves all of those having any responsibility for educational facilities to conduct in-depth studies in this changing role of the teacher so that resultant buildings properly accommodate the form and purpose of life that the building is meant to house.

The trend I choose to call *learning experiences in the community* has great implication. The condition of isolation within which most education operates is not suitable to meet the needs of today and the future. I will not attempt to state the case for education moving out of its buildings and becoming community oriented, for the reasons seem obvious as we hear the many comments on the relevancy of today's education. If one carried this concept far enough, it is possible to envision that the high school of 1980 might not even be a place, but rather, would be more of a social condition.

It appears that education in the future will actually become part of life and part of the community—perhaps as I mentioned earlier, almost life itself. No matter where a school is located, surrounding it is a community of people, of business, of life itself. To be truly relevant and meet the needs of individual students, it seems mandatory that valuable learning experiences available in this surrounding community be utilized. The process of individualized learning and the new role of the teacher, combined with immensely flexible schedules, will make utilization of these community learning resources possible.

Development and use of these resources will again vary from community to community. Perhaps one of the strongest reasons for a community oriented program will be motivation of individual students. Actual use of various experiences will vary according to the needs of the individual student. For educators to develop this concept fully, it requires new understanding and new cooperation on the part of the lay and business communities. It appears that communities are ready to assume these responsibilities and fulfill their obligation to assist education in reaching this new goal.

Another important trend to note can be termed *the learning path of a student.* Previously discussed trends on individualized learning, the changing role of a teacher and use of learning experiences in the community certainly indicate some different happenings as each student pursues his process of learning. It is obviously important to understand this learning path and to obtain a visual picture of it. Earlier I said one of my most common requests when I was trying to learn about education 1980 was "Please describe to me what the teacher does each day and what the student does each day." You have a glimpse of what a teacher does, but emphasis must also be placed upon what a student does.

You will recall that curriculum materials, in a broad sense, have been broken down into many small pieces so that facts can be learned on an individual basis. Units of curriculum will come in a variety of forms that will include learning activity packages, a vast variety of teaching machines, computer-assisted instruction and individuals involved in "hands-on" experiences with equipment and the real world. It is probably difficult to estimate how much of a student's time will be spent as a single individual learning in an individual setting, but it appears this could be up to 50 percent of a student's time.

Beyond this we find the student involved in a variety of group sizes under a variety of conditions. Certainly students will be found discussing information gained in their individual learning experiences in small groups. This could be two to six students. There will also be times when these groups will begin to increase to 15, perhaps to 30 or even more. Remember, schedules are flexible and teachers, in their management roles, are moving the learning process in different directions and in different modes as required by the learning needs of their individual students. Thus, although much of the learning will be done individually, education will be taking place in a whole variety of group sizes.

It is interesting to note that at times the old traditional class size comes into being as a logical size group to be involved for some experiences. In this new form of education, if this size group applies, then certainly it will be used.

It has been noted that the teacher, essentially, does no lecturing. This is probably true as far as delivery of facts pertaining to a particular subject area is concerned. It does not, however, rule out the possibility that the teacher will assemble larger groups for delivery of a short, highly motivational presentation concerning a particular subject area. Also, there are times when it will be necessary to have meetings of larger groups for organizational purposes. Speaking of organizational patterns in schools, students will be grouped administratively in different ways. A term that is appearing more and more to describe student organization is the word *house*. This administrative grouping will be discussed under a separate trend.

As you become more involved with these various trends and begin to understand what is happening inside the building, you will realize that there is need for great variety in the sizes of spaces for education to take place. The nature of a presentation held under large group settings should be carefully noted because it has considerable significance to design of facilities. It has been common in the past few years to place sophisticated spaces for large group instruction in secondary schools. These spaces were equipped with a vast array of audiovisual devices to facilitate carefully prepared presentations by master teachers to a large group of students. Many times these spaces were divisible into several smaller units, each still handling what would be termed a large group. This type of space was often very expensive when compared to other portions of the school, and it does not appear to be a part of the school facility of 1980. The spaces for grouping students into various sizes, including large groups, need to be far more flexible, more casual, more quickly obtained and certainly more simple than the heretofore large group spaces.

The learning paths of the student also take him in and out of the building as he becomes involved in the previously mentioned learning experiences in the community. Thus we see a very flexible, ever-changing condition as the student of 1980 goes about the learning process. It is distinctly different from what happens in most schools today, and unless you have some understanding of it, you can't possibly comprehend education 1980.

The trends of *Individualized Learning, the Changing Role of the Teacher, Use of Learning Experiences in the Community and*

*Learning Paths* have a profound effect upon the functional
relationship of almost every activity in the school building and,
thus, the facility's architecture. The condition and trend I will
describe next I term *Flow, Not Surge.* The learning path of the
students indicates a totally different people movement situation
within school buildings. Within the schools of 1980, you will no
longer find classes which cause set numbers to move "en masse"
from one situation to another at a designated time. In lieu of this,
you will find rather quiet flowing situations with students coming
and going individually and in small groups. This change is
extremely significant to architecture, for it makes available a
whole variety of new choices regarding shapes, spaces and plan
usage. It will greatly increase the efficiency of school facilities
because it will not be necessary to turn over upwards of 15
percent of the building for passage of students. In our practice, we
now have a building that commits only 7/10 of 1 percent of its
total area to space to be used exclusively for circulation of
students. In fact, in this particular facility—an elementary
school—it was found that when all of the educational functions
seemed to be accounted for, there were almost 8,000 square feet
of space remaining to be used for other purposes that would not
have existed in a traditional building . . . space that had normally
been used simply for corridors. This particular school is based
upon all of the concepts I have discussed and would be termed, in
today's language, an "open plan school."

Transportation to and from the schools will be drastically
affected. Students will be coming and going individually or in
smaller groups at all times throughout the day. Not all students
will start school at the same time in the morning. Students will go
to and from the school at different times throughout the day as
they are leaving their base of operations to move out into the
community to become involved in various learning experiences. In
most communities in America today, many school buses arrive en
masse at a set time in the morning and leave again en masse at a set
time in the afternoon. This condition probably will not exist in
1980. When schools buses are used, they may very well move
continuously throughout communities travelling on regular

schedules and making regular stops throughout the day—perhaps in a manner similar to present-day bus systems. Maybe other means of transportation to and from the school will replace the bus entirely. The center for learning will then become, in essence, a docking station. In 1980 probably most students will spend one-third or more of their time away from the school itself.

It should be evident why the schoolhouses of 1980 will not contain boxes called classrooms and crowded highways called corridors to connect them. In this context, it is difficult indeed to comprehend the statistic that, while our national investment in school facilities each year now approaches 8 billion dollars, the majority of the new educational facilities being constructed are many years obsolete the day they open the doors. The wasteful expenditure of these amounts of money alone is a national scandal, but the greatest crime involved is the deterrent effect it has upon achieving new forms of education. It can only be assumed in these cases that people—be they architects, educators or demanding, misinformed lay people—simply have made no attempt to truly examine the educational systems as related to the needs of today and the tools available.

You will note in the trends discussed that, in theory, the need for buildings decreases. As education moves out of the buildings, leaving them basically a center for operations, building needs diminish. If every school moved 25 percent of its program out into the community, it would reduce buildings needs by 25 percent in America. This would be an astronomical figure. Also, I have mentioned the new efficiency of building which indicates smaller buildings or the ability for a facility to handle a greater number of students. This flow and surge characteristic, in which up to one-third of the students will not be in the building at any given point of time, indicates more space available for others. Others might be more students of the same age levels, adults, or people of all ages who come to utilize this facility which really, in the final analysis, is simply an assembly of many varied types of learning devices and learning tools.

Educational facilities of 1980 will probably have primary missions to fulfill, and, when these are taken care of, the facilities themselves will become available from early morning until late at night as centers for learning for people of all ages. For example, a secondary school would have as its primary mission the responsibility of providing a secondary level education for a certain group of students. As long as this primary mission is met, then anything in the facility or the educational system that is not being used would be available from when the school opens in the morning until it closes late at night. Thus, we see people of different ages learning side by side. This further reduces the claim that education is not relevant, for it helps break down the isolation factors so prevalent in schools today.

The last trend I will discuss is that of *open space planning*. I have deliberately left this until last because open plan schools are a frequent subject of discussion, and, frequently, a source of conflict in many communities in America. Tragically, many people, including architects, educators and lay people, approach the subject of open space completely backwards. You are aware that a school building is only an interpretation of the educational process—the life and the form of functions that are going to take place in it. It is ridiculous to talk about an open space school simply on the basis of open space. What should be talked about are the educational concepts and what is going to happen in the facility from an educational standpoint. Whenever this is done reasonably well, you will probably arrive at only one general conclusion, and this is an open plan facility. If you approach it this way, you will then understand what is happening, and the foolish waste of time discussing the pros and cons of purely open space will be eliminated.

I feel it is important to clarify that when I refer to an open plan school, by no means does it mean all of the walls are left out. It could be a building where there are essentially no walls, but this is not necessarily true in every case. Most of all, it is a school where there is tremendous flexibility and adaptability because spaces flow smoothly from one to the other, usually without doors or fixed closures. There can be, however, some subtle breaking points to create nooks and crannies, provide some quiet places, prevent noisy equipment from interrupting others and meet other similar needs. Thus, we are not talking about a wide open warehouse.

The point that we live in a changing world has been stressed, and we know education is not left out of this changing scene. This has great implications for buildings and explains to some extent why open space in the end is a very reasonable conclusion. Though these trends are the basis of a prediction as to education 1980, they certainly are not an accurate road map, and it is obvious there will be many adjustments and many unknown changes.

Education must be able to move in different directions very quickly as the situations demand, and must never again permit itself to become locked. It follows that the facilities that house the educational process must be equally ready to run in any direction that is necessary. They should in no way inhibit or restrict the educators from trying new forms and new ways in their educational systems. Thus, the time has come when we must stop just talking about flexibility and adaptability, stop simply giving it lip service only, and deliver the kind of facilities that have real flexibility and adaptability. Along with the concepts of open space planning, it seems important to place a horizontal slice of open air, either over or under the entire facility. As architects, we refer to the space when it is overhead as a loft plan building. Its great value to the educator is that it is a place where different kinds of things and services can be moved about and brought to different points in the building if necessary. Certainly walls of a permanent nature should be almost totally eliminated. Schools should be compact . . . should put all possible area in one large unit under one roof. Building with many small pieces of open space in separate buildings finds the educators involved in head-on collisions with the exterior walls. Again, they are locked. Essentially there will be no offices.

One of the problems now occurring in open space planning is that many architects and educators have the feeling it is the thing to do, and, therefore, they must have an open space school. Again, in these cases, they often approach the problem backwards by attempting to take a traditional concept of education and start leaving out some walls and putting in folding partitions. The usual outcome is a tragic failure, and the end result is a clash of events and circumstances that can cost superintendents their jobs and bring considerable turmoil to an entire community. These architects and educators are the copiers. I can report to you that we now have this group abroad in America, and we are already seeing some tragic cases of what people call open plan schools.

The first open planned schools emerged as a result of in-depth discussions and planned processes where educational systems were examined and very carefully projected into the future. Planning was done by a sensitive, articulate process, and the buildings that resulted had much meaning and generally worked quite well. Unless you arrive at your own plan through this kind of a process, you are probably headed for great trouble. You must have an understanding of what is really going to happen educationally if you are to successfully create the kind of educational facility that will respond to the function of life it will contain.

# 20

## Architectonics of the Mind

Daniel Melcher

In a recent education journal article, Dr. Francis A.J. Ianni, director of the Horace Mann-Lincoln Institute at Teachers College, Columbia University, was quoted as warning that: "Companies and teachers who depend too much on books had better start looking for a new job... With tapes, sound projectors and pictures, the ear and eye naturally assimilate information much more readily than deciphering the code of written words."

This, of course, is outrageous nonsense. Anyone who has gotten past the stage of "Look, Jane, look," knows that reading is not "deciphering" letters any more than listening is "deciphering" sound vibrations. Most of us can read any message much, much faster than anyone can read it *to* us. In fact, anyone who can't read at least three times as fast as he can listen needs to go look up Evelyn Woods.

The preeminence of the book as a means of input to the mind is so self-evident to most of us that I wouldn't dream of taking your time to examine the fallacies in Dr. Ianni's claims if it were not for the fact that they are doing a lot of mischief, and, I may say, badly misleading companies like Raytheon, Xerox, General Learning, IBM, etc. We can all applaud the idea of giving the newer media their chance. But let's remember that the use of automobiles did not cease when the helicopter was invented.

Reprinted from *School Library Journal,* Vol. 94, No. 18, January 1971, by permission of author and publisher—R.R. Bowker (a Xerox Company) copyright © 1971, Xerox Corporation.

We have listened politely for years while "experts" held forth on what their new educational technologies were going to do in the schools, and their promises and predictions sound just as empty today as those made by the Pentagon about what their new military technologies were going to do in Vietnam. It is time, and past time, to do a little counter-attacking.

I would like to explore three points:

First, whatever Dr. Ianni thinks, books *have been* and remain the number one mainstay of the learning process. Education without machines and teachers is possible, but education without books is unthinkable.

Second, books are *not* on the defensive against the newer media in the overall context of today's learning activities. In certain special situations they yield to certain kinds of audio and motion devices, but in general they promise to be with us long after many highly touted competitors have failed to get their grant renewed.

Third, books are apparently about to get a huge boost from the new sciences of brain mechanics. We're being told scientifically what we always knew but couldn't prove, namely that the way we *like* to read books is the *right* way to read books. We like to browse, nibble, pick up, put down, race ahead, refer back, ponder, skip, etc., and now they tell us that this is infinitely more in tune with the way the brain actually works than any externally programmed learning or lecturing. It is beginning to appear that all of us instinctively know more about how to instruct ourselves than about how to instruct others. I will come back to this.

I do not deny other technologies their special capabilities. The Link trainer long ago carved out a niche for itself in the teaching of flying and driving, where the problem is coordination of mind and muscle. In areas like music or foreign language pronunciation it would certainly be going the long way around to start with the eye in order to train the ear. There are good and valid roles for the film and for all kinds of lab equipment, including the computer.

But, as a general-purpose teaching—or, as I prefer, *learning*— machine, the book can outperform virtually every more recent competitor.

The book is, after all, the original data bank. In the jargon of the computer boys, it is on-line, real time and random access. You can interrogate it without learning Fortran, Cobol, or Algol. You can process it without paying or sharing a king's ransom in monthly rental fees. You can work in either the digital or analog mode—in simple English, you can have not only words or pictures, but both intermixed. You aren't limited to semi-legible roman letters, not to mention Russian and Chinese. You can even have small letters instead of just caps. In fact, the book is the standard of legibility by which other devices are judged—and usually found wanting.

The book handles symbols, diagrams and pictures, presents them in color as well as black and white. It has fast forward and review capabilities and much faster retrieval action than most computer data banks. By virtue of existing bibliographies and library catalogs it is cross-linked to 11 million similar data banks located in the special information centers called libraries, all over the world.

The book requires no electric connections; it has no moving parts breaking down, needs no darkened room or screen and can't be accidentally wound backward.

It can be used to feed 30 students the same message simultaneously, or 30 different messages.

It has been tested and debugged over 500 years. It is used and recommended by every major company and organization. It is so simple a child can operate it and so cheap you normally own it rather than rent it from a distant materials center. It poses no problems of incompatibility with other equipment. It has an hourly operating cost too low to permit accurate measurement.

Someone may say, "Ah, but can it store 20 million characters on a single reel of magnetic tape and access any of them within two minutes, on equipment renting for as little as $1,000 a month?" We can answer, why that's *nothing*, nothing at all. *We* can give you 20 million characters in a simple college dictionary and access to any of them in a fraction of a minute, with no more than the rent-free equipment you were born with.

Lest I fall into the trap of ridiculing another man's agreement rather than rebutting it, perhaps I should go back to Dr. Ianni's statement and try to find at least a kernel of truth in it. We have already granted the value of the audio approach in ear training. Let us ask ourselves, *are* there important areas where input to the mind by way of words-in-print should yield to input by way of pictures, i.e., nonprint visual images?

There are many such cases. It's why books have illustrations. This is no argument against the book. In fact there is really only one kind of visual data not easily presented in book form—namely motion—and even here unconscious tribute is paid to the book each time a projector manufacturer trumpets that his machine can *stop* the motion and give you time to study the still.

In this connection let me cite another quotation, from a recent article in *Forbes* magazine. Educators, it says, are coming to realize that "a student working on his own and at his own pace can usually learn more and faster than he can by simply listening to a teacher." So far, so good. It follows, they say, and this is what I regard as the massive *non sequitur*, that the answer is individually programmed instruction by *automation*.

The assumption concealed here is very insidious. For a split second you think that the scales have suddenly fallen from the eyes of the "I-teach-you-listen" crowd, and they have finally sensed the infinitely richer potential in the "one-reader-one-book" confrontation—but oh, no, they're not going to bring in the book, they are going to automate the teacher. Johnny is not to be allowed to go at his own pace after all, but instead is to be "programmed."

By common consent, our whole present educational structure is under attack—by students, by employers, by parents and by many faculty members. But it hardly follows that machines are the answer. In fact the machine approach, in education as so often in business, opens the horrid possibility that we will end by automating the trouble instead of curing it.

Before we go out looking for new devices, maybe we ought to see whether the trouble might lie in how we use the resources we have. If our children aren't learning effectively from their teachers, there are at least three other highly promising avenues crying out for greater utilization, namely, learning in the home, learning from other pupils and learning from books.

I think this is the heart of the dilemma that has been frustrating the big companies. They are looking for a big new thing to sell, like the automobile, or television, or air conditioning. Something patentable, something involving engineering and manufacturing, and big sales and service organizations, perhaps a sort of combination between a Xerox copier and a sauna bath; put the pupil in and bake until done in a carefully controlled atmosphere of geometry.

What about the assumption that people like Dr. Ianni often make, namely that *nobody reads unless forced to?* Many kids do reach college with a conditioned reflex against doing any *assigned* reading, but it may not follow that sloth is the natural condition of man. The resistance may not be inherent in either the student or the book, but rather in its content and presentation. Before we throw in the sponge and say, "Well, they just won't read, we'll just have to reach them some other way," hadn't we better find out what bred their resistance to assigned reading?

Our typical student reads unwillingly because he knows he'll be examined on it to prove he read it, and that's no fun. He can't just read it for what it has to say to him; he's got to spot and memorize everything in it that the *teacher* is going to consider important, or be made to feel stupid. In his entire school career he may *never* be allowed to read an assigned book for the simple excitement of what it says to him—as distinct from what he thinks it has to say to the teacher.

We have long been told that this memorize-and-regurgitate method of learning is nevertheless a necessary process—that children must learn to remember what they read. Must they? I have always liked the little poem by Robert Frost which goes:

> *Nobody was ever meant*
> *to remember or invent*
> *what he did with every cent*

It is not only more joyous to read a book for whatever part of its message sticks by you naturally without conscious effort; it may also be more efficient, in terms of input and memory.

Imagine this situation. Two students spend three hours in a library or bookstore. Each may choose any book he wants, but one faces an exam tomorrow on his comprehension of it, while the other has no assignment or quiz. Who learns more? Too many educators will still answer, "The disciplined one, of course."

"Wrong," say an increasing number of others.

The procedures by which we all taught ourselves to walk and talk are so fantastically more successful than those used later in school, that we must bow in reverence to Nature's instinctive methods, and try to emulate them. Every child learns his native language and learns it perfectly, or at least as perfectly as it is spoken by those around him. It is a fabulous achievement. Yet he does it on his own, without structured assistance.

No one says, "Learn this word first. You aren't ready for the others." In a lively family they throw the book at him—long and short words, simple and complicated sentences, indicative and subjunctive, present, past and future tenses—and as it flows over him, his brain, uncoaxed, uncudgeled and undirected, clarifies and sorts and sifts the gibberish until suddenly he has a word. Then four words. Then 64. By the time he reaches school he has literally thousands of words, including not only "cat" and "dog" but probably also "bandersnatch," "jabberwocky," and of course such complicated multisyllabic concepts as "chocolate," "vanilla" and "strawberry."

Then at school they say: "Start with 'dog' and 'cat'; wait a bit for the big words like 'mother' and 'father.' "

The newer voices are saying *let him do his later learning the way he learned to talk*—by total immersion. The brain will sort it all out; that's what brains are for.

This theory is worth a double-take! Every child teaches himself to walk and talk by his own methods, with a sureness and ease never even approached when his instinctive methods are replaced by the "scientific" methods of the schools.

Does Nature know something we don't know about how best to feed information to the brain? If the best learning we ever did was when we were following our natural instincts, are we paying enough attention to these instincts later in life? John Holt says, quite seriously, "If a child was taught to talk the way he is taught to read, he'd never learn."

The child learns to talk by sorting and winnowing out, from a torrent of spoken words in action, his own usable vocabulary. It is rare for a child to be given comparable exposure to a torrent of *printed words in action*. But we are told that those who get such exposure learn to read just as easily and instinctively as they learned to talk.

The situation recalls the old story of the bumblebee. According to accepted aerodynamic theory the bumblebee cannot fly: he has too large a body and too small a wing area. Educational theory, similarly, tells us that the two-year-old cannot possibly learn to walk or talk by the methods he uses. Fortunately for both bumblebee and child, they do not know this, so they go ahead and do it anyway.

I dwell on this matter of random vs. sequential learning because while the book as written is perhaps the very prototype of sequential presentation, *the way it is read* is often quite the reverse—and it lends itself admirably to the random approach. Do you ever start a book in the middle? Do you sometimes start at the end and work toward the front? Or just nibble here and nibble there? Or gallop through half the book in half an hour, then spend two hours on ten pages? Or lay out half a dozen books at once for comparison? Try doing that with most audiovisual aids. Yet you *can* with books.

If we could drop the memorize-then-regurgitate approach to learning and get our children back to the excitement of finding things *beyond* what the teacher told them to find, we might see a phenomenon that would make book consumption take off like a rocket.

First, educators in increasing numbers now believe that I.Q.'s are *not* fixed but are environmental. One report prepared for President Johnson said that if we would fully exploit the average child's natural urge to learn in the preschool years, we could reasonably hope to raise the average I.Q. by 30 points. We could raise the average I.Q. from 100 to 130. Some think 30 points might be high, but virtually no serious investigator puts it lower than 20.

Second, most of these educators now believe that from the very start of formal instruction we have been making a very fundamental error in assuming that the only way to learn a subject is to start with the foundation and work methodically upward. Much new light is being thrown on the mechanics and dynamics of information input to the brain—or perhaps more accurately, certain old themes are gaining new acceptance. These theories assume two levels of memory in the brain, just as in the computer: one temporary, the other permanent. One is like a blackboard. The other is like an ever-expanding jigsaw puzzle, to which you can effectively add only at the perimeter, but where a new piece that fits is retained.

In the infant the jigsaw puzzle is just starting. For practical purposes he *has* only the temporary kind of storage. He records everything he hears, however, instinctively classifying like with like. A word is heard and it leaves a trace, though one that is sublegible. When the word comes again the trace gains strength. On the tenth or 100th hearing, the cumulating impressions strengthen the trace to the point of retrievability. The child *knows* the word, and not only in its most recent or most common context, but with overtones of all the other permissible contexts. All have left their trace, the formerly sublegible traces becoming accessible through the more dominant record. Related words and phrases take related places, intricately cross-linked to each other, or "locked in." What began as a blackboard notation evolves into an important part of the jigsaw pattern. Some later words or ideas arrive to find places waiting for them. They stick durably and almost instantly. Others too strange and new to be fitted in immediately go into a sort of purgatory awaiting either oblivion or reinforcement.

It follows that new learning must either be wholly temporary, in the sense that you may now recall my last few words, or it must be at the perimeter of the already known.

Generations of students have viewed the exam with hostility, sensing that memorizing is simply not the same thing as learning, even though it passes for learning the morning after the cram session. This theory gives them new support.

This analogy, if valid, tells us also much about why textbooks have such a reputation for being dull and hard to learn from. You have all, I am sure, noted how hard it is to learn a completely unfamiliar word from the dictionary. The brain is supremely able to generate its own working definition from an accumulated store of varying citations in context, but whereas the definition is implicit in the citations, the citations cannot be derived from the definition.

In general, the brain abhors generalities, except as they serve to unify or explain particulars already in memory. The brain must work from the specific to the general, since it can understand the specific without the general, but never the general without the specific. Codified education on the other hand delights in the very generalities, conclusions, summings up, that the brain rejects.

As Paul Goodman has observed, the dropout who can't add and subtract can nevertheless make change for a dollar.

To a brain just eagerly sensing apperceptional breakthroughs on some frontier of its knowledge, it is no good saying, "Here, don't improvise some new subjective organization of this area, relevant only to the happenstance of what you already know about it. That would be like building a house starting with a window frame instead of with the foundation. Here's a better way."

The brain's proper answer may be: "Foundations be darned. I am a brain, not a house builder. I don't *have* to start with a lot of concrete-pouring I can't yet see the use of. I am damn well *going* to start with the window. Time enough to build back toward the basement if I like the view. This is my structure, not yours, and I am building it on my land, not yours, and if I don't build it my way, it won't fit in with the structures I already have. Give me what I ask for, but don't tell me what I want. I may be farther along than you think."

And this is where books excel. You can call on them for help, without danger of their pressing help upon you. You cannot hurt their pride. If occasionally they hurt your pride, the hurt is private, and such hurts are easy to bear. They are ready when you are, but they do not waste your time, nor can you waste theirs.

In terms of whether the book is obsolete we might also note that a population which reads earlier has a higher I.Q., thus earns more and is going to read a *lot* more.

The fact that all this *should* happen does not, of course, guarantee that it *will* happen. The book has many enemies, notably those with something more expensive to sell.

It therefore behooves those of us who grasp the potential of the book to speak up for it. We are not the custodians of a dying technology. Ours is a product which has already changed the world, but whose greatest of triumphs are still to come. In the gallery of great inventions, the book is second only to speech. By contrast, most of its competitors rank at best alongside the electric carving knife.

If the ferocious drive to learn which we observe in all preschoolers could be preserved into adulthood so that people would read eagerly instead of reluctantly, think of the relief to the overburdened teacher. Think of the relief of the frustration now underlying unrest.

Under this approach we will not say to a group of students, "Here are 1000 facts. Everybody learn them." We will rather say, "Here are 100,000 facts. Explore whichever interest you, and sing out if you want more of anything. Skip, skim, jump around as much as you want. If you find a book dull, why, drop it and try another. Start at the beginning or start in the middle, it doesn't matter."

Is this chaos? Not if it works, and it *is* the way we all learned to walk and talk, and pretty much the way we tend to tackle our hobbies.

# 21

## Technology in the Individualized PLAN System

Robert A. Weisgerber

As the result of 3½ years of developmental effort on the part of the American Institutes for Research and the cooperation of fourteen school districts across the country, a comprehensive individualized learning system was made fully operational in 1970.* The system, called PLAN (Program for Learning in Accordance with Needs), spans grades 1-12 in Language Arts, Social Studies, Mathematics and Science. Altogether some 4,500 learning objectives are included in the instructional modules, called teaching-learning units, which comprise the heart of the system. Each module specifies the learning activities, materials and media which are appropriate to learner attainment of a particular set of objectives. A number of guidance or career-related objectives are integrated into the curriculum, helping students to gain goal-setting and decision-making skills and other self-enhancing behaviors which complement their mastery of subject matter.

### Application of Technology

Charles Hoban has defined technology as "the management of ideas, procedures, money, machines and people in the instructional process" (Hoban, 1968). PLAN fits this broad definition of

---

*The PLAN system is now being marketed by Westinghouse Learning Corporation, Palo Alto, California, and approximately 25,000 students were using the PLAN materials in the 1971-72 school year.

Reprinted with permission of the author.

*251*

technology for it involves much more than the use of instructional hardware and materials in the classroom. In PLAN provision is made for a wide range of support services outside as well as inside the classroom. As an example of services outside the classroom, school administrators receive special training as do the teachers before PLAN is introduced into a new school. As another example, the acquisition and replacement of instructional materials and equipment (a 1970 catalog listing of items exceeded 1,200 pages) is facilitated by the use of a large-scale computer. More important, although the computer is located in mid-continent, remote terminals in the participating schools across the country make it possible to use the computer to score progress tests overnight, prepare daily class status reports for the teacher and generate recommended programs of study for individual students, that is, to suggest sequences of instructional modules suitable for a student's needs, abilities and interests subject to teacher concurrence.

### Facilities Design

PLAN has been implemented in diverse schools ranging from traditional classroom configurations to modern designs. In both the older schools and in the newer schools the main emphasis in the classrooms is on providing (a) open space for student movement, (b) flexibility in the use of furniture, (c) easy access to equipment and materials and (d) an acoustically and visually desirable environment for learning to the extent possible. A number of PLAN schools have established learning centers as extensions of the regular classroom. In such schools the students move freely to the learning center as they seek the materials appropriate for their teaching-learning units. In a few traditional schools this has necessitated some modification of the physical structure but more often it has simply meant a reallocation of space. Typically, the newer schools have been designed with a centralized resource area that all classes share. In the text *Perspectives in Individualized Learning*, Weisgerber (1971b) has suggested a school design that uses the principle of contiguous classrooms with retractable walls to facilitate individualized learning.

Teachers in PLAN classrooms have organized their students' seating in many different ways but the most typical approach is to cluster the seating according to function. If certain seats are set aside for private study or for testing, they are situated away from the main area of activity where distractions will be minimal. Similarly, an audiovisual "cluster" frequently is situated near electrical outlets, often with side-by-side seating in order that pairs of students can share the equipment.

**Equipment Provision**

An important component in the PLAN system is the provision of a variety of audiovisual equipment. Because the media are used in an integral way and, like verbal material, help the student to attainment of educational objectives, it is essential the equipment be (a) reliable, (b) safe, (c) easy to operate, (d) economical, (e) durable and (f) appropriate for individualized study. (A filmstrip previewer is more appropriate than a filmstrip projector because the image is brighter and large images are unnecessary.) During the developmental years, when PLAN was being field tested in the cooperating school districts, project staff experimented with various equipment configurations to determine the combination(s) that best met these criteria. Based on feedback from teachers and records of use (and abuse), a number of changes were made. Some examples of changes were:

(a)  use of rubber drive rather than sprocket drive filmstrip viewers to avoid filmstrip damage,

(b)  use of cassette rather than open reel tape recorders to avoid handling of tape and inconvenience of threading,

(c)  use of earphones with straight rather than coiled wires to avoid tangling when earphones are stored,

(d)  use of earphones which fit over rather than in the ears to minimize the time and effort expended for cleaning the earphones and

(e)  use of brands or models that do *not* have prominently exposed screws (which encourage playful disassembly) or delicate plastic controls and switches (which are prone to breakage).

Because students of all ages directly access audiovisual equipment without prior scheduling, it is important that effective procedures be instituted to keep the equipment in functioning order. In that regard, a "back-up" machine should be available for temporary use while any repairs on the regular equipment are accomplished.

Weisgerber (1971b) has explained the many considerations that are involved in purchasing or leasing a sufficient amount of equipment to meet class needs. It is essential that costly surpluses be avoided while at the same time minimizing the possibility of shortages, so that the students will not have to wait too long for equipment when they should be moving ahead in their teaching-learning units.

## Materials Access

Students in PLAN classrooms obtain (and return) specified instructional materials as they progress through the learning activities in their teaching-learning units. Accordingly, various techniques for keeping materials organized and easily accessible were tried out during the developmental years. Color coding, picture symbols and a modification of the "buddy system" seemed to be the most practical ways to surmount this problem at the primary grade levels. Of course, secondary students are able to work with numerically coded materials. Separation of materials according to subject areas is recommended at all grade levels. An effective control system for support materials (IBM test cards, etc.) is essential so that the teacher's time can be spent on students' learning problems rather than on managing supplies or being preoccupied with administrative details.

## In Review

PLAN is, as indicated previously, a comprehensive techno-logical system for individualization. A thorough description of the PLAN system as well as other national systems of individualized learning can be found in *Developmental Efforts in Individualized Learning* (Weisgerber, 1971a). A complete set of the behavioral objectives in PLAN's four subject areas has recently become available (Flanagan, Mager and Shanner, 1971).

Adaptability to local budgets, facilities and resources has been a stated goal in PLAN. In general, this has been accomplished successfully; however, overall effectiveness cannot be assured unless administrators and teachers take steps to see that the dynamic interface between student, teaching-learning units and instructional resources is accomplished with ease. Aside from the multi-purpose computer, with remote terminals in the schools, the equipment and materials in PLAN are purposely simple and inexpensive. Visitors to PLAN classrooms are not immediately awed by a rich array of audiovisual equipment. Rather, they notice that a variety of activities are going on and that students move from texts to filmstrips to experiments to workbooks to audio cassettes, and so on, quite freely and with assurance. It is evident that students in PLAN not only are learning subject matter but they are also learning *how* to learn on an increasingly self-reliant basis.

## References

Flanagan, J.C., Mager, R.F. & Shanner, W.M. *Behavioral Objectives: A Guide to Individualized Learning (Four volumes: Social Studies, Mathematics, Language Arts, Science).* Palo Alto, California: Westinghouse Learning Press, 1971.

Hoban, C.F. Man, Ritual, the Establishment and Instructional Technology. *Educational Technology,* October 30, 1968, 8 (2), 5-11.

Weisgerber, R.A. (Ed.). *Developmental Efforts in Individualized Learning.* Itasca, Illinois: F.E. Peacock Publishers, 1971a.

Weisgerber, R.A. Media, Facilities and Learner Options. In Robert A. Weisgerber (Ed.), *Perspectives in Individualized Learning.* Itasca, Illinois: F.E. Peacock Publishers, 1971b.

# 22

# Learning Centers and Stations:
# A Different Concept

Paul R. Daniels

When the learning center concept began to be felt in elementary schools it was looked upon by many people as a panacea. Others, more realistically, looked at it as an aid to individualizing instruction. However, it has not met either expectation.

One of the first problems that developed was that hardware became the fashion. Too frequently software was designed for the hardware rather than focusing on the instructional needs of the children. Therefore, children were involved with materials they could not use or did not need.

This problem developed because few school districts invested time or money to develop their own diagnostic tools and skill sequences which generally grew out of the feelings and needs of the staff. The program, in all of its ramifications, was packaged, received as a package and used as a package. In many cases there was no more understanding of learning and teaching than there is of the complexities that must be organized to permit a light bulb to glow because a switch is thrown. This is exactly how teachers looked at the learning center. It was to operate the same way as a light bulb.

It seems that if this concept is to work, then a definition of learning center must be developed. Hardware and the accompanying software must take a supporting role to the overall concept.

To me a learning center is an organized group of activities

Reprinted from *Audiovisual Instruction*, Vol. 15, No. 9, November 1970, p. 29, by permission of author and publisher.

that lead to the acquisition of an ability or increased information. The stations in a learning center are the activities that lead to the mastery of a skill or set of data. Thus, we may have a learning center on syllabication which contains four learning stations which represent the four major syllabication principles. We may have a learning center on linear measurement.

To foster individualization of instruction, each station is predicated on the idea that there must be multiple opportunities to learn and a consistent system for evaluating the learning. Each station, as conceived here, would contain five opportunities to acquire the skill. Each station would require that the learner demonstrate mastery on two consecutive correct reproductions.

Learning stations and centers should also be constructed so that they can be used in classrooms, pods or halls. In this way, scheduling of children becomes a rather minor problem in so far as each teacher, or team of teachers, will be able to decide when children should be using learning station activities within specific blocks of time. For example, a child can understand that he is free to use his assigned or free choice station at any time it is available and he is not scheduled to work directly with a teacher.

This learning center concept allows for improved classroom control in a number of ways. Children can be dispersed into small groups or individually, which helps keep the noise of competitive talking at a lower level. Children can be assigned tasks at a level where success is nearly guaranteed. Specific skills can be attained on a needs basis no matter what developmental program might be in progress. The child is very involved in evaluating his progress in that correction of errors and the opportunity to learn from these errors is built into each station of a learning center. Finally, each child is allowed to move at his own pace in acquiring a skill. If he needs five opportunities to learn something even though another child needs only two experiences, no one knows this and there is no stigma attached.

Many of our present schools are criticized for not individualizing instruction when they state this policy as a part of their philosophy. Too frequently the philosophy was developed because people were led to believe that the "new media" were going to help provide the guidance. Unfortunately, packaged materials have a rigidity about them that does not lead to true individualization. Too frequently the content of these materials does not fit the curriculum being pursued. A true learning center should provide for skill development but should not conflict with the goals of the school.

The materials should be drawn from the content and vocabulary of whatever units are being pursued, or a standard vocabulary used to express the content and also be the basis for skills development.

It seems that a true learning station should be just that. In skills learning, children should be presented with materials that lead inductively to the concept. They should be helped to verbalize the concept and then they should be given the opportunity to apply the concept deductively to problem activities that are appropriate to the curriculum.

If the children are studying clouds in a weather unit, the term "cirrus" is just as useful and helpful in discovering the "s" sound value of "c" as in the word "circus." Frequency is too frequently equated with ease of learning. "Cirrus" and "circus" are both easy if you know them.

In summary, learning stations for reading skills are helpful when they allow a teacher to teach those things for which she is essential. Secondly, offer her help in classroom management. Thirdly, provide independent learnings that do not require a teacher. Fourthly, foster individual learning.

These goals are best accomplished in light of children's, teachers' and schools' purposes. Certain types of media can help supplement the program. It would appear that once the media become the program, the learning center concept is unorganized and therefore of little value to children.

# 23

## Design Follows Concept:
## A Case Study of Facilities Development

R.S. North

In 1962, when Oklahoma Christian College first started planning for a new library, ideas were running along very conventional lines. The building would seat 25 percent of the student body, accommodate initially about 50,000 books, have open stacks and be expandable as the College developed. Then some new concepts began to creep into the discussions—carrels, new media, recordings, dial-access, individual study spaces, learning center. As each of these was investigated, the concept of the OCC library was vastly changed, and with it the proposed design of the facility.

### Each Student His Own Carrel

The first major decision was that better study space be provided for all students. A survey revealed that about sixty percent of the students were doing most of their study in their residence hall rooms. But these rooms were also the center of many other types of activity, most of which were not compatible with serious study. Since college learning is supposed to be largely done "outside the classroom," OCC decided that in addition to providing better classrooms, something should also be done to improve the space a student has for learning out of class.

Why not give each student his own carrel? This would encourage him to study, and give him a more quiet and private place than his room. His carrel would become his "office" in

Reprinted from *Educational Technology*, Vol. 9, No. 12, December 1969, pp. 69-71, by permission of author and publisher.

which he could do all types of study and from which he could move to various nearby campus locations—library, classroom, laboratory, chapel, or the student center.

The second major decision was based on the belief that much greater use could be made of recordings for instructional purposes than previously had been made. After some experimentation and further study, it was determined that each student would need access to recordings from his own carrel. A dial-access position for each carrel proved to be the best way to provide this, since it would allow the student to select any one from scores of audio tapes available simultaneously.

With a million dollars to invest in the new learning center, which had to provide space for the library, some faculty offices and a thousand carrels with associated electronic equipment, careful planning and efficient use of space was required. After almost two years of design and construction, in September, 1965, the new learning center was finished and by January, 1966, all the electronic equipment was installed and in full operation. The first floor contained the collection of books and periodicals, with seating space for about 100. The second and third floors each had space for 508 carrels, making a total of 1016, and each had a dial and headset for listening. The control room—with the computer, switching equipment and tape players—was on the third floor. Adjacent to the control room were two recording studios and a production facility.

**Instructional Materials and Philosophy**

Through careful planning, and use of workshops and special project funds, the faculty was ready with materials when the new facility opened. Within a year, over half the classes were utilizing some special feature of the learning center—recordings, single concept films, special conference rooms, viewing room.

The instructional program was undergoing considerable change. No longer did every three-hour class meet for three hours a week. Some met only once or twice, with the students spending additional time in their carrels listening to music, poetry or drama, interviews, historical events, speeches, exercises, recordings of themselves, or special programs prepared by their own teachers. Teachers began using more overhead projection and films in class. More independent study projects developed. Some courses met in large groups for one purpose and in small discussion groups for others. An audio-tutorial laboratory was added.

Overall, a new instructional philosophy was developing: no longer did teachers have to be the primary source of information; no longer did students have to be in the classroom a set number of hours a week; no longer did all students have to be lock-stepped into doing exactly the same things at exactly the same time. Now the teacher had greater flexibility in designing his program; and the aim was learning, not meeting the rigid restraints of pre-established patterns. Now the teacher was managing the learning process rather than just preparing lectures. Now the teacher had a wider range of media at his disposal. Now more attention was being given to personalizing the learning experience by meeting individual needs more effectively.

## Need for Expansion

By 1968, the continued growth of the student body required the planning of new buildings. The most pressing needs were for more carrel space, more classrooms, more offices, more laboratories and more activity space in physical education.

With the school's program having developed along a philosophy of flexibility, it seemed imperative that the added instructional space have that same flexibility. With the program seeking greater personalization, greater allowance for individual needs, and a wider variety of media, all of these must also be considered in the new design.

Lessons which had been learned from three years of operation of the learning center also must be taken into account: carrel space should be as acoustically "dead" as possible; putting carrels in smaller groupings would be advantageous; the basic carrel design had proved successful; dial-access was most useful for large classes, since its greatest value was in handling heavy usage; more conference space per student was needed; having teachers' offices near carrels was beneficial.

## The Instructional Module

Out of all of this came the idea of a new unit of design—the instructional module. First a list was made of the various personal relationships which were needed:

one student working by himself
a small group of students by themselves
one student working with a teacher
two or three students with a teacher
a seminar group with or without a teacher
a group of up to 40
a group of up to 80
a group of up to 200
a group over 200

Then the possibilities for various types of learning experiences were listed:

students with each other
students with the teacher
filmed materials
printed materials
audiotapes
videotapes
overhead projectors
slide projectors
filmstrip projectors
film loop projectors
movie projectors
specialized equipment such as computer terminals, calculators, laboratory equipment

Out of these concepts came a design. Teachers with their offices were set at the heart of the plan. Around them were placed the various types of space which would be needed to accommodate the various personal relationships and the various types of learning experiences—student carrels equipped with multimedia;

seminar rooms accommodating up to 20; classrooms designed for all types of projection, dial-access and flexible in size; a room for using specialized equipment according to specific needs of the area being served; secretarial and storage space; and a lounge area (see Figure 1). This combination of spaces would provide for all the necessary personal relationships and all of the various types of learning experiences except specialized laboratories and group meetings of over 80. And these would be located as near as possible and be shared by several modules.

*Figure 1*

*Functional Relations*
*Between Elements*
*in a Typical Module*

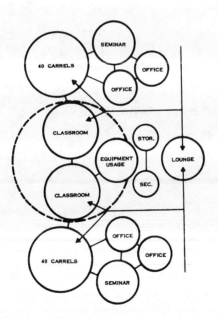

*Figure 2*

*Actual Floor Plan*

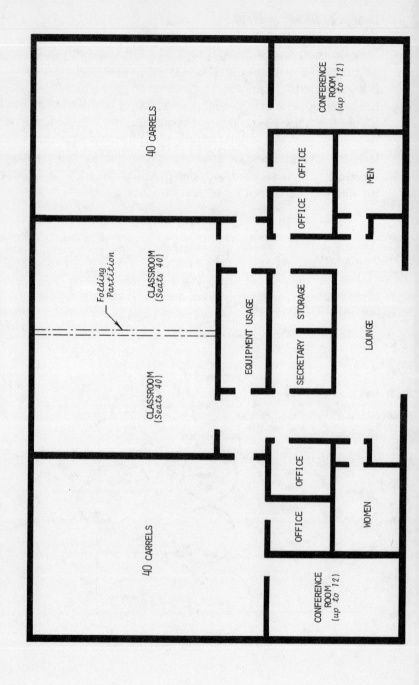

40 CARRELS

CLASSROOM
(Seats 40)

Folding
Partition

CLASSROOM
(Seats 40)

40 CARRELS

CONFERENCE
ROOM
(up to 12)

OFFICE

OFFICE

MEN

EQUIPMENT USAGE

SECRETARY

STORAGE

LOUNGE

OFFICE

OFFICE

WOMEN

CONFERENCE
ROOM
(up to 12)

In an instructional module, therefore, would be four teachers, 80 student carrels, two seminar rooms, two classrooms, an equipment usage room, secretarial and storage areas and a lounge—literally a microcosm of all the campus except the living area. As shown in an actual floor plan (see Figure 2), the overall area required for one module was found to be about 100 feet by 65 feet when all the required elements are combined. Such modules were placed in all three buildings to be constructed—two in the science building, two in the American Heritage building and one in the physical education building.

## Conclusion

Again, at OCC design had followed concept, form had followed function. While no one can foresee what may develop in the future of education, Oklahoma Christian College is firmly committed to flexible, functional buildings shaped by the design of its instructional program.

# 24

## Educational Futurology

Richard Hooper

Educational technologists love talking about the future. Frustrated by the slow rate of advance with the new media in education today, the educational technologist is quick to seize a chance to eulogize the future of satellites, educational television, video cassettes, computer-assisted instruction, holography. It is here that all the dreams can be indulged in, uncontaminated by the colder realities of the present, forgetting some of the more spectacular failures of the past. The future is undifferentiated—short term possibilities fading into longer term dreams.

Looking at the state of education today there are a number of current trends which seem likely to shape future developments:

- The teacher's role is changing from information transmitter to manager of learning resources.
- Group-paced, group-prescribed instruction is giving way to individualized instruction where learning goes on in groups of different sizes, according to the needs of individual learners and different subject matters.
- The school is opening up, with space (classroom boxes) and time (45 minute periods) being used much more flexibly.
- Comprehensive reorganization of education is leading to learners with mixed abilities being grouped together.

Reprinted from *Educational Broadcasting*, Vol. 5, No. 3, September 1971, pp. 151-154, by permission of publisher.

- Educational "permissiveness" is on the increase with learners demanding greater participation in their own education. The belief that adults "know what is good for children" is being eroded.
- Education across the world, and at all levels up to and including higher/further education, is coming to be seen as a more *accessible* commodity, more open to more people.
- Demand for education is growing exponentially across the world, creating real and continuing problems of finance and resources.

These movements in educational thinking will have significant implications for the role of the new media in education. While the media such as television and film have a real job now of supporting and enriching traditional educational procedures, their future might be more assured if they took over a radical function—acting as catalysts and enabling agents for educational change and renewal.

### Teacher's Role

In the traditional classroom the teacher is the fountain of wisdom, from whom—with the exception of the textbooks—all formal instruction comes. With the rapid expansion of new knowledge in many areas of the curriculum, this exclusivity of the teacher is no longer desirable, nor actually possible. No teacher can be expected to keep up-to-date with all current developments in his own field. With the task of information transmission shared by other media—including, of course, books—the quality and topicality of information being communicated in the learning situation will be radically improved. The teacher today has so much content to cover—especially with examinations bearing down upon him—that almost all his student contact time is spent on this task. Other equally important teacher roles, such as motivating the student to learn and getting him to apply acquired knowledge in new situations, are neglected.

If the new media can relieve the teacher of some of the

information transmission (and there always will be information transmission of sorts, however discovery-oriented learning becomes), then the teacher's real job may be made possible. This is important because, in the design of conditions of learning, the various communications media must—in theory at least—be used for what they do best. Much information can be transmitted as efficiently by various types of machine. Some would argue that they miss vital links in the argument. But the task of getting students to apply knowledge creatively and to solve problems is difficult to program from a machine, but ideal for the live human teacher. Any rigorous analysis of the information transmission that goes on in the classrooms would yield a number of benefits. Taken-for-granted content would be questioned, quite a bit of it reduced, and much of it put across to the learner in less time. The time saved would be more than filled by the new role of the live teacher. There is one final reason why the new media are in the future likely to play an important part in the information transmission area of education. Thousands of different teachers all over the country teaching the same bit of subject matter over and over again to different groups of learners is a highly unproductive use of the *human* resource.

## Individualized Instruction

Perhaps the major contribution of psychologists to the educational debate has been the identification of the wide range of individual differences among learners. The differences span ability, pace of learning, learning style, choice of subject matter, level of motivation, linguistic skill. Thirty children of the same age in the same class demonstrate these differences acutely—yet we continue in many schools to try to teach them as a group. They enter school at the same age, move from class to class together, go on to the next school at a specific chronological age and irrespective of ability, take a rigidly defined number of years to get a degree. It can be argued that group-paced, group-prescribed instruction is all but inevitable when the communications media available for use by education are restricted to human teachers and books. Given a wider range of media, group instruction can give way to a more individualized approach. This does not mean that all learning is done on an individual basis. If only for financial reasons, this possibility is ruled out. It does however mean that the size of the group can and should differ according to the characteristics of the pupils and the subject matter being taught. There is a strong argument for making much work in mathematics an individual situation, with the learner working through materials at his own pace. Work in the arts area, on the other hand, demands group interaction and discussion as an integral part of the learning process.

The new media have a key role in making possible the individualization of instruction. There is a clear-cut need for small, robust, cheap, easy to operate audio and audio-visual equipment for use by individuals, small and large groups. The child who is a good reader will want to get his information one way, the poor reader another. One student will want to handle equipment immediately, another look up results at second hand. Diversity and richness of approach will be made possible by a sensitive use of the newer media.

**Open School**

The move towards more flexible use of time and space in schools is part of the trend towards greater individualization. Under a group-paced system, time and space have to be divided up rigidly. There is little possibility of letting individuals make personal choices about *what* they want to learn and *when.* But given that the teacher can be joined by other teaching machines, then the tyranny of time and space can be partially overcome. The leading specialist in a given subject has long been able to distribute himself through time and space via books and articles. This distribution is given new potency by the addition of film, television, radio, gramophone. The live lecture is the exclusive right of a particular group of people who meet at a certain location at a certain point in time. The same lecture recorded is no longer restricted to just one time and space slot—it can be experienced, depending on the particular recording technology used (print, video tape, film, etc.), by masses of people at any number of different times and places. While the recorded lecture will not have the power of the live occasion, its substance can be shared more widely. In this sense the new media will *open* up education. The notion that formal education can only proceed inside classrooms is no longer taken for granted. The notion that learning can only proceed in the presence of something called a teacher is dissolving.

## Comprehensive Learning

The move away from the segregation of learners into ability groupings (streaming, tracking, setting, separate schools) and towards comprehensive types of education poses a whole set of new problems for the teacher. New strategies are required in the comprehensive situation. Paradoxically, the move to individualize instruction could lead to new types of ability grouping. One bright child, for example, learning by himself, constitutes in one sense an ability grouping. How can curricula be individualized, yet learners of different abilities be encouraged to learn together? American experience with games and simulation shows this technique to be a useful medium of instruction with learners of differing abilities. The game does not put at a disadvantage the poor reader, for example. Mixed ability teaching requires access to sophisticated remedial learning packages, as well as good diagnostic tests that show where individuals are having trouble.

The comprehensive school requires a wide curriculum with large areas of choice. At present in Britain, for example, only the big comprehensive schools can afford wide curriculum offerings and sixth forms—with the result that children in the smaller school away from populated areas are discriminated against. This will continue until educational media—not just teachers—are given emphasis. Curricula will have to be widened without the addition of more specialist teachers. The comprehensive school faces another curriculum problem—the content of education. In the academic grammar schools the content is taken for granted—with emphasis on verbal and intellectual skills and the dominant importance of abstraction. Given a population of learners with mixed ability this content may not be so immediately appropriate.

There is a growing feeling that education has been dominated for too long by abstraction and verbal intellectualisms. The need for greater relevance in the curriculum of tomorrow's world, greater emphasis on emotional development, greater involvement of all the senses, more *active* learning experiences—all of these point to new roles for the new media. The highly verbal content of all curricula must, in part at least, be the product of educational reliance on teacher and book—both predominantly verbal media. In the not too distant future, the teenager loath to express himself in written essays may be stimulated into working with a cheap 8mm camera or a cassette tape recorder. At the moment the latter media are barely respectable for English language classes (on a more practical level they are also far too expensive for all but the most affluent schools). There are numerous examples where the academic bookish curriculum developed for the elite is not suitable for the mass. If different curricula for different groups of learners are acceptable to society (and this could be the ironic result of any radical individualization of instruction, as already noted), then there is no problem. But if this is considered unacceptable because, for example, of its certain bias in favor of middle-class children, then the future must see urgent searches for methods of learning *and* subject matter that are useful for, and attractive to, different abilities within the same school. The challenge to the educational technologist, film-maker, television director, is a major one.

## Educational Permissiveness

The progressive movement, though scarred, would still seem to be one of the strongest factors in the future development of education. In a period of swift social change, the role of the teacher in specifying and controlling educational objectives is under question. Children getting their information from sources such as the mass media are increasingly knowledgeable about areas in which the teacher may have no interest or training. The monopoly of education held by the triumvirate—home, school and church—has been broken. If the idea of learners being encouraged to specify their own educational objectives is accepted, the live teacher plus the normal range of textbooks just cannot handle the resultant demand. Whereas all pupils in a conventional class are prescribed a text, the children in a freer situation will prescribe themselves different ones. The load that this lays on the communications media within the school is enormous. Children moving into areas of knowledge outside the competency of the actual teaching staff must be catered to (this has always been accepted in post-graduate university education).

The implications for the future development of media in education are clear. The learning situation must include well-designed and equipped library resource areas where both teachers and students can find and study materials. The notion of resource areas to which only teachers have access is out of date (and, incidentally, a good example of innovation being distorted back in the direction of the *status quo*). The building up of library resource centers, with well-catalogued materials in different media, and well-maintained hardware for showing the materials, is the key task of the educational technologist. Diversity of method without adequate diversity of content is likely to prove insufficient. The instructional materials need to be developed along modular lines—so that both teachers and learners can form their own personal combinations to suit individual needs. The modular construction of the curriculum allows the learner to become involved in his own education. Instead of being told of relationships between areas of knowledge he is encouraged to make his own connections. Education passes from memorization of content to the structuring of content—from a low-order to a high-order skill.

## Equality of Educational Opportunity

Education has traditionally been a restricted commodity—restricted to particular social classes, to particular geographical areas within countries, to particular age groups. All sorts of visible and invisible selection mechanisms have been used to perpetuate these restrictions and legitimate them. Technology's greatest promise is perhaps its ability to help break down these restrictions.

Technology has a democratizing influence. As with the printed book for centuries, television today allows many to share experiences previously enjoyed only by the few. The small village gets the same quality of television performance as the big city. The President of the United States gets knowledge of his own election no quicker than the lowliest member of the population—they are both watching the same channel. In Britain, via the Open University's multi-media courses, students in remote areas can now take degrees without moving from the house. Technology allows us to develop mass education because it widens the influence of small numbers of good teachers.

Continuing education throughout life—vital in today's world—cannot in the future be achieved solely by recourse to traditional means. The adult working in full-time employment must be able to pursue home-based studies as well as the more conventional institution-based updating courses. Looking ahead, educational technology may find its strongest role in the area of adult education—literacy, health and welfare, agriculture. Technology has that distinctive ability to take education outwards to where people are. Traditionally education has required people to come inwards to where teachers are. It can be argued that the traditional twosome—teacher and book—in the formal classroom has led to over-emphasis on formal education to the neglect of the more informal requirements of adults. In terms of developing a nation's potential, investment in adult education may prove every bit as worthwhile as the more obvious investment in children's education. In fact the influence of the home environment on the child's school attainment has been demonstrated to be so powerful, that school reform without "home" reform is unlikely to succeed.

### Educational Demand

Demand for education is constantly outstripping the national resources to supply it. The crunch point has been reached and it is becoming clear that education cannot proceed along traditional lines. Productivity must be increased and educational budgets must go further. This again is a key area for the development of educational technology. Mass education requires economies of scale and productive use of the human resources in the system. Both these aims can, for example, be met by broadcasting. The potential contribution of satellites is immense. The economics of education will sooner or later force us to ask awkward questions. Can a teacher be permitted to spend x hours preparing a piece of live instruction to which only a handful of learners has access, when a similar piece of instruction recorded would reach many more learners? Can every individual country afford to spend its resources preparing instructional materials (for example, in science) which duplicate what is being done in many other countries? The differences between nations—most obviously language—are too often used as a defense against pooling of resources. Just as medicine and agriculture have across the world made large-scale—often co-operative—applications of technology to meet the problems of quantity, so it seems that world education will be forced to follow suit.

Technology can perhaps help to solve the paradox of modern education. The use of mass media of instruction to meet the required economics of scale seems at first sight to go counter to the use of individualized media of instruction designed to cater to individual learners. Can in the future individualized learning materials be mass-produced? Can mass media of instruction such as television—ideal for large group viewing—be combined with individualized media, such as textbooks and teachers, for example, to achieve a realistic balance of resources? Or does it mean that only affluent countries and affluent schools can have the privilege of individualized instruction because of favorable teacher-student ratios, while the developing countries and the poorer schools within developed countries are condemned to mass instruction?

## Trends

Any prediction of possible futures for educational technology should start with an examination of educational trends, not with the bits of audiovisual machinery. Designing the technology to enable changes to take place in the school which would otherwise be impossible, seems to be the most positive strategy to pursue.

Perhaps the most obvious trend in educational technology is this move away from a preoccupation with machinery. Educational technologists are trying to become systems designers—specifying educational objectives that can be measured, attempting to make rational choices of media on the grounds of cost, effectiveness and availability, designing evaluation and feedback procedures so that the learning system can be steadily improved. Much of the experience here is patchy and much of the evidence on which to base systems thinking inconclusive. But here the educators and the educational technologists (if these ever should have been seen as discrete categories!) are in tune. From both camps comes an increasing desire to formulate objectives that go beyond the generalized and largely unexaminable aim of "developing individual potential." Education has for too long been an amateurish business where art is too often given the benefit of the doubt. The arrival of expensive satellites and computers demands a more sophisticated approach to education. The trouble is that—as with so many educational innovations—systems analysis has become a fashionable commodity. Systematic thinking and systemic thinking are easily confused. The hard and rigorous analysis that systems analysis could bring to education is quickly lost. One of the safest predictions that can be made about education is that it will not lose its genius for transforming innovatory ideas into harmless fashions. In many of the new open schools now springing up, much of the authoritarian, rigid and group instructional tone of the closed school is still present—but camouflaged by "in" terminology, a scattering of audiovisual aids, and better architecture.

The short term future for educational technology is not rosy. For years Britain has spent more money on providing free milk for school children than on school textbooks. The percentage of the recurrent budget spent on instructional materials is minute and has recently in Britain declined slightly. Innovation costs money—innovation with the newer media costs lots of money. In developing countries the message of educational technology may be better understood than in industrial countries which can still just about afford not to change. The key historical trend in modern society—the replacement of human labor by the machine—is not likely to find in education an exception. The machine will sooner or later replace the teacher—in some of his or her many functions.

# BIBLIOGRAPHY

## Media in Individualized Instruction

Ahl, David and Bailey, James. "Computers Are for Kids—Not for Geniuses," *School Management*, Vol. 15, April 1971, pp. 26-28.

Allen, David. "Reach Many Senses with Multi-Media," *Educational Screen & Audiovisual Guide*, Vol. 48, No. 12, December 1969, pp. 14-15 and 27.

Banister, Richard E. "What Does Multimedia Have to Offer?" *Educational Media*, Vol. 1, No. 2, May 1969, pp. 10-12.

Banister, Richard E. "Writing and Illustrating Multimedia Lessons," *Educational Media*, Vol. 1, No. 4, July-August 1969, pp. 19-21.

Barnes, Jarvis. "Instructional Media and the Teacher-Learning Process," *Educational Technology*, Vol. 9, December 1969, pp. 59-62.

Borowski, J.F. "Low Cost Study Carrel Stations in Materials Centers," *Audiovisual Instruction*, Vol. 14, No. 3, March 1969, pp. 98-99.

Bretz, Rudy. "An Independent-Access Instructional Television System," *Educational Technology*, Vol. 10, No. 12, December 1970, pp. 17-22.

Butler, Lucius. "Self-Instruction Lab Teaches Communication Skills," *Audiovisual Instruction*, Vol. 15, No. 2, February 1970, pp. 55-56 and 60.

Camp, Susan. "A-V Media Support Children's Literature," *Instructor*, Vol. 79, No. 3, November 1969, pp. 64-66.

Coffelt, Kenneth and Hudson, Kenneth. "The Cassettes Can Go Rolling Along," *Educational Media*, Vol. 1, No. 5, September 1969, pp. 8-9.

Cooley, William W. and Glaser, Robert. "The Computer and Individualized Instruction," *Science*, Vol. 166, October 31, 1969, pp. 574-582.

Cypher, Irene F. "Media Memos for the Seventies," *Instructor*, Vol. 80, No. 10, June-July 1971, pp. 32-35.

Dalgo, Rodney C. "Dial Access Retrieval System: Is It Worth It?" *Educational Media*, Vol. 2, No. 3, May 1970, pp. 18-19.

Deep, Donald. "The Computer Can Help Individualize Instruction," *The Elementary School Journal*, Vol. 70, April 1970, pp. 351-358.

Diamond, Robert M. "A Feasible Approach to an Independent Study Facility," *Educational Technology*, Vol. 10, No. 12, December 1970, pp. 29-31.

Dible, Isabel W. "Individualizing Instruction Through Direct Dial Access," in *Individualizing Instruction in Science and Mathematics*, Virgil Howes (Ed.) New York: Macmillan, 1970.

Dible, Isabel W. "The Teacher in a Multi-Mediated Setting," *Education Digest*, Vol. 36, No. 6, February 1971, pp. 26-28.

Drowne, Frances. "Individualizing Instruction Through the Use of Tapes," *Audiovisual Instruction*, Vol. 14, No. 5, May 1969, pp. 41-42.

Duffey, B. "Individualizing Mathematics: Tape Helps Each Student Do His Own Thing," *Audiovisual Instruction*, Vol. 14, No. 2, February 1969, pp. 55-56.

Dunn, Rita Stafford. "Individualizing Instruction—Teaming Teachers and Media Specialists to Meet Individual Student Needs," *Audiovisual Instruction*, Vol. 16, May 1971, pp. 27-28.

Elkings, Floyd S., Rabalis, Michail J. and Gaby, Ewin. "Make Media a Systemized Learning Experience—Part 1," *Educational Media*, Vol. 2, No. 2, May 1970, pp. 16-17.

Fisher, Jack R. "Audio-Visual Sources for IPI Mathematics," Philadelphia: Research for Better Schools, Inc., 1969.

Fleischer, Eugene. "Systems for Individual Study; Decks, Cassettes, Dials or Buffers?" *Library Journal*, Vol. 96, No. 4, February 15, 1971, pp. 695-698.

Gausman, C.H. and Vonnes, J. "Single-Concept Film: Tool for Individualized Instruction," *American Vocational Journal*, Vol. 44, January 1969, p. 14+.

Gilkey, Joseph W. "Pick Media by Objectives, Not by the Numbers," *Nation's Schools*, Vol. 88, No. 4, October 1971, pp. 68-70.

Gilstrap, D.B. "Elementary School Media Programs: An Approach to Individualizing Instruction," National Educational Association, 1970, 32pp., ERIC No. ED047521.

Giorgio, Joseph F. "Mediated Self-Instructional Mobile Unit," *Educational Media*, Vol. 1, No. 4, July-August 1969.

Gottardi, Leslie. "Instructional Media Center Services in the Nongraded Elementary School," *Audiovisual Instruction*, Vol. 16, No. 4, April 1971, pp. 30-32.

Gunselman, Marshall. "What Are We Learning About Learning Centers?" Oklahoma Christian College, Oklahoma City, 1970, 213 pp., ERIC No. ED053536.

Hatfield, Frances. "Using Media in Our Teaching," *Instructor*, Vol. 80, No. 3, November 1970, pp. 58-59.

Hollick, H. Eugene. "The Future—Now!!" *Educational Television*, Vol. 2, No. 6, June 1970, pp. 11-15.

Houser, Ronald L. and Van Mondfrans, Adrian P. "Selecting Media to Present Basic Concepts," *Educational Technology*, Vol. 10, No. 12, December 1970, pp. 40-43.

Isaacs, Dan Lee. "A Self-Instruction Laboratory Teaches Audiovisual Equipment Usage," *Audiovisual Instruction,* Vol. 16, No. 3, March 1971, pp. 70-71.

Jacobs, Don. "Staying One Century Ahead," *Educational Media,* Vol. 2, No. 1, April 1970, pp. 16-17.

Johnson, Ted. "Learning How to Apply the First True Random Access Learning System," *Audiovisual Instruction,* Vol. 16, No. 8, October 1971, pp. 78-81.

Lambek, Marcia and Lorentzen, Maude. "Learning Resource Centers in Every Classroom," *Instructor,* Vol. 81, October 1971, p. 88.

Lewis, Philip. "Multi-Media Packages Aid Instructional Flexibility," *Nation's Schools,* Vol. 84, No. 4, October 1969, pp. 88-92.

Linck, Norman. "Educational Media and Independent Study," *Audiovisual Instruction,* Vol. 15, No. 2, February 1970, pp. 36-37.

McBride, O. "Learning Through Media in the Library," *Audiovisual Instruction,* Vol. 14, January 1969, p. 69.

McPherson, Ann, Krulils, Stephen and De Flandre, Charles. "Media and Mathematics Curriculum Change." *Audiovisual Instruction,* Vol. 16, April 1971, pp. 24-25.

"8mm Cartridge Films Aid in Individualized Study," *Business Education World,* Vol. 49, November 1968, pp. 2-3.

Murray, J. Robert. "Instructional Technology: Tape Cassettes," *Today's Education,* Vol. 59, No. 8, November 1970, pp. 36-38.

Porrin, D.G. "Role of Media in Individualized Instruction for Teaching the Deaf," *American Annals of the Deaf,* Vol. 114, November 1969, pp. 912-919.

Pratte, Richard. "Media Revolution: Its Educational Implications," *The Clearing House,* Vol. 45, No. 4, pp. 207-211.

Schommer, R. Jerome. "Materials for Individualized Instruction," *Wisconsin Library Bulletin,* Vol. 66, No. 3, May 1970, pp. 147-149.

Schultz, Susan Polis. "Toy Technology Aids Teachers, Benefits Children," *Educational Media,* Vol. 1, No. 7, November 1969, pp. 20-21.

Snow, Richard E., Tiffin, Joseph and Scibert, Warren. "Individual Differences and Instructional Film Effects," *Journal of Educational Psychology,* Vol. 60, June 1969, pp. 153-157.

Swyers, Betty. "Teaching with Technology—Get It on Tape," *Teacher,* Vol. 89, No. 3, November 1971, pp. 4-8.

Tanzman, J. "Individualized Instruction and Media: A Double Pay-Off," *School Management,* Vol. 14, December 1970, p. 30.

Tanzman, Jack. "Individualized Instruction Requires Media Training," *School Management,* Vol. 15, No. 3, March 1971, p. 28.

Tunks, Roger. "A-V Media and the Performance Curriculum," *School Shop,* Vol. 27, April 1968, pp. 11-83.

Turner, William E. "Individualizing Spelling with 600 Students," *Instructor,*

Vol. 80, August 1970, p. 142.

Twyfold, L.C., Jr. "Educational Communications Media," in R.L. Ebel (Ed.), *Encyclopedia of Educational Research,* 4th edition, American Educational Research Association, Macmillan Co., 1969, pp. 367-379.

Valentine, Thomas J. "Proper Tools Can Substitute for Teacher Background." *Educational Media,* Vol. 10, No. 5, September 1969, pp. 14-15.

Walton, W.W. "Computers in the Classroom: Master or Servant," *National Association of Secondary School Principals' Bulletin,* Vol. 54, Fall 1970, pp. 9-17.

Weisgerber, Robert A. "PLAN is a Project Halfway There," *Educational Screen & Audiovisual Guide,* Vol. 48, No. 7, July 1969, pp. 12-13 and 29.

Werner, Sister Marijane. "Computer-Assisted Planning and Scheduling of Individualized Programs of Study in Science and Mathematics at the Secondary Level," *Journal of Educational Research,* Vol. 64, No. 3, November 1970, pp. 127-131.

# PART 4

# THE EVALUATION OF
# INDIVIDUALIZED INSTRUCTION

# PART 4

# The Evaluation of Individualized Instruction

The selections in Part 4 present several of the problems relating to individualized instruction programs and suggest some possible solutions. Also included is information concerning teachers' attitudes toward their roles in individualized programs.

The first article in this section, written by Davis and Kirby, begins by reviewing the major characteristics of packages and then discusses some of the problems and concerns with packages such as inflexibility, availability, teacher education, adoption procedures, marketing, experimentation and cost. The authors discuss packages, not as a new idea, but rather in terms of maturation.

Keuscher reveals that because individualization is "in," most teachers will claim that they are individualizing to some extent. However, in most cases, if we evaluate what is going on, we find very little effective individualization. Keuscher states that teachers must be very cautious, since many of the commercially available individualized kits, packages and programs are ineffectual, and in some cases may even stifle the learner's initiative and creativity. He encourages individualized instruction where instruction becomes a matter of activity and meaningful experience. He makes an argument against teachers deluding themselves and the indoctrination provided by some of the packaged materials. In short, Keuscher is striving more for personalized teaching.

Wang and Yeager emphasize that conventional systems of evaluation may not always apply to individualized instruction programs. Conventional systems are primarily designed to measure achievement within a specific time period and usually do not

287

consider individual differences in learning rates. Wang and Yeager discuss the various problems encountered in evaluating the progress of the individual student in relation to his own previous performance, the amount of time spent on a given task, and the level of achievement demonstrated. In their conclusion, the authors are unable to offer any definite standards to be used in evaluation.

Lindvall and Bolvin evaluate the role of the teacher in an IPI system of individualized instruction. They break down and explain the three major functions of an IPI teacher and then proceed to list the seven basic aspects needed by teachers to make the system function. The authors conclude by suggesting that preparation of teachers to carry out these new roles should provide a new focus for professional programs of teacher training.

The last two articles in this section summarize two studies which were conducted to determine how teachers perceive their role in an individualized instruction program.

Flynn and Chadwick, in the first study, report on a comparative survey of classes using LAPs, individualized instruction but not with LAPs, and classes which were traditional. After listing the findings, the authors expand upon them to strengthen their argument that, in a changing system, it is vital to provide a model of teacher role behavior—not leaving the behavior to chance.

In the second study, Steward and Love report the findings of a survey conducted with teachers who had worked in a high school that had incorporated an individualized program. The authors provide tables ranking the teachers' responses. The survey showed that individualization provides high levels of teacher satisfaction, but demands a tremendous amount of extra effort. Teachers did not indicate a loss in status, but suggested the need for more precise role designation.

# 25

## The Package:
## A New Way of Life

O.L. Davis, Jr. and
Paul W. Kirby

The Age of the Package is one way to know these times. Its signs
are abundant. Notice, for example, vacation plans, financial
proposals and arrangements, teacher negotiations, book clubs and
the six-variety pack of cat food. Note also the accumulating litter
of packages. For, in truth, the package is that contained and its
container. The package also is the way it is used.

The package is a concept already materialized in education.
Once considered alien, some packages are recognized as having a
solid, even respectable place in school programs. Packaging,
indeed, is so common in the general culture that it is expected by
many to contribute dramatically to educational improvement.
Without doubt, the package seems likely to be a feature of
educational life and for some time to come.

Packaging concepts did not enter the educational scene
abruptly. Incomplete concepts have been standard for many years.
The textbook is one such package. The textbook package contains
an instructional message, segmented into "lessons" or "units,"
accompanied by visuals, exercises, activities, bibliography and even
answers to questions. These components are encased by a binding
sturdy enough to withstand a variety of abuses. Merchandising for
these packages has insisted upon their validity, usefulness and
potency. Frequently, such packages have been parts of a larger
system, a textbook series.

Reprinted from *Educational Leadership*, Vol. 27, No. 8, May 1970, pp.
767-771, by permission of authors and publisher.

The textbook package, however, represents an incomplete packaging concept, incomplete at least by contemporary standards. It is only one, however major, of many materials that are or may be appropriate for instructional purposes. Likely, it was developed independent of other materials, even if additional media (for example, films, apparatus, ditto masters) accompany it. The textbook probably was developed first and, characteristically, was designed for principal use, with other media cast clearly in supporting roles.

**Major Characteristics of Packages**

More complete packages being merchandised in schools these days seem recognizable by three prominent characteristics. Common as they seem, they exist in differing degrees.

First, packages are conceived as program, not materials. The purpose is the creation of a new curriculum and its necessary, not interesting, accessories. Perhaps the concern is physics or reading or geography or oral language. The genesis of the package is curriculum. Many of the popular packages have been financed by massive federal government funding, some from private foundation sources. The past decade saw a spate of such curriculum developments, each with its cryptic alphabetic name. While the rate of establishment of large-scale projects may decrease in this decade, smaller, less grandiose projects probably will be stated. Curriculum concerns likely will remain central to educational package development.

A system of instructional media and materials is the second feature. The first major projects, conventionally ambitious, set out to put the newly fashioned curricula into a traditional textbook package. Yet, as work proceeded, the developers seemed to recognize that convenient carton as unsuitable for the product on which they labored. Indeed, the "product" began to be conceptualized as a system of closely related materials, each serving a particular purpose. Thus, while a textbook was developed, so were films, exercises, laboratory notebooks, paperback booklets, inexpensive equipment and recordings. The textbook may have been a principal component of the system, but the other materials were not seen as supplementary; like the textbook, they were essential.

Each component is integral to the system; omitting one would be to deny the validity and frustrate the impact of the whole. A key to the entire system of materials seems to be the plan for their use. The restrictiveness of some plans has caused their systems to be tagged "teacher-proof." This derision has prompted most subsequent plans to be less detailed and to provide guidance for flexible use. Even so, the system is real and holds together. It is another type of product, basically unlike a collection of related materials grouped together for sales purposes or because they "could be used together." The package is itself a viable system.

The third characteristic element of packages appears to be their pattern of developmental tryout and distribution. Packages usually receive rather extensive field testing under project supervision. Teachers selected to use the package in its early form receive special preparation to understand both its substantive content and pedagogic rationale. At times, this in-service education has been coupled with materials design and development over a summer; on other occasions, in-service preparation has continued regularly over an entire year.

Important to understanding the package is the fact that teacher education is a component critical to its success. Limited availability of the materials during field testing is also a feature. When news breaks of a new package being developed, requests for specimen sets of materials pour into the project. But the package, being highly commercial, is not distributed to all those interested. Descriptions and general project plans may be circulated, but not the materials. When the package has been field tested and is about ready for marketing, it may be purchased but, even then, usually with some restrictions on use.

These features are drawn from available packages. Most have been financed by public (government) funds, and public accountability, however minimal, is necessary. As private, commercial enterprise produces increased numbers of packages, from conception through distribution, these three features may be altered and others added.

## Small Packages: A Concern
## About Inflexibility

One vexing issue currently is the degree to which the package should be used flexibly in the school situation. This concern, a recurrence of the "teacher-proof" charge, now involves the matter of "pupil-proof," as well. Packages which are seen as quite self-contained primarily are more limited in scope than the large curriculum systems. These small packages have an integrated design and usually are implemented by a coordinated set of audiovisual media. Employing these packages in a school program, teachers need make few or no instructional decisions. Pupils are bound to the package also. For the package's purposes, popularly derived and published as statements of expected pupil behaviors, the system is complete: the substantive material is treated more adequately than in other and available forms; other materials and modes of discourse are not only unnecessary, they are seen as liabilities by system designers.

Too little evidence is available for adequate judgment and generalization about this type of instructional package. Nevertheless, a few preliminary reflections may be helpful in considering the potential impact and usefulness of such tightly conceptualized and instrumented products. The specter of arrogant, omnipotent and omniscient designer-producers, frightening enough, seems unlikely in any real sense. Competitive marketing of packages, on the other hand, seems a special necessity. With different ideas implemented and on sale by different firms, options for choice and consumer direction remain potent.

Teacher militancy and negotiations relating to instruction may be seen as inhibiting schools from buying into instructional packages which restrict teachers' professional expertise. Yet, teachers should be expected to demand packages which enable them to perform more professionally. Generally increasing education costs seem another reason that large, controlled systems of small, self-contained packages may be more fanciful visions than realistic possibilities. Too, packages must account for the enthusiasm of eager pupils to seek additional sources of information beyond those available.

Concern for reversing observed school procedures which tend to dehumanize the educational process may blunt efforts that act on people rather than make possible people's acting on things. Noting these observations, however, is not to deny the possible widespread usefulness of many small, self-contained packages. Also, using them probably will not subvert the schools. And those pupils needing limited, special programs based on restricted and specific objectives likely will profit from this type of package.

## Some General Problems and Prospects

Availability and use of instructional packages probably will increase. Packaging processes, employing systems design and product engineering techniques, may be expected to yield more complete packages. Large-scale packages should continue to be developed, but the small package field may soon burst with activity. Such projections are easily framed. Other prospects and some attendant problems, not so superficially apparent, merit consideration.

Attention to instructional packages in teacher education programs is an obvious necessity. After a decade of major curriculum developments, systematic consideration of their materials systems seems rare in most undergraduate programs. Candidates seeking teaching posts, consequently, may have heard about the AAAS elementary science program, but do not know the system and its materials and have not worked with children using this package. Or, knowing the AAAS program, candidates do not know another science program. As projects have multiplied, the problem has grown more serious. Undergraduate preparation programs probably should not be captured by one of several competing programs, but should afford candidates opportunities for intensive familiarization.

In-service programming seems an appropriate strategy for deliberately attending to a specific program in a school system. Too long dependent on training grants, themselves never sufficient for the need, teachers must receive their needed preparation to teach particular instructional systems in programs financed and directed by local schools. To adopt a package without making provisions for the required teacher education seems wasteful, at best. So, local schools must budget sufficient funds for in-service education, not an inexpensive enterprise, and, perhaps, mandate participation as a condition of employment.

Major barriers in teacher education domains must be dismantled before even the best-conceptualized and instrumented instructional systems will have substantial payoffs. These tasks will not be concluded with ease, but they must be begun and soon.

Adoption procedures for instructional materials warrant review and, in some cases, revision. Too frequently, in all probability, adoption of packages is inhibited by regulations established for choice and purchase of textbooks. These rules usually permit only the textbook from a larger system to be considered, thereby reducing the entire package to shambles. Some elements may be considered later and by other groups and apart from the textbook. In such events, the materials developed as a system seldom can be regrouped meaningfully. An entire package should be considered on its own merits. If this were done, even more systems would be produced and more appropriate materials would be available for pupils.

But adoption rules are not all the problem. The pervasive mythology enveloping a single material must be destroyed. Most teachers probably expect to use only a textbook as the principal instructional source. When thinking about and examining new materials, they probably pay closest attention to the textbook and see other materials, even those in a system, as useful but not integrally necessary, perhaps only decorative. Teacher education has a role to play in the demythologizing process. So, too, do local supervisory and administrative practices. And merchandising must play a role as well.

Marketing of instructional packages currently follows traditional forms. Textbook publishers produce and sell textbooks as other traditional producers and distributors make and market films, transparencies and equipment. Since rules and myth restrict usual choice to textbooks, materials more appropriate to other media are issued in bound book form. And other materials in the instructional systems are left to founder by themselves. Needed, it would appear, is a new kind of commercial enterprise. Perhaps the new educational conglomerates may serve in this capacity. The distributor of the package would subcontract the production of all materials in the system but would market the package only as a complete system. Negotiation with local schools could yield different contract specifications for purchase of system components. Purchase of textbooks or films (or a film) alone simply would not be possible. If the package is viable as a whole, it deserves marketing which emphasizes and capitalizes on that feature. This new educational marketing agency very well might include in or with the instructional package a teacher education component. Thus, schools buying the package would also purchase time, materials and consultants for the adequate preparation of their staff to use the package well.

The "match" between various packages in a total instructional design seems quite troublesome. In the past decade, complaints were commonplace about the lack of "match" between different modern mathematics programs. The elementary mathematics program may have lacked a close match with the junior high program and the senior high program may have been built on bases other than those programs coming earlier. Not the least difficult, of course, was that pupils in the system became confused. Problems of selection and placement of topics, sequence and articulation were highlighted. The match between "Man: A Course of Study" and the "other" years of social study, for example, may become a mettlesome complication and frustration. Surely, the notion of match between the new package and other program elements cannot be ignored.

Additional models of package development should be sought. The patterns of the national curriculum project (for example, BSCS, HSGP) and small-scale packages probably do not exhaust viable possibilities. Available and apparently successful, they are most easily copied. As other models appear, attention should be directed to several important features. One is provision for flexibility. Another might relate to the extent of specification of learner behaviors in instructional objectives. Local production of particularly relevant materials (for example, a film loop showing neighborhood street signs, a tape recording of local speech patterns) should be encouraged by special suggestions, plans and directions. Master tapes, prints and transcripts that may be reproduced locally should also be components in new package development plans. Alternative models, seriously considered, will represent considerable and useful variety.

Cost undoubtedly will persist as a major problem. Budget restrictions and rising expenses make necessary more frugal operations. And a tempting portion of every budget are the already meager lines for instructional resources. Purchases of materials may be cut further than already anticipated. Since packages usually have a high initial cost, they may face drastically decreased sales. Yet, because of their conception and development, and with greater attention to marketing, packages could benefit from current budget restrictions. The argument could be, simply, that the package is a better instructional system and the more economical choice would be a decision based on demonstrated quality. Such an argument, however cleverly merchandised, must still be accompanied by products at reasonable costs. Extravagance has never been a hallmark of school business management, in spite of a few excesses and some inflammatory publicity. Costs must be reduced for widespread adoption and use.

Greatly needed are data useful to the possible adopter about the package. Advertising and artful merchandising, in this respect, are obscurant. Empirical data about initial and replacement costs and equipment up- and down-times, as well as about pupil learnings, will be helpful. Records kept by teachers about instructional problems, pitfalls and successes with specified and described pupil groups probably are more valuable to the adopter than a list of towns in which tryouts were held. Critiques of the package by several experts will provide perspective and highlight attention to important concerns for substantive and pedagogic validity. Accounts of patterns of use in different schools will demonstrate the flexibility possible or rigidity required. Indeed, attention to these matters of evaluation permit the practical expansion of evaluation activities and theory and provide relevant, usable information for those who are interested in the package.

This Age of the Package is not a new era. Rather, it seems to be the present state of maturation of a posture about instructional media and materials. The new way of life is here, to be sure, but it is not here for all, in every school. Continuing to emerge as only dimly seen here, this age presents possibilities only dreamed about in days past. But dreams, like metaphors and labels, are not the reality of bustling pupils working on important matters. Seizing the possibilities of instructional packages is a current opportunity for living in these days.

# 26

## Individualization of Instruction: What It Is and What It Isn't

Robert E. Keuscher

There are several generalizations one can make about individualization of instruction today. First, it's "in." Everyone is in favor of individualizing. Second, most teachers will look you squarely in the eye and tell you they are individualizing instruction to some extent in their classrooms. Which leads naturally to the third generalization, that there are easily as many definitions of what individualization is as there are people attempting to do it. Fourth, every major producer of instructional materials and equipment in this country is peddling one or more sure-fire gimmicks to enable teachers to individualize. And last, but surely the most disconcerting, is that very few, if any, of the different modes of individualization or the kits, packages and programs purported to help teachers individualize do much of anything for the individual; in fact, they may do much to stifle the learner's initiative, his creativity and his independence.

### Individualization Is "In"

It is easy to account for enthusiasm for individualization of instruction. Primarily, it is a natural reaction against the impersonal, mass-production methods we have been using in education. The idea of a teacher standing before a class of 30 or more

Reprinted from *California Journal of Instructional Improvement*, Vol. 14, No. 2, May 1971, pp. 53-59, by permission of publisher and author, who is with the International Center for Educational Development, Encino, California.

youngsters attempting to teach the same lesson to all of them at the same time is preposterous. It defies all we know about the wide range of differences that exist within the group. It negates what we know about motivation, about children's needs, their interests, their creative capabilities. Nor does dividing 30 kids into 3 groups do anything to make instruction more effective. The teacher must get closer to the individual pupil than that—at least ten times closer!

If learning is to be meaningful to children they need a voice in deciding what they study and when and how they study it. Children must see the utility of what they are learning. We're a long way down the road from the time when adults (curriculum committees, textbook writers, teachers) can play God, handing down the decisions as to what students must study "from on high." All we've done with that kind of behavior—and educators are beginning to realize it *finally*—is turn kids off, make exhortation the number one task of teachers, and increase classroom discipline problems. Older students are complaining about "relevancy." The younger children would, too, if they knew the word. Far too much of what we have been handing out as required curriculum is not relevant to children at the time we confront them with it. The term "individualize instruction" to me means bringing the decision-making about curriculum closer to the individual learner. Unless he participates in the decisions, the planning, the goal setting, let's not pretend we are "individualizing" anything. The term just doesn't apply.

## Teachers Delude Themselves

Most teachers recognize the myriad of differences that exist among children, but they have never really faced the possibility of adequately meeting such a great range of diversity. Rather, they tinker with the organizational structure of the assignment requirements and honestly believe they are individualizing.

It is very difficult for most teachers to visualize a classroom where everyone is busy working alone, in pairs or in groups of three to eight on a variety of projects spanning several subject areas at one time, while the teacher moves freely about the classroom lending a hand here, making a suggestion there, asking an appropriate question or two here, receiving a progress report there. Teachers who work in this manner tell me they have never known their students so well and have never seen boys and girls so excited about schooling.

Teachers have to quit kidding themselves about how individualization takes place. To really do it, they must know their children as they've never known them before. This means listening to students much more than they have previously, observing students more than they have in the past, and permitting students to incorporate their own needs and interests into the instructional program. The teacher will do far less "teaching" in such a program and much more facilitating, or helping learning take place.

## Most Programs Miss Their Mark

With so many different versions of what constitutes individualized instruction, it is inevitable that most individualized programs fall far short of their mark. One thing is increasingly clear to me as I visit so-called individualized classrooms. There is no possibility of attending to the diversity we find there without increasing many times over the number of options available to students. Children must have choices as to what to study and how to study it.

Providing alternatives for students dictates a different kind of classroom environment than the desk- and textbook-dominated rooms we now have, most of them so tidy and formal that they bore the teacher as well as the pupils. "Chalk and talk classrooms," one visiting British educator dubbed these unexciting boxes we cage our children in while we talk and they sit passively and listen. And then we wonder why they begin to turn off as early as second or third grade and learn to dislike school!

Learning should be an exciting activity and to make it so, schools have to be exciting places. There have to be projects for children to do, problems for them to investigate, ideas for them to read and write and calculate about, activities that are fun as well as educational, and experiences to whet the interest of pupils of different levels of maturity, of different backgrounds and cultures. There should be books and books and books—not textbooks, but library books—books so plentiful, so colorful and so broad in their interest appeal that one would almost defy a child not to find several that turn him on. There should be interest areas for science, including experiments with plants and animals, a microscope, a dry cell battery or two, mealworms, tropical fish, perhaps a salt-water aquarium, small animals, rocks, shells, insect collection boxes and a lot of common, inexpensive science supplies.

There should be a mathematics center. Here is a place where students can weigh, measure, time and graph their data. It contains yardsticks, tape measures, rulers, a click wheel, balances, two or three different kinds of scales, a stopwatch or two, and of course things to weigh and balance—beans, pebbles, nuts, blocks. Also found in such a center are paper, yarn, and other materials necessary for pictorial representation of findings.

There should be a language arts center with all kinds of suggestions and incentives to help motivate children to write. An old typewriter or two is a must for this center as well as the materials needed to make hard-back covers for the "books" children will write.

There should be a quiet corner for research or just plain reading. A piece of used carpet, an old sofa or rocking chair, and several large pillows can make this area the most popular in the room.

Other attractions might include a junk art area, the "tinker table" where children dismantle old clocks, radios and electrical appliances that the teacher has picked up at the repair shop where they were about to be discarded. Also one might find a puppet theater or drama corner, a sewing or knitting center, an educational game area.

Where does one find room for all of this? In the regular classroom! But most or all of the students' desks are removed. Bookcases and tables properly placed divide the room into the various areas and students keep their belongings in tote trays or individual cubby holes in a cabinet along one wall.

Students are encouraged to bring materials for the room.

Parents get in on the act. It's surprising what an exciting environment can be built in a short time when everyone pitches in. Surprising, too, will be the different attitude students have about the room when they feel it is "their" room.

It won't take a lot of money to set up a room along the lines suggested. In fact, you will find it much less expensive. The classrooms I visited in Great Britain were simply "rich" with materials for children to work with despite the fact that the expenditure per pupil is only a small fraction of what we spend in this country.

One thing is certain. You will not need to purchase many of the products currently appearing on the market and advertised as facilitating individualization.

## Gimmicks and Packages
## Aren't the Answer

Most materials and programs marketed in the name of individualization do very little over and beyond adjusting the pace with which the student wades through the prescribed assignments. Everyone covers the same material (what allowances for differences exist here?)—some just go through faster than others.

Another indictment of most programmed or computer-assisted materials is that they teach only those facts and understandings that are going to show up on the tests. Both information and answers are decided beforehand by some "all-knowing" person or group of people who, although they do not know, have never seen, nor ever will see the pupil, have decided what he should learn and the manner in which he should learn it.

Let's face it! What programmed materials do is indoctrinate, with no concern whatsoever for the individual's rights in the matter. And they can indoctrinate for any purpose desired. I'm sure that Adolf Hitler, if he were alive and training German youth today, would be using many of the same kinds of materials and methods that are being urged upon teachers in this country as aids to individualization. Proponents claim their programmed materials and methods to be a more efficient way of educating. They may be right, if we are willing to accept the premise that what we are trying to do is get our students to learn a specified, fixed block of knowledge. But is there such a block of knowledge that everyone must have? If so, who determines what that knowledge is? And is our methodology in exposing the child to that knowledge going to accomplish what is intended? I'm fully convinced that in our zeal to teach some children to read through the high pressure tactics of computer assistance, systems approaches and programming, we may be raising reading scores but turning children so against reading that they will never enjoy it again as long as they live!

Individualizing instruction along the lines of diagnosis and prescription, pre-testing, and post-testing, through behavioral objectives, is a manipulative method of teaching. It stresses what is to be taught and how it is to be taught with little or no regard for the feelings of the individual. He becomes a pawn in the process. There is NO way we can develop a zest for learning, self-confidence, rational thinking, independence and responsibility through the programmed approach to learning.

Educators who grasp such methods hoping they'll solve all problems ought to be smarter than that. They should realize that all they are going to reap is more disinterest and alienation. If there is anything children DO NOT NEED at this time, it is more manipulation, more distance between pupil and teacher. Schooling is far too impersonal now. What we need desperately to do today is to PERSONALIZE our teaching.

### It's What Happens to the Person That Matters

Most attempts at individualization fail to do much, if anything, for the individual, his self-concept, his feeling about school. I'm convinced we must start with the learner before we worry about reading or mathematics. If a child doesn't feel pretty good about himself, have some confidence in his ability to succeed, and if he doesn't feel good about school, enjoy being there, look forward to returning each day, find it an exciting, fun place to be, we aren't going to accomplish much with reading or any other content we try to teach. *We must work on first things first.* The child's feelings about himself and about school precede all other concerns.

This cannot be accomplished with a machine, nor can it be programmed. It takes a teacher who gives primacy to the feelings of his children and to the personal development of each member of his class to turn students on to learning. Place that teacher who is personalizing his instruction in the rich environment that every teacher owes his pupils, and learning is going to take place. There is no way to prevent it! Furthermore, creativity will flourish, relationships between students (a great concern to many of the teachers I know today) will become less aggressive and more warmly cooperative, and boys and girls will not only learn to read but learn to love reading!

Personalized teaching (I prefer that term over individualized) is not a program; it's a way of performing in the classroom, based on a set of values about children and schooling. It's not a method; it's an attitude.

Most British schools have moved dramatically in this direction, and I have never seen more turned-on, happy, productive students than those I saw there on a recent visit. Over there, they call it Open Education and I recall one primary school Head who told me, "It's not a program we have, it's a way of living!"

I think it is a way of life based on a genuine concern for our most precious resource, our children. Whether we call it Personalized Instruction or Open Education or stick by the oft-misused term Individualized Instruction, it is urgent that we educators re-examine our programs with special concern for one question regarding what we are now doing—"What is happening to the person in the process?"

## References

Association for Supervision and Curriculum Development. *To Nurture Humanness.* ASCD Yearbook, 1970.

Holt, John. *What Do I Do Monday?* New York: E.P. Dutton and Co., Inc., 1970.

Howes, Virgil M., Darrow, Helen F., Keuscher, Robert E., and Tyler, Louise L.

*Individualization of Instruction: Exploring Open-Structure.* Los Angeles: ASUCLA Students' Store, 308 Westwood Plaza, Los Angeles, California 90024, 1968.

Howes, Virgil M., ed. *Individualization of Instruction. A Teaching Strategy.* New York: The Macmillan Company, 1970.

Kohl, Herbert R. *The Open Classroom.* New York: The New York Review, 1969.

Rogers, Vincent R. *Teaching in the British Primary School.* New York: The Macmillan Company, 1970.

Silberman, Charles. *Crisis in the Classroom.* New York: Random House, 1970.

# 27

## Evaluation Under
## Individualized Instruction

Margaret C. Wang and
John L. Yeager

During the past decade, increasing attention has been given to the
development of instructional systems designed to accommodate
the individual needs of the pupil.[1] Many classroom teachers are
seeking new techniques and materials that are responsive to the
needs of individual pupils. Large scale classroom innovations are
being introduced to meet individual needs. Among these innovations are programmed instruction, individually prescribed instruction and Project PLAN.

Because of the increasing emphasis on the individualization
of instruction, methods of assessing pupils' learning need to be
revised. Under conventional instructional procedures, pupils are
required to master particular lessons within a given time interval,
and each pupil is expected to proceed at the same pace.
Conventional procedures do not take into account individual
differences in rate of learning. A pupil's success or failure in school
learning is judged in terms of his achievement when learning time
is held constant. Achievement is usually measured by standardized
achievement tests or by tests that the teacher has constructed.

The recent emphasis on programs that provide for individual
differences has resulted in a number of procedures which permit
pupils to progress through a given set of learning tasks at
individual rates. In a discussion on individualization of instruction,
Bloom calls attention to one basic assumption in these programs:

Reprinted from *Elementary School Journal*, Vol. 71, No. 8, May 1971, pp.
448-452, by permission of authors and publisher.

if we can find ways and means of helping each pupil, all pupils can conceivably master a given learning task.[2] It must be recognized that some pupils will require more effort, more time and more help to achieve mastery than other pupils, but given sufficient time and appropriate types of assistance, the majority of pupils can achieve mastery. Under these circumstances, individual differences are expressed in the amount of time the learner requires to master a particular learning task. Under most plans of individualized instruction, the level of mastery each pupil exhibits on a test does not provide a valid indication of the pupil's progress since all pupils are required to attain a specific level of mastery before continuing in the program.

Let us say that a criterion level of 80 percent is specified for a particular test: all pupils must achieve a minimum of 80 percent before moving on to a new area of study. Under this arrangement, variability in achievement is limited. However, since each pupil is permitted sufficient time to meet this criterion level, the amount of time pupils require to meet the criterion varies. Some pupils may require three days; other pupils may require ten. One reasonable solution to the problem of measuring pupil achievement when individual rates of progress are permitted to vary is to use rate of learning as an achievement measure—that is, to use the number of lessons mastered, the number of tests passed, or the amount of time required to complete a given task. In brief, a pupil's achievement can be measured by his performance on a particular test and the amount of time required to master the given activity.

Research studies on learning, in particular, report substantial differences in rate of learning among pupils. The differences have been found in school situations as well as under experimental laboratory conditions.[3-7] These differences in individual learning rates are related to characteristics of the learner, to the learning task and to the learning environment.[8-13] Some studies indicate that learning rate is related to typical aptitude measures.[14-16] Other investigations indicate that rate does not have any simple relationship to measures of aptitude and is not consistent over many units of work.[17/18]

Why do some studies show no relationship between a given rate measure and pupil's aptitude and no consistency of the rate measure over a number of tasks? Perhaps the materials and the lessons are more suited to some pupils than to others. Under these circumstances, a measure of learning rate may be biased.

The writers working in an individualized instructional program—the Individually Prescribed Instruction Project[17]—investigated the relationship between a number of indices of pupils' rate of learning and selected measures of pupil aptitude and achievement, as well as certain measures of classroom performance.

The results of these studies indicate that no one measure of learning rate is superior to any other; nor does there appear to be any simple relationship between rate of learning and selected pupil characteristics. On the basis of these studies, it would seem that rate of learning is specific to a given task and is not a general factor that characterizes pupil performance in all learning situations. Furthermore, the results suggest several possible reasons why various measures of rate of learning have not been found to be consistent and why related or predicting factors have not been clearly identified.

School learning situations are complex. This fact poses many problems in measuring learning rate. The problems can usually be classified into two major categories: problems associated with the measure used and problems associated with the many variables that probably affect rate of learning.

A major problem in measuring rate of learning arises from the definition of *rate*. *Rate* may be defined as the amount or degree of anything in relation to units of time, that is, rate equals amount or degree divided by time. The main problem here is to determine the amount or degree of learning (the numerator in the equation).

Should the amount to be learned be specified in terms of the number of discrete skills to be mastered over a short period of time, such as a few hours of work? Or should the amount to be learned be represented by longer periods of time covering larger areas of content? Should the skills and the attitudes that the pupil brings to the learning situation be taken into account? What type of measure should be developed to account for and describe the learning rate of two pupils, each working on the same task, when one pupil had mastered 40 percent of the task before he began work and the other pupil had mastered none of the task before he started? These are technical problems associated with the development of any measures of achievement; yet the classroom teacher must recognize the difficulties when evaluating pupils' performance.

The writers believe that the basic problem in studying pupil's rate of learning and the factors related to it is to specify the characteristics of the learning situation itself. In the writers' judgment, before any consistent relationship can be established between measures of rate and the learning task and pupil variables that might be related to these measures of rate, a careful study should be made of the nature of the learning task itself. In other words, it is essential to examine the learning objectives and the types of skills to be learned in each unit of the individualized curriculum. After this step has been taken, the relationship between pupil's rate of learning and the type of tasks to be learned can be specified.

Once the nature of the task to be learned is specified, the next major problem is to identify classroom procedures that will help each pupil master the specified task to a degree commensurate with his abilities. It should be recognized that the relation between pupil variables and rate of learning may be influenced greatly by the effectiveness of the instructional system. Pupil's rate of learning in school varies with the nature and the quality of instruction. Carroll has suggested that the effectiveness of instruction determines rate of learning.[9]

Therefore, one major task in solving the measurement problem in assessing pupil's rate of learning in school is to develop an instructional system that provides optimal learning conditions for each pupil. Only when each pupil has maximum opportunities to learn can one realistically investigate the pupil's rate of learning in school situations. Only then can one study the nature of the relationship between rate and factors related to pupil's rate of learning in schools under an individualized instructional system.

In summary, scores on achievement tests, by themselves, do

not describe the progress of pupils in an individualized system of instruction. The seemingly obvious alternative—to measure learning rate—also poses major problems. Even so, teachers who are working in classroom settings that permit each pupil to progress individually through a sequence of learning experiences must consider two measures of pupil progress—degree of mastery achieved on tests and the rate at which the pupil masters a given task. If one or the other of these measures is missing, there is little chance that the assessment will be meaningful.

## Notes

1. The research reported herein was supported by the Learning Research and Development Center supported as a research and development center by funds from the United States Office of Education, Department of Health, Education, and Welfare. The opinions expressed in this publication do not necessarily reflect the position or policy of the Office of Education.

2. B.S. Bloom. "Mastery Learning for All." An invited address presented at the American Educational Research Association Annual Meeting, Chicago, February 1968.

3. J.O. Bolvin. "Report on Individualized Instruction Project." Presented at the Board of Visitors Meeting, Learning Research and Development Center, University of Pittsburgh, April 1965 (mimeographed).

4. R. Kalin. "Development and Evaluation of a Programmed Text in an Advanced Mathematical Topic of Intellectually Superior Fifth- and Sixth-Grade Pupils." Unpublished doctoral dissertation. Tallahassee: Florida State University, 1962.

5. D.L. Nicholas. "The Effect of Pacing Rate on the Efficiency of Learning for Programmed Instructional Material." Unpublished doctoral dissertation. Bloomington: Indiana University, 1967.

6. P. Suppes. "Modern Learning Theory and the Elementary School Curriculum," *American Educational Research Journal*, 1 (March 1964), 79-94.

7. J.L. Yeager. "Measures of Learning Rates for Elementary School Students in Mathematics and Reading under a Program of Individually Prescribed Instruction." Unpublished doctoral dissertation. Pittsburgh: University of Pittsburgh, 1966.

8. R.B. Allison. "Learning Parameters and Human Abilities." Unpublished doctoral dissertation. Princeton, New Jersey: Princeton University, June 1966.

9. J.B. Carroll. "A Model of School Learning," *Teachers College Record, 64* (May 1963), 723-32.

10. J.P. Guilford. "Three Faces of Intellect," *American Psychologist, 14* (August 1959), 469-79.

11. D.D. Sjogren. "Achievement as a Function of Study Time," *American Educational Research Journal, 4* (November, 1967), 337-43.

12. J.T. Smith, M.D. Ruter, F.M. Lackner, and D.S. Kwall. "Academic Sociometric and Personality Variables in the Prediction of Elementary School Achievement," *Proceedings of the 75th Annual Convention of the American Psychological Association,* Vol. II, pp. 339-40. Washington, D.C.: Merkle Press, 1967.

13. C.J. Spies. *Some Non-Intellectual Predictors of Classroom Success.* Technical Report No. 10 Office of Naval Research, Contract No. NOR 816 (14) Naval Air Technical Training. Washington, D.C.: Department of Naval Research, October 1966.

14. A. Jensen. "Learning Ability in Retarded, Average and Gifted Children." In *Educational Technology,* pp. 356-76. Edited by J.P. DeCecco. New York: Holt, Rinehart and Winston, 1964.

15. R. Glaser, J.H. Reynolds and M. G. Fullick. *Programmed Instruction in the Intact Classroom.* Project No. 1342, Cooperative Research, United States Office of Education, Pittsburgh, Pennsylvania. December 1963.

16. G.L. Gropper and G. Kress. "Individualizing Instruction through Pacing Procedures," *Audiovisual Communication Review, 13* (Summer 1965) 165-82.

17. M.C. Wang. "An Investigation of Selected Procedures for Measuring and Predicting Rate of Learning in Classrooms Operating under a Program of Individualized Instruction." Unpublished doctoral dissertation. Pittsburgh: University of Pittsburgh, 1968.

18. C.M. Lindvall and J.O. Bolvin. "Programmed Instruction in the Schools: An Application of Programming Principles in Individually Prescribed Instruction," *Programmed Instruction,* p. 217. Sixty-sixth Yearbook of the National Society for the Study of Education, Part II. Edited by Phil Lange. Chicago: National Society for the Study of Education, 1967. (Distributed by the University of Chicago Press.)

# 28

## The Role of the Teacher
## in Individually Prescribed Instruction

C.M. Lindvall and John O. Bolvin

The current renewed attention to the problem of individualizing instruction in the schools is probably the result of a variety of factors. One of these is the fact that the development of new media and new modes of instruction offers unique possibilities for adaptation to individual differences. Also, some of the better applications of programmed instruction in the schools have demonstrated the feasibility of a certain type of individualized instruction. Certainly one of the major reasons for this attention to individualization is the growing recognition that some type of individualized instruction is becoming a necessity.

Today's student not only has much more to learn than the student of past eras, but also is faced with more options for alternative areas of concentration. This dictates that classroom instruction must become much more efficient; that the classroom activity of each student be based on his unique needs and interests. We can no longer afford classroom situations where more than 50 percent of the students may be listening to a teacher making a group presentation on a topic that they have already mastered. Perhaps an even more important consideration is that each student's school experience must prepare him to become a life-long learner. Continuing rapid advances in technology make it likely that a person's occupation may be abolished once or more during his adult life. In view of this situation, it is imperative that

Reprinted from *Educational Technology*, Vol. 10, No. 2, February 1970, pp. 37-41, by permission of authors and publisher.

most adults be equipped to carry out self-initiated and self-directed study which will equip them for a new occupation. That most citizens have the skills and the inclination to be life-long learners seems essential, also, to the satisfactory solution of many of our current major social problems. Achieving such solutions seems possible only if citizens are willing to study the problems, to become familiar with the issues, and to work out answers.

In view of these needs, *the goal of a system of individualized instruction must be to develop persons who seek opportunities to learn, and who have the capabilities for setting their own goals, planning an instructional program, and evaluating and monitoring their activities as learning progresses.* Available techniques of instruction, lesson materials, diagnostic tests, etc., should not be permitted to determine the nature of an individualized system. The nature of the system must be assessed in terms of the extent to which it gives promise of achieving the goal presented above. The teacher's role and all other aspects of instruction must be designed to enhance the achievement of this kind of instructional situation.

It would be possible to develop an individualized system in which maximum control came from outside the student himself. The simplest to describe would be the situation where there is one teacher per student and where all planning and control is exercised by the teacher. Another equally extreme example would be a computer-assisted instruction system where all decisions were built into the system itself. Presumably it would be possible to build systems of this type that, while individualized, exercised maximum external control on student plans and student progress. These systems might be highly efficient in some respects, but in the light of the goal described above they would be entirely inadequate. The desired type of individualized instruction requires a program in which pupils can take part in meaningful learning activities adapted to their own requirements and to a considerable degree directed and managed by each individual student. This is a basic and ultimate goal of the program for Individually Prescribed Instruction (IPI), an effort at individualizing instruction in the elementary school that is being developed at the Learning

Research and Development Center at the University of Pittsburgh and the Baldwin-Whitehall Schools, and which is being field tested and disseminated by Research for Better Schools, the Philadelphia-based Regional Educational Laboratory.

### IPI As an Instructional System

A basic assumption of IPI is that the desired type of individualized instruction is feasible in a typical school situation only when careful structure and guidance is provided through a carefully defined educational system. The history of our schools indicates that individualization is not achieved by telling the teacher to "pay attention to individual differences." This has been preached to teachers for decades; little individualization has resulted.

The teacher needs to be assisted by a system which makes individualization feasible. He needs materials that permit a great amount of independent study, diagnostic techniques that provide information as to what a pupil is ready to study, a procedure for monitoring pupil progress, and detailed guidelines that the teacher and pupils can follow to make the total system operate. Only with this type of assistance is it possible for the typical teacher to individualize instruction. But this system is not an end in itself. That is, the goal of a structured program such as IPI is not to put a pupil in an efficient system. The system is only a means to a goal. The goal is to have each pupil operating as a self-directed learner within an individualized instructional program. The system is only one major factor in permitting the achievement of this goal.

### The Role of the Teacher in IPI

What is the role of the teacher in the IPI classroom? What is the teacher's part in helping to achieve the overall goal of this individualized system? One way of describing this role is to outline it in terms of three major functions. These are:

A. The teacher's role in operating the system.
B. The teacher's role in supplementing the system to enhance adaptation to individual needs.
C. The teacher's role in providing for the achievement of goals possible only with teacher intervention.

Obviously, these three points do not cover the total role of the teacher. They make no mention of the teacher's role as a developer and evaluator of the system, nor of the role of the teacher as a member of a total school faculty. These three points are intended merely to cover key aspects of the teacher's role when functioning within the classroom.

## The Teacher's Role in Operating the System

In brief, Individually Prescribed Instruction is based on a structured curriculum involving a detailed specification of instructional objectives which are organized in terms of levels and topics. Some conception of what this involves may be gathered from Table 1. This presents the overall organization of the IPI Mathematics Curriculum. Mathematics has been broken into

*Table 1*

*Number of Objectives in Each Topic at Each
Level (or in Each Unit) of the IPI
Mathematics Curriculum*

| Topic | Level | | | | | | |
|---|---|---|---|---|---|---|---|
| | A | B | C | D | E | F | G |
| Numeration | 12 | 10 | 8 | 5 | 8 | 3 | 8 |
| Place Value | | 3 | 5 | 9 | 7 | 5 | 2 |
| Addition | 3 | 10 | 5 | 8 | 6 | 2 | 3 |
| Subtraction | | | 4 | 5 | 3 | 1 | 3 |
| Multiplication | | | | 8 | 11 | 10 | 6 |
| Division | | | | 7 | 7 | 8 | 5 |
| Comb. of Processes | | | 6 | 5 | 7 | 4 | 5 |
| Fractions | 3 | 2 | 4 | 5 | 6 | 14 | 5 |
| Money | | 4 | 4 | 6 | 3 | 2 | |
| Time | | 3 | 2 | 10 | 9 | 5 | 3 |
| Systems of Measure | | 4 | 3 | 5 | 7 | 3 | 2 |
| Geometry | | 2 | 2 | 3 | 9 | 10 | 7 |
| Special Topics | | | 1 | 3 | 3 | 5 | 4 |

several topic areas, such as Numeration, Place Value, Addition, Subtraction, etc., and each such topic area has been divided into levels which are roughly equivalent to grade levels. A typical student progresses through the curriculum by mastering the objectives for each topic at level A, then moving on to the topics at level B, and so on. All of the objectives for a given topic at a given level, such as C-Addition, constitute a unit.

For each objective or skill, instructional materials have been identified that permit the student to master the objectives on a relatively independent basis. This outline of objectives organized in terms of topics, levels and units provides the overall framework for the Individually Prescribed Instruction system. Other elements of the system include a placement testing program, which places the new student at the proper unit level in each of the topic areas; unit posttests, which diagnose the student's needs as he enters each new unit; a system for developing individualized plans of instruction or prescriptions; and a testing and evaluation procedure for monitoring the student's progress as he moves through each objective and each successive unit. This total system has been described in detail elsewhere.*

A basic aspect of the teacher's role in IPI is to make this system function. This must include such aspects of the system as the following:

1. *The evaluation and diagnosis of the needs and the progress of each student.* The IPI procedure calls for the use of placement tests to identify the unit with which a student is to start his study and unit pretests to provide diagnostic information for prescription writing. As the student works through a unit, he takes a

*C.M. Lindvall and John O. Bolvin. Programmed Instruction in the Schools: An Application of Programming Principles in Individually Prescribed Instruction. *Programmed Instruction.* Sixty-Sixth Yearbook of the National Society for the Study of Education, Part II. Chicago: University of Chicago Press, 1967.
C.M. Lindvall and Richard Cox. The Role of Education in Programs for Individualized Instruction. *Educational Evaluation: New Roles, New Means.* Sixty-Eighth Yearbook of the National Society for the Study of Education, Part VII. Chicago: University of Chicago Press, 1969.

Curriculum Embedded Test (CET) to check his mastery of each objective and a unit posttest to assess his command of the total unit. All of these tests and the procedures for using them are key aspects of the IPI system, and the teacher is responsible for seeing that they are used properly.

2. *The development of individual study plans or prescriptions.* The essential element in individualizing the program of each student is the unique prescription of learning activities designed to meet his special needs. Such prescriptions may be developed by the pupil, or the teacher, or as a cooperative effort. The IPI system provides forms and procedures for making the necessary data available, and includes guidelines for prescription development.

3. *The development of immediate and long range plans for the total class, which take individual needs and plans into account.* In planning a daily class schedule, the teacher makes use of information concerning the placement of every pupil and concerning current problem areas. In some implementations of IPI such data are provided as a part of a computerized system for data collection and analysis. This information is used in grouping students, in providing for peer tutoring, and in planning for total group seminars.

4. *The planning and organization of the classroom and the class period to create an effective learning environment.* Even though study is carried out largely by having each pupil pursue a unique set of activities, it is necessary for the IPI teacher to give careful thought to his own schedule of classroom activities. He must allocate time for general supervision of activities, for small group instruction, for individual tutoring and for counseling. The teacher must also be concerned with such details as seating arrangements, the accessibility of supplies and equipment and the availability of supplementary learning materials. Planning for all of these details of classroom operation is essential to the effective implementation of IPI.

5. *The development, in cooperation with other members of the professional staff, of plans for any necessary large group instruction.* The successful operation of IPI typically demands full cooperation of teachers at a given grade level or adjacent grade

levels. If time is to be found for all of the needed individual tutoring and counseling, activities such as group instruction must be planned on a cooperative basis. To achieve this, the IPI system calls for regularly scheduled planning sessions involving all teachers who constitute an instructional team.

6. *The supervision of the work of para-professionals such as technicians and teacher aides.* Under present IPI operating procedures, every classroom teacher has the services of a teacher aide who carries out such duties as scoring tests, assembling records and distributing supplies. The aide is an essential part of the classroom instructional system, and it is the responsibility of the teacher to see that these activities are effectively integrated into the overall operation.

7. *The study and evaluation of the system so as to improve its operation in the classroom.* As the foregoing points indicate, the total IPI classroom operation involves many elements that must be coordinated if the system is to function effectively. It is the teacher's responsibility to evaluate the entire operation on a continuous basis and to take steps to correct any instances of malfunctioning.

Making the system function also requires that the teacher train pupils to manage their own activities. Pupils must be taught to evaluate their own lessons and assess their progress. They must learn how to overcome learning difficulties by means other than always asking for teacher help. This will include learning to use a variety of supplementary materials and to obtain appropriate help from a fellow student. The effective functioning of the IPI system requires that pupils accept major responsibilities, and a key role of the teacher is to guide pupils in developing the ability to function in this way.

Experience has indicated that the starting point in the implementation of Individually Prescribed Instruction must be to make certain that teachers can make the basic "mechanics" of the system operate. Of course, IPI, or any other structured program for individualizing instruction, would be relatively narrow and sterile if the structured system is the only part of the program that operates. But emphasizing the fact that "operating the system" is only one part of the teacher role should not cause one to lose sight of the fact that this is an essential role.

## Supplementing the System to Enhance Adaptation to Individual Needs

Schools using a structured system such as Individually Prescribed Instruction quickly find out that despite the lengths to which materials and procedures are developed to permit pupils to progress on an independent basis, there are many aspects of instruction that cannot be carried out effectively without the personal intervention of the teacher. To really adapt instruction to individual needs, it is essential that certain aspects of evaluation, diagnosis, prescription and instruction be carried out by a trained teacher. Certainly this is true, for example, in assessing individual learner characteristics. Test results and records of past performance of pupils can be very important in identifying certain needs of the learner, but there are many other variables defining the learner's needs and aptitudes that at present can only be identified through the day-by-day interaction between teacher and learner. Another function demanding the personal attention of the teacher is that of adjusting learning programs to meet the characteristics of the learner. Such personal intervention by the teacher may involve providing personal tutoring or some other type of personal instruction for the student. It may involve a decision to set up peer tutoring: arranging for one student to instruct another. Frequently it will result in the decision to use small group or large group instruction, when either is deemed to be the most effective procedure for achieving certain goals.

Another essential role of the teacher is in taking exceptions to the system when this is necessary. The idea of adaptability to individual differences would seem to require that with any system, no matter how carefully developed or how fully variations in procedures are provided, there is still provision for variations based upon on-the-scene decisions of the teacher. One example of this would be a decision to lower the mastery requirement on a skill or unit for a given pupil. Another might be the decision to have a student skip certain units. The teacher always remembers that the goal of instruction is the growth of the individual pupil, not the completion of skills or units, and modification of the system to enhance this type of growth is an essential aspect of individualization.

In summary, experience with Individually Prescribed Instruction has indicated that the teacher role in supplementing this system is absolutely essential for an individualized instructional program; it will probably be a growing role in any procedure that attempts to meet the broad goals of individualized education.

## Providing for the Achievement of Goals
## Possible Only with Teacher Attention

If a program for individualized instruction is to achieve the basic goal of developing students who have an interest in learning and who have the capacity for setting goals and carrying out a self-directed study program designed to achieve those goals, it is important that the system provide for a number of experiences that can only be carried out through personal involvement of the teacher. Certainly one of these personal roles demanded of the teacher is that of being a counselor or a listener. Many of the things that it is important for a teacher to take into consideration in helping the student adjust his program to his needs are the kinds of things that can only be obtained by personal interview with the student. This means that, when the teacher is moving around the classroom and interacting with the students, an important aspect of this interaction must be an attentiveness to the concerns and the problems of the student. If the student is to become a willing and interested learner, it would seem to be important that his experiences with learning be in situations where he feels an attentiveness and a receptivity to his particular needs. A part of this must be having a teacher who is willing to listen to him.

To carry this further, the counseling role should probably involve such things as helping the student to set realistic goals for his program of study. At early levels this may merely involve discussing with the student how much work he expects to accomplish in a day or how long he thinks it will take him to cover a certain type of assignment. At higher levels it will involve assisting him in writing his own prescriptions. At still higher levels it could include helping him to map out the path that he hopes to follow in working through a unit, or assisting him in making decisions concerning what kind of study he needs to carry out to supplement that which is found within the system. These types of experiences should be major contributors to a pupil's becoming a self-activated and self-directed learner.

Another important role that the teacher can play in developing a desirable learning atmosphere is that of being an agent for selective reinforcement of desirable types of pupil activity. At early stages of the program, this type of reinforcement may be associated with such simple behaviors as attending to the learning task and showing simple types of self-initiative in solving simple problems. At later points, reinforcement might be used with more sophisticated types of self-directed, self-managed and self-motivated behaviors. Certainly, if the student is to develop the appropriate attitudes toward learning and the appropriate abilities with respect to carrying out the learning task, it is important that he be encouraged and reinforced for any evidence of the appropriate type of behavior. In this connection, the so-called behavior modification systems may have much to offer. First steps have been taken in the IPI Project for exploring the use of these procedures, and results up to this point have been quite encouraging.

Situations involving individual instruction present unique opportunities for the teacher to become aware of each pupil's progress in the development of important types of attitudes, values and personal-social skills. As has been stressed earlier, these learnings are major aspects of the real goals of individualization. If the teacher is not prepared to enhance the achievement of these learnings, programs of individualized instruction will fail to reach their potential.

## Conclusion

It is to be anticipated that expanded work on a variety of programs for individualized instruction will lead to a greater clarification and an expansion of the role of the classroom teacher.

This type of study of the teacher function is an essential aspect of the continuing development of IPI. When the teacher is freed from the task of serving as a continuing dispenser of learning content, as is true in most individualized systems, he then has the opportunity of devoting his energies to more important functions. He can become a counselor, a diagnostician and a prescriber of individualized learning experiences. He also has the time and opportunity to assist students in the achievement of important personal-social goals which are too frequently neglected.

It might well be suggested that the preparation of teachers to carry out these new roles should provide a new focus for professional programs of teacher training, both pre-service and in-service. In fact, it is probably the theory, the technique and the skills associated with the performing of these roles that constitute a major component of the content of professional education. As long as the teacher's task is looked upon largely as being that of lecturing on the content of mathematics, history, science, or economics, there is probably no real need for providing any type of professional education for teachers. A teacher need only be a mathematician, an historian, a scientist, or an economist. Professional preparation becomes necessary only when there is truly a professional content needed by the teacher. Work on the identification of this content can be a major contribution of the current emphasis on individualized instruction.

# 29

# A Study of Teacher Role Behaviors in an Innovative School

John M. Flynn and
Clifton B. Chadwick

As our educational system continues to evolve through the introduction of innovative learning methods and new technological developments, the role of the teacher is also evolving. However, the exact direction in which the role of the teacher has changed and is changing is not always well specified by the changes in other aspects of the system, nor is it always directly related to other changes.

In the implementation of changes in the schools, several possibilities are available in handling the teacher's role. One possibility is that teacher role behaviors (i.e., the behaviors characteristic of the role of the teacher) can be omitted from consideration in the system changes, and thus left to evolve without planning (i.e., the teachers can be left to follow whatever course *they* happen to choose deliberately or assume tacitly). This is the most frequent course; it has inherent dangers, since it is unlikely that any of the teachers in a given school have been trained to perform under the new conditions imposed by system changes. Consequently, each teacher's personality and background will dictate his role behaviors, and a variety of roles can be expected to emerge, many of which may counter the effects of system changes. For example, when new curricula are introduced which emphasize new methods, teachers frequently continue teaching the content by the old methods, thus negating the

Reprinted from *Educational Technology*, Vol. 10, No. 2, February 1970, pp. 49-55, by permission of authors and publisher.

possible benefits of the new program. Expecting the teacher to develop new role behaviors unaided as the system changes does not seem to be an efficient way to improve education.

If the teacher is not to find his own way as the system changes, then some guidance and direction must be provided for him. In some innovations, new or revised characteristics of the teacher's role have been outlined; and occasionally training is provided for the teachers. But frequently the changes in the role and the concomitant training are *ad hoc* and not well integrated into the teacher's total role. In many cases an administrator dictates what the role should be—based upon his visceral reactions to the matter. Thus, such role specifications are frequently based largely on opinion, with little supporting evidence.

Another approach to the problem is to systematically study the situation to determine the teacher role behaviors which are indicated by the total system configuration. With this method, the various requirements of the system can be taken into account, and efforts can be made to maximize the system's chief output—the education of children. This, of course, is a systems approach to defining the role of the teacher. Utilizing such an approach, a model of a teacher's role behaviors can be constructed which will optimize the objectives of education *within* the limits of today's knowledge and the constraints of the environment.

A first step in constructing such a model is to analyze the existing teaching system to determine the current role behaviors and system constraints. Perhaps a model could be developed without this step, but the implementation of any role model should take into consideration where the teachers are now so that changes can be effectively implemented. An administrator who hands his teachers a list of new behaviors, and tells them that tomorrow they are to act in these new ways, cannot realistically expect to effect the new model. Rather, he must systematically implement the model, providing necessary training and incentives to ensure that each step of the transition is orderly and effective.

Another reason for analyzing the existing system before constructing the model is to determine the relevance and relative effectiveness of the various existing activities of teachers. Much that teachers are currently doing might remain in a new model of teacher role behaviors. Many current behaviors, however, may be either ineffective or non-relevant to the outcomes of education. Perhaps by studying the existing system, these ineffective behaviors can be eliminated, and the necessary but non-relevant behaviors can be reassigned to other personnel. Still other behaviors may be both relevant and necessary, but do not require the talents of a *teacher*. Hopefully these also can be identified and reassigned to non-professionals.

A final reason for studying the system is to identify the system constraints which exist so that these can either be removed or taken into account in the model. A model which ignores the realities of the system cannot be satisfactorily implemented.

**The Existing System**

This article is a summary report of efforts to study teachers in existing school systems as a prelude to formulating one or more role models of teacher behaviors for individualized instruction. The schools studied were those in the Nova public schools complex in Fort Lauderdale, Florida, which is comprised of two elementary schools and one junior-senior high school.

Many of the classes in the Nova complex have increased the degree of individualization through the preparation and adoption of Learning Activity Packages (LAPs), which permit the student to have greater autonomy in his learning experiences than normally provided by more traditional methods of instruction (see McNeil and Smith, 1968, and Wolfe and Smith, 1968, for detailed descriptions of the LAP).

The LAP is a form of organized instruction ordered in units of effort which can be completed by students in varying lengths of time. The *ideal* LAP is organized to contain a clear statement of objectives, alternate routings through the presented materials *and* opportunities for student self-evaluation and teacher evaluation. While there are several variations in practice, the student in a LAP class can work largely on his own at a pace which is appropriate for him; and when he completes an assigned unit, he can move on to a new one.

The Nova schools provide an interesting setting for studying the effects of individualization of instruction on the teacher because only *some* of the classes are individualized, while others remain more or less traditional. At the time of the study there had been only limited in-service training of teachers for the utilization of the LAP in the classroom, and much of the in-service training which did occur did not deal directly with teachers' classroom behaviors, but with more peripheral activities. Consequently, teachers in LAP classes in general had assumed roles which were not clearly prescribed by the administration, but were largely ones which the teachers themselves devised or assumed.

**The Study**

Extensive observational data were gathered on many teachers at grade levels 1 through 12 in the Nova schools. Two observational instruments which provided structured forms of specimen description recording were developed. One of these instruments, the $RO_1$, was used to observe teachers, and the other, the $RO_2$, to observe students (see Flynn, Chadwick and Fischler, 1969). Supplementary data were also collected with Flanders' Verbal Interaction Scale (Flanders, 1966) and Honigman's Multi-Dimensional Analysis of Classroom Interaction (Honigman, 1967). Anecdotal information was collected through interviews with teachers and staff. Also, three teachers were commissioned to keep daily diaries, which provided a running account of their classroom situations. These latter two types of data collection were used primarily to familiarize the project staff with the school environment and to provide background for the observational data.

Some observational data with the $RO_1$ instrument were collected on 109 teachers, or about 48 percent of those in the Nova schools, but a random sample of 36 teachers was studied intensively, and this provides the basis for most of the findings reported in this paper. Trained resident observers spent most of each day for a period of about four months in the schools. Additional observers were used for brief periods, with the other observational instruments mentioned above.

One hundred and six $RO_1$ observations were made on the 36

teachers who comprised the core sample (1 to 5 observations per teacher, with a median of 3). These observations are categorized according to four types of teaching situations: classes using LAPs; classes not using LAPs but in which the teacher works with students on an individual basis (Non-LAP Individualized or NLI); non-individualized classes in which the teacher typically works with the entire class as a group (Traditional); and mixed classes (Mixed) in which none of the other types were clearly predominant. For the purpose of this report, the Mixed classes are ignored. The classes studied cut across all grade levels and major subject divisions in the school. There was a tendency for some academic departments to be more dependent upon the LAP than others, so some of the comparisons between LAP and non-LAP classes tend to be confounded by subject matter differences.

The findings which are reported here are considered as a first step in determining the role of teachers in individualized classrooms. The data are not to be considered as specifying what the teachers' role behaviors should be, but rather what they were in the Nova schools at the time of the study. Many additional inputs will be required to develop an adequate model of what the teacher's role should be.

It would be particularly desirable to relate teacher behavior to student subject matter performance for the ultimate in a "payoff" analysis, but the data collection design necessary to determine such a relationship may be impossible to develop and implement in regular classrooms. Students cannot be tested or queried after each small segment of teacher behavior, and comparisons of student performance data gathered at realistic intervals cannot be related to specific teacher behaviors. Consequently, only overt and observable student behaviors were recorded and analyzed in the study. Hence, no statements can be made regarding the relative effectiveness of various teacher behaviors on student subject matter acquisition.

The data collection and subsequent analyses emphasized the managerial aspects of the teacher's role in the classroom. That is, the teacher was looked at as a manager of the instructional environment, in which he arranged for the student to be instructed by various methods—including himself (see discussion by Chadwick, Tosti and Bell, 1968).

Under the managerial rubric, the observed teacher behaviors were grouped into three general categories. These are cognitive activities, educational environment activities and affective and social activities. Cognitive activities are those in which the teacher is concerned with some aspect of the cognitive educational processes of the students. Most activities which are typically thought of as teaching are in this category. Educational environment activities are primarily those related to maintaining the system; they are, in general, supportive of the outcomes of education, but are not directly related to those outcomes. Activities such as providing supplies and cleaning facilities are included here. The last general category is comprised of activities which deal with the affective and social lives of the students rather than the cognitive. Included are career planning, clubs and patriotic activities.

## Findings

The data were quantified in various ways, but the principal analyses dealt with the percent of time a teacher engaged in various types of observed events. The techniques utilized in examining the data included discriminate functions, pattern analysis and visual comparisons of percentages and means (see Flynn, Chadwick and Fischler, 1969). To determine the effect of individualization, comparisons were made with Traditional classes. To determine the particular effect of LAPs, comparisons were made between LAP classes and NLI classes.

For the purposes of this report, differences between the elementary schools and the high school and differences among the academic departments in the high school are not discussed.

Various comparisons of LAP classes to Traditional classes were made, and the results are briefly summarized below. Compared to teachers in Traditional classes, LAP teachers spent:

    (a)    less time presenting subject matter information to students;

   (b)  less time in the management of cognitive activities through the use of non-cognitive directions, requests, etc;

   (c)  more time in traffic control (e.g., taking roll, directing students' whereabouts, etc.);

   (d)  more time using various non-instructional materials to aid in the management of students;

   (e)  more time getting supplies and materials for students;

   (f)  more time making evaluative comments about students;

   (g)  more time giving grades to students and discussing grades;

   (h)  more time in housekeeping chores such as cleaning equipment;

   (i)  more time giving directions to students regarding aspects of the educational environment;

   (j)  more time directing students to do logistical tasks (e.g., having students get supplies);

   (k)  more time in events coded as "no observable relevant activity";

   (l)  less time asking questions and selecting students to answer questions; and

   (m)  less time interacting with the whole class.

An interesting finding was that LAP teachers and Traditional teachers both spent about the same amount of time interacting with individual students. Yet Traditional classes were so categorized because the teacher characteristically worked with the entire class as a unit. The explanation seems to be that in Traditional classes the teachers tend to interact with individual students in front of the entire class while in LAP classes they interact without involving the other students.

Differences were also found between the behaviors of *students* in LAP classes and those in Traditional classes. One area in which differences were determined was in the interactions with the teacher. In the LAP class, an average of 52 percent of the interactions with the teacher were initiated by the student. In the Traditional class, an average of only 34 percent of all interactions were initiated by the student. Hence, in the LAP classes it would appear that the student is more in charge of his own learning activities than in the Traditional class. For comparison purposes the NLI class had 54 percent of the student-teacher interactions initiated by the student. This exceeds that for the LAP classes so it would appear that not the LAP but rather the *individualized nature of the class* is responsible for this student initiation.

Since the students in individualized classes tend to initiate the interactions, a problem of queuing, waiting for the teacher's attention, frequently occurs. A student was considered to be waiting for the teacher's attention if he made an overt sign or attempt to get her attention and continued that sign for at least 15 seconds (reported by $RO_2$ observers). In LAP classes an average of 24 percent of the students had to wait 15 seconds or longer for the teacher's attention, while in Traditional classes only 6 percent of the students had to wait 15 seconds or longer. However, in the NLI classes 46 percent of the students had to wait 15 seconds or longer (which might suggest that the LAP did increase the teacher's ability to control the class).

Also from the data, a picture emerges of how the teacher's role in LAP classes differs from the role in the NLI classes. Table 1 summarizes how the teachers in the different situations divided their time across the three general behavior categories. In terms of this time allocation, LAP teachers spend slightly less time in cognitive activities than do their counterparts in NLI classrooms. LAP teachers average 62 percent of their time in cognitive activities, while NLI teachers average 68 percent of their time in such activities. The difference is made up in the educational environment activities, where LAP teachers spend 36 percent of their time compared to the Non-LAP Individualized teacher's 29 percent. Both average 2 percent in affective and social events. (There are, of course, individual variations within groups, and the reverse trend could be observed for a given pair of teachers.) It is suggested that the reason for the tendency of LAP teachers to spend less time in cognitive activities is that the LAP performs some of the instructional duties of the teacher in the LAP classroom. Since the LAP is intended to perform instructional tasks, it is noteworthy that the difference between the groups is not larger.

*Table 1*

*Mean Percent of Time LAP and NLI Teachers*
*Spent in Cognitive, Environmental and*
*Affective-Social Activities*

|  | LAP | NLI |
|---|---|---|
| Cognitive | 62% | 68% |
| Educational Environment | 36% | 29% |
| Affective-Social | 2% | 2% |

It would appear, then, that the LAP provides some structure to the role of the teacher that would otherwise be absent. However, it does not necessarily increase the teacher's freedom in the sense of being able to determine his own activities. The percentages of self-initiated activities were compared for the two situations (see Table 2), where a self-initiated event is defined as one which the teacher undertakes without being directly requested by a student or person immediately prior to the event (the observers, of course, were unaware of requests which were made at some time prior to the event). In LAP classes 24 percent of the teacher's events were self-initiated, while in the NLI classes, 34 percent of the events were self-initiated. This implies that the LAP structures the teacher's role in such a way that it provides less freedom for personal initiative than in the Non-LAP Individualized classroom.

When the type of events which were self-initiated are examined for the two groups, the LAP teachers are seen to initiate more environment events than cognitive ones, while the NLI ones initiate about equal numbers of the two types. As seen in Table 2, the LAP teacher's self-initiated events are 40 percent cognitive, 57 percent environmental, and 2 percent affective and social. The NLI are 49 percent cognitive, 48 percent environmental and 2 percent affective and social. Again, the differences may be explained by the structure provided by the LAP. The LAP assumes some of the instructional role otherwise undertaken by the teacher; thus, proportionately more of the teacher's self-initiated activities are system supportive, rather than instructional.

*Table 2*

*Mean Percent of Events LAP and NLI*
*Teachers Self-Initiated*

|                                | LAP | NLI |
| ------------------------------ | --- | --- |
| Self-Initiated Events          | 24% | 34% |
| Types of Self-Initiated Events: |     |     |
| Cognitive                      | 40% | 49% |
| Environmental                  | 57% | 48% |
| Affective-Social               | 2%  | 2%  |

Part of every classroom's activities are traffic control events, which include roll taking and giving students permission to go somewhere. One LAP teacher remarked during the project that all he did was take roll and permit students to go to the restroom. This prompted an examination of the relative frequency of traffic control events across the two individualized situations (see Table 3). It was found that LAP teachers averaged 8 percent of their time on such events, while NLI ones averaged only 3 percent. Since traffic control is a function of the number of students involved, an average percent of time per student was calculated for the two groups. For the LAP classes this figure was .28 percent, while for the NLI it was .09 percent. Thus, even when corrected for the number of students, LAP classes involve more traffic control than NLI classes. The percentage was greater for all types of traffic control events, but more so for directing students signing out to leave the classroom than for other types. This is perhaps because LAPs stress more independent work on the part of the student, and frequently necessitate his utilization of resource centers or other places for aspects of his work.

*Table 3*

*Mean Percent of Time LAP and NLI Teachers
Spent in Traffic-Control Events*

|  | LAP | NLI |
|---|---|---|
| Time Spent in Traffic-Control Events | 8% | 3% |
| Average Percent of Time Per Student Spent in Traffic-Control Events | .28% | .09% |

While the comparisons of teachers' behaviors in the various situations discussed above have emphasized *averages* across teachers, there is also considerable intra- and inter-teacher variation within the different situations. For example, using a pattern analysis technique, the LAP teachers were found to have a tendency toward similar patterns in the relative amounts of time spent in logistic and maintenance events, but they had dissimilar patterns in the relative amount of time spent in affective events and reward and punishment events.

Illustrative comparisons were also made between two teachers who were teaching similar subjects in the same department, both using LAPs, and between two classes taught by the same teacher using LAPs. On the comparison between the two teachers, the observational data were averaged over several classes for each teacher. Teacher A interacted with over three-fifths of the students in the class, while Teacher B interacted with less than one-fifth, and in both cases the students initiated over half of the interactions. In Teacher A's class, 57 percent of his time was related to cognitive activities, while only 40 percent of Teacher B's time was related to cognitive activities. Similarly, Teacher A spent 41 percent of his time in traffic control events, and Teacher B spent about 12 percent of his time in such events. Teacher A averaged about 11 discipline events in his classes, while Teacher B had only 2 such events. Other differences were observed in other types of activities, and collectively these tend to point out that inter-teacher differences do exist.

A comparison was made for Teacher A in the above illustration between two classes taught sequentially on the same day, and several differences were found between these two classes. For example, in the first class, the teacher interacted with about 86 percent of the students, while in the second class he interacted with only 40 percent. In the first of these classes, 41 percent of the interactions were initiated by the students, while in the second class 65 percent were initiated by the students. Of the total events in the class, the teacher spent 53 percent in cognitive-related activities for the first class and 62 percent for the second class. In the first class he spent 46 percent of the time in educational environment activities, and 38 percent in the second class. In the first class he spent 6 percent of his time in traffic control, and 82 percent in the second class. In the first class he had 16 incidents of discipline, and in the second class only 6 such incidents.

Thus, while there is a tendency to consider teacher behaviors in one type of class as being consistently different from those in another type of class, there are also differences among the classes within types and even among classes taught by the same teacher. Apparently various other considerations influence the teacher's behaviors in addition to the general teaching method. This, of course, does not deny that mean differences do exist across situations; it merely suggests there is a wide spread of teacher behaviors within each of the various situations.

## Summary and Conclusions

This paper has presented highlights of the findings of an observational study of teachers in innovative situations in the Nova public schools. The study was undertaken as an initial step in the development of a model of teachers' role behaviors for individualized instruction and is considered descriptive in nature. Inferences should not be readily made from these findings to other individualized situations.

The individualization program of the Nova schools, centered around the Learning Activity Package (LAP), appears to structure and control the classroom to a discernible extent. As a result of this structure, the teachers in the LAP classes tend to have less direct control over the subject matter acquisition aspects of the class (particularly information dispensing) than their counterparts in the more conventional classrooms. On the other hand, the teachers in the LAP classes spend more time in housekeeping and logistical chores than do teachers in the other situation. It is doubtful that the LAP imposes these tasks on the teacher directly, but by freeing the teacher from instructional tasks he is given extra time, with which he tends to do mundane chores.

The comparison of LAP Teachers A and B reported above demonstrates differences between teachers on performance which may be the result of different reactions by the two teachers to the requirements of the LAP classroom. Teacher A tended to use his time engaging in cognitive acquisition events, and thus had a higher percentage of such events and a lower percentage of environmental events than did Teacher B. The LAP by design should minimize the teacher's effort in the cognitive area, and therefore it appears that Teacher A, relative to Teacher B, may have tried to resist or compete with the LAP's intended function as the information dispenser. This attempt is also reflected by the larger fraction of students with which he interacted. The anecdotal records associated with the two teachers also illustrate the differences between them. For example, Teacher A is reported as stating that he wants to interact with all the students and that he feels he can never see enough of them. Teacher B, however, wants the students to seek his assistance and is concerned when they do not ask him questions. Thus, Teacher A has adopted an active role with the students, while Teacher B has adopted a passive role.

The use of the Learning Activity Package as the central unit of the individualization process in these schools shows that the organization of the classroom for individualization increases the occurrence of, and possibly the requirement for, systems supportive of logistical tasks, and tends to reduce the occurrence of cognitive acquisition tasks—particularly of information dissemination. A decrease in information disseminating activities is also suggested as a product of the Individually Prescribed Instruction classroom and of the CAI classroom.

It seems apparent that an increase in the degree of staff differentiation with a higher and broader use of personnel primarily trained to perform the systems supportive tasks could release the professional teacher from the tasks which are not directly relevant to education (e.g., getting supplies, cleaning equipment, etc.). However, such increased staff differentiation will require the redefinition of the role of the professional teacher. For example, in light of the findings of this study, it would appear that training a teacher in information dispensing and large group activities is not appropriate; instead, emphasis might be given to training in the diagnosis of student learning problems, grading and quality feedback techniques, analysis of student performance characteristics and understanding of a facility for utilizing instructional media.

As the previous paragraph suggests, and as was discussed in the introductory section of this article, the next step following the study of existing teacher role behaviors is the construction of a well-defined model specifying what the teacher's role behaviors should be. This model building should begin with a list of clear and precise statements of the expected outcomes of education for the students. These outcomes should be stated in unambiguous language and should represent measurable objectives. Second, the experiences which are required for the students to achieve these outcomes should be clearly delineated. Third, the various activities and activity sequences which must be supplied by the system in order to provide the students with the necessary experiences must be specified. These will include both activities which directly come in contact with the student and activities which are required for the support of the student's learning experiences. The next step is to allocate each of the various activities to the component of the system which can best perform them, adding new components where necessary. Hence teachers, para-professionals, clerical personnel, computers and other people and machines will each be assigned the activities they are best equipped to handle. A final step would be the development and implementation of training programs to provide each person with the skills necessary to adequately perform the activities assigned to him.

While this process is easy to envision, it would not be easy to complete because of the many gaps which exist in the present level of knowledge. It would require extensive reliance on existing research and perhaps new research. Further, the process, if adequately completed, would require much time and large amounts of money. However, it is needed to maximize the functioning of the schools. Studies such as the one reported above can at best tell us where we are; much additional work is required to tell us where we should be going.

## References

Chadwick, Clifton B., Tosti, Donald T. and Bell, D. Scott. "Instructional Management: A Refined Role for the Teacher." *NSPI Journal,* 1968, 7, pp. 5-7.

Flanders, Ned A. *Interaction Analysis in the Classroom.* (Revised Edition). Ann Arbor: University of Michigan, 1966.

Flynn, John M., Chadwick, Clifton B. and Fischler, Abraham S. *An Analysis of the Role of the Teacher in an Innovative Prototype School.* Final Report, February, 1969, Nova University, Contract No. OEC-0-8-080421-4466(010), Bureau of Research, U.S. Office of Education.

Honigman, Fred A. *Multidimensional Analysis of Classroom Interaction (MACI).* Villanova University Press, 1967.

McNeil, Jan and Smith, James E. "The Multi's at Nova." *Educational Screen and Audiovisual Guide,* 1968, 43, pp. 16-19.

Wolfe, Arthur B. and Smith, James E. "At Nova, Education Comes in Small Packages." *Nation's Schools,* 1968, 90, pp. 48-49.

# 30

# The Teacher's Response to Technology and the Individualization of Instruction

Judith R. Steward and W.A. Love, Jr.

Innovation has become the watchword in American education. Since Russia sent Sputnik into orbit, we as a nation have developed a powerful sense of urgency in regard to the improvement of our educational system. Tremendous stress has been laid upon technological improvement in the teaching process. Because of the rapid tempo of change, attention has been focused upon the technology itself, rather than upon the people involved. As a result, it is much easier to make definitive statements about the quality and extent of educational technology than it is to make definitive statements about the humans manning the systems.

At present, we stand between two widely divergent positions. On one hand, we have the old system in which the teacher was personally responsible for most of the educational processes, including testing, planning, imparting information to children and discipline. On the other hand, we have the new system in which the teacher's role is that of a specialist. He evaluates and makes prescriptions for the individual student on the basis of a variety of instantly accessible data about the student, and then selects curriculum from a wide range of prepared courses and materials. The alternatives available to the teacher usually involve a multiplicity of instructional modes and media.

For the teacher, the new technology represents a plethora of changes. In the old system, the teacher's role was fairly well

Reprinted from *Educational Technology*, Vol. 10, No. 2, February 1970, pp. 56-61, by permission of authors and publisher.

standardized and accepted. In the new system, his role must be redefined to meet the changing technology.

In a classic study by Woodward (1965), it was found that the organizational structure of industries tended to reflect the technological differences. Certainly, the old organization will not be adequate for the new technology. What is the role for the teachers in the new technology? Are they technicians or possibly storekeepers passing out materials? Will there be satisfactions in the new role equal to those in the old? What will happen to the status of the teacher in the eyes of the students and the community?

In order to obtain some understanding of the ways in which the teacher's role has been modified by the new technology, the investigators obtained permission to study the professional personnel of an innovative school, which we will refer to as Central High School. Certainly, the literature of organizations is replete with studies demonstrating the importance of such things as status, specialization, job satisfaction and their impact on people and work (Katz and Kahn, 1966; Herzberg, Mausner and Snyderman, 1967). Philosophically, Central High School is devoted to the goal of individualized instruction. Such things as closed-circuit television, language lab tapes, a central testing center, modular scheduling (as developed at Stanford University) and the Learning Activity Package (as developed at Nova High School) are utilized.

In the Learning Activity Package (LAP), behavioral goals are identified, and appropriate materials are selected to enable the student to meet the goals. The LAP informs the student of the aims and purposes of the activities, the readings involved and the behaviors expected at the end of the lesson, and refers the student to resources available to help him meet the behavioral goals.

As we began planning the study, we felt that there were two types of questions which should be answered. The first type of question is, "How does the teacher feel about working in a school that stresses individualized instruction?" Since the technology is changed, and since the teacher's role has had to change to meet the technology, the question of teacher satisfaction became paramount. How do they like it? What are their problems?

The second question of interest is more specific. Exactly what do they mean by *individualized instruction;* what are the components of individualized instruction? At the outset of the study, we interviewed individuals who had intimate knowledge of the Central High School system. The interviews were semi-structured (i.e., while certain questions were on the protocol, any divergent path could be followed by the interviewee, and all the information possible was collected; the interviews tended to run several hours each).

We interviewed consultants who had worked with the school and teachers who had been employed at Central in the last two years, but did not work there currently. The latter group was selected to avoid contamination of the sample of current Central teachers. From these extensive protocols, we set about developing a set of research instruments that would obtain the information necessary to answer the specific questions we posited. A number of forms finally emerged from the interview protocols. Those that will be of interest in this report are a 45-item attitude paper that utilized a seven-point scale, which ran from "Strongly Agree" to "Strongly Disagree," with four as a neutral point. For the present study, only twelve of the items are directly applicable. From these items, plus the interview data, we are able to obtain a picture of the teacher's satisfaction and the problems she saw in the system.

A second set of data was also derived from the interview protocols. We identified the five definitions of individualized instruction that occurred most frequently. These five were placed on a form, and the teachers were asked to put them into rank order according to the importance of each for an individualized system.

The data that will be reported here do not include the responses from administrators and supervisory personnel. The data include information given by the teaching staff and by the five guidance counselors.

Our first area of concern was: how comfortable are teachers working in the Central High School system? Does this highly developed technology create a sensation of discomfort on the part of the teachers? It should be noted that, in some of the preliminary interviews, one of the comments we frequently heard was, "I feel like a storekeeper. I pass out the materials; and when the students are through, I pick them up." Because of this statement, we developed a set of items that dealt with how well the teachers agreed with the Central philosophy; how well they fit in; and how much satisfaction they expressed. The results, in general, seem to be positive. The 12 attitude items that bear on this question are shown in Table 1. For ease of interpretation, the seven-point scale is condensed into Agree, Neither Agree nor Disagree and Disagree categories.

The first statement, "My philosophy of education is the same as the Central High School philosophy," produced overwhelming agreement. Ninety-one teachers indicated that, indeed, their philosophy was in agreement, 21 teachers said they neither agreed nor disagreed, and only 11 took the position that they were in disagreement with the high school's philosophy. Since the teachers in the sample had all been working at Central High for at least a year, it is impossible to tell whether they were won over to the Central High philosophy by their experiences, or were selected for the Central staff because their ideas were originally congruent with the philosophy of the school. Whatever the reason, the teachers working in this situation overwhelmingly endorse the individualized philosophy, which leans heavily on technology and individualized instruction.

## High Level of Satisfaction

The general level of satisfaction expressed by the teachers is quite high. On Item 2, "I would recommend Central High as a good place to work," 94 agreed with the statement, 15 neither agreed nor disagreed and 14 felt that they could not recommend Central. A similar question, "Central High is a satisfactory place for teachers," yielded 102 agreeing with the statement, 17 able neither to agree or disagree and 4 in disagreement. Of course, it is possible that teachers like Central in spite of its innovative aspects, and the positive responses reflect satisfaction derived from other components of the system. A question dealing with this specifically, "I would prefer to stay at Central High rather than transfer to

## Table 1

### Teacher Opinion Questionnaire

| | Agree | Neither Agree nor Disagree | Disagree |
|---|---|---|---|
| 1. My philosophy of education is the same as the Central philosophy. | 91 | 21 | 11 |
| 2. I would recommend Central as a good place to work. | 94 | 15 | 14 |
| 3. Central is a satisfactory place for teachers. | 102 | 17 | 4 |
| 4. I would prefer to stay at Central rather than transfer to a comparable traditional school. | 112 | 8 | 3 |
| 5. Compared to the traditional system, the Central teacher finds that her position has been eroded. | 18 | 48 | 57 |
| 6. It requires more effort on my part to function in the Central setting than at the traditional school. | 93 | 15 | 15 |
| 7. The extra effort that it takes to make the Central system function produces results that make the extra effort worthwhile. | 99 | 15 | 9 |
| 8. The Central system maximizes my opportunity to be creative on the job. | 107 | 4 | 12 |
| 9. What is expected of the teacher is much less clear at Central than at the traditional school. | 57 | 21 | 45 |
| 10. Central teachers should receive more in-service training than teachers in traditional schools. | 90 | 19 | 14 |
| 11. Every teacher should prepare her own curriculum materials. | 28 | 17 | 78 |
| 12. There is no substitute for a warm interpersonal relationship between the teacher and student. | 107 | 4 | 12 |

N = 123

a comparable traditional school," gave weight to the notion that the innovative component of the system is providing satisfaction. One hundred and twelve of the 123 teachers agreed with this statement.

## Loss of Status

As was mentioned before, in the preliminary interview we heard comments indicating that some teachers felt they were losing status. It should be noted that the teachers we originally interviewed had left Central, presumably for a reason, and as a result differential selection was operating in our interview sample. However, we developed an item to test this hypothesis specifically with the teachers currently at Central. Item 5 reads, "Compared to the traditional system, Central teachers find that their positions have been eroded." Only 18 teachers agreed with this statement, 48 were unable to make a decision and 57 disagreed. While the data indicate that most teachers either were neutral or disagreed, the defense of the Central system is not as overpowering here as it was in the general satisfaction items. A factor to be considered is that many of the teachers indicated informally that they checked the middle category because they had come directly from teachers' college to Central High and did not have enough experience in a traditional school to make a comparison. It is clear that among those who felt able to discriminate, the Central teacher has not lost status. If we disregard the middle category, the ratio is approximately four to one.

## Extra Effort Required

While the teachers may not feel that they have lost status, they clearly feel that they have to work much harder in a system like Central High School. Ninety-three of the 123 agree with the statement, "It requires more effort on my part to function in the Central High setting than in the traditional school." The paradox is resolved to some extent when additional responses are considered. Item 7, "The extra effort that it takes to make the Central system function produces results that make the extra effort worthwhile," produced 99 agreements from 123 teachers. Even more interesting in the light of expressed concerns about teachers being deprived of their opportunities to make a creative and professional contribution to the educational process is the fact that 107 agree with the statement, "Central maximizes my opportunity to be creative on the job." These findings are consistent with the work of Herzberg and his two-factor theory of job motivation (1967). Herzberg finds that job satisfaction is much more related to the ability to be creative, to feel that one is functioning well on the job, than it is to what he has called "hygiene factors," which are the human relations values stressed in most organizational research. At Central High, we find a high correlation existing between this feeling of expressing one's creative self, of doing well on the job and job satisfaction.

However, all is not "sweetness and light." In reviewing the responses to the previous item, it must be concluded that the teachers' responses are primarily positive to the innovative situation. On the other hand, we had information from our interviews indicating that there was a considerable lack of role clarity. Teachers were simply not sure of what they should be doing. As a result, we inserted two questions dealing with clarity of the teacher's role and the amount of in-service training necessary.

## Lack of Role Clarity

In response to "What is expected of the teacher is much less clear at Central High than at the traditional school," 57 of 123 teachers agreed with the statement, 21 were unable to make a discrimination and 45 disagreed. Item 10 also bears on this point: "Central High teachers should receive more inservice training than teachers in traditional schools." Here 90 of 123 teachers are in agreement, 19 are unsure and only 14 disagree. When these two points are taken together, a picture begins to emerge. While there is a great deal of satisfaction, there are also marked feelings that role clarity is lacking and teachers are simply unsure of what is expected of them, which creates anxiety. Collateral information is available to support this interpretation, both from the interviews and from other instruments utilized in the study. Our most significant finding was that the greatest area of dissatisfaction is the teachers' lack of knowledge of what is expected of them. Throughout the protocols and interviews we were impressed by the strong need the teachers feel for guidance and help in working in the new system. It should be pointed out that the lack of clarity is something of a two-edged sword. On the one hand, the lack of structure allows the teachers to express their own creative urges without the usual constraints inherent in the locked-in textbook approach. On the other hand, the same lack of guidance and structure creates feelings of anxiety. In traditional settings it becomes obvious fairly soon which behaviors are acceptable and which behaviors are not. In a situation like that of Central, the unpredictability can be uncomfortable. This notion about role clarity has some components of Erich Fromm's thesis that freedom enables man to be maximally self-actualizing, but at the same time threatens to give the individual more responsibility than he feels he can cope with (1968).

### Preparing Curriculum Materials

One of the factors that may be related to the teachers' feelings concerning creativity is the development of curriculum materials. In the science-oriented areas particularly, there has been a de-emphasis on lectures and strong emphasis placed on writing LAP materials. In other words, the teacher's role has been defined as a creator of curriculum materials. Question 11, "Every teacher should prepare her own curriculum materials," yielded a surprising amount of disagreement. Only 28 teachers felt that every teacher should produce her own curriculum materials, 17 neither agreed nor disagreed, and 78 disagreed. Again, collateral sources of information help us to interpret this finding. It seems that a limited number of teachers have become extremely active in producing curriculum materials; and, in the innovative situation, this has become a method of obtaining status. For those who like to write curriculum materials, it is a highly satisfying way to express their own creativity. In the case of the teacher who rejects this activity, anxiety is produced. Status accrues to teachers as a result of curriculum writing; yet they do not wish to engage in this activity. As a result, they find themselves in something of a dilemma. When we refer back to the question dealing with the chance to express themselves, we find that even among those who do not feel every teacher should be a producer of curriculum materials, this system does allow them to express their creativeness more fully. Even those who do not wish to be preparers of curriculum materials have indicated strongly that they do not wish to go back to a classroom-lecture approach.

## What Is Individualized Instruction?

In the design of the study, the second set of questions dealt with definitions of individualized instruction. It became apparent early that many definitions were used. We identified the five most common ones, and asked the teachers to rank these statements in the order of their importance in creating an individualized instruction system. The statements were: (1) Students select the materials on which they will work; (2) students progress through learning materials at their own rate; (3) teachers spend a good bit of time on individual consultation with each student; (4) students work by themselves out of the regular classroom situation; and (5) many paths are available to reach the same educational objectives and the best one may be selected for each student. After all the statements had been ranked, the procedure outlined by Kendall (1962) was utilized, and the average rank was found for each statement. A coefficient of concordance was computed and found to be significant beyond the .001 level. In dealing with ranked data, if the coefficient of concordance is significant, then the average ranks may be considered as representing the true ranks.

As shown in Table 2, the statement "Many paths are available to reach the same educational objectives, and the best one may be selected for each student" was ranked first. This, of course, is consistent with the technologically intensive philosophy espoused by Central High. Since it is a multi-media, multi-model situation, we may conclude that the teachers have essentially viewed this as the kernel, the most important part of an individualized instruction situation. The statement that received the second rank, "Students progress through learning materials at their own rate," is characteristic of ideals espoused by Central. In the utilization of LAP packages, one of the assumptions is that since the student is working independently and is not in a lockstep, he will be able to progress at his own rate. As a matter of fact, the ranks for these two statements were very close to a tie.

*Table 2*

*Ranking of Components of Individualized
Instruction According to Importance*

RANK

Many paths are available to reach the same educational objectives, and the best one may be selected for each student.                                                                                      1

Students progress through learning materials at their own rate.                                                                                                                                          2

Teachers spend a good bit of time on individual consultation with each student.                                                                                                            3

Students select the materials on which they work.                                                       4

Students work by themselves out of the regular classroom situation.                                                                                                                               5

In the previous section, we found that teachers agreed strongly with the Central High philosophy. This is another manifestation of the phenomenon in that the Central High philosophy emphasizes these two points, and they are the most highly selected statements. These choices are especially interesting because they imply maximum replacement of the teacher's didactic role by enhanced technology.

The statement ranked third, "Teachers spend a good bit of time on individual consultation with each student," may be a key. As we can see in the first two ranks, teachers have played down the classroom lecturer role. The third-ranked statement stresses a great deal of time on individual consultation with each student. In the preliminary interviews, we heard a great deal of stress placed on what we began to call the "guidance function," the need for individual guidance, both in the academic and in the socio-personal area. In the attitude scales, question No. 12, "Teachers feel that aiding in the student's personal development is at least as important as imparting information," was agreed with by 93 of the 123 teachers. Thirteen neither agreed nor disagreed and only 17 disagreed. Of special interest here is the manner in which the distribution broke down. While we have only been reporting three-point scales, the data were originally collected on a seven-point scale. Forty respondents agree strongly, meaning that almost half of those who agree, agree in the most extreme position, whereas of the 17 who disagree, 10 "tend to disagree." From these data, it seems to the investigators, we may conclude that the emerging role of the teacher is not only one of prescribing specific learning tasks for the students, but also one in which the guidance function in socio-personal development will be stressed. The development of curriculum which can be used over and over again with little effort on the teacher's part frees the teacher to help students with difficulties they encounter in academic areas or in the socio-personal realm. This philosophy came through very strongly in the interviews. Most teachers felt that while this is the goal for which they should strive, this function is not yet being handled well because of the scrambling that is still going on to create appropriate curriculum materials.

There was a significant and predictable reordering of ranks by the guidance function to the number one position. With this exception, their other rankings were like those of the other respondents.

This finding fits in well with the expectations placed upon the schools by our society. We emphasize mobility. The child must be prepared for roles other than those of his parents, and the educational institution is responsible for bridging the gap between parental training and the ultimate social demands to be made upon the child. Since the school has been entrusted with a large part of the child's socialization, the teacher must guide parts of this socialization process in such a way that the values, attitudes and intellectual skills which the student acquires will be those he needs to cope with our society, but has not acquired at home.

While this is reminiscent of the "whole child" approach of the forties, it is actually quite different. The role of the school in the child's personal development is emphasized, but it is based on the functional needs of the society as well as the needs of the individual child. While it might seem the new technology, and the casting of the teacher into a role as one who diagnoses and then directs the child to the suitable learning resources, would forestall the teacher's development of this kind of interpersonal role, it seems in practice that it has freed the teacher's time and given her a chance to do things the older system did not allow. The evidence presented here indicates that the teacher may utilize the opportunity and the freedom inherent in the new technology in order to emphasize other aspects of her role.

**Summary**

The teachers at Central agree with the Central High philosophy. In other words, they approve of the notion of individualized instruction. They feel that Central is a good place to work and that it maximizes their creativity. While they feel that the core of individualized instruction is that the teacher diagnoses and prescribes for the individual student working at his own pace, they do not feel that they should be the primary developers of curriculum. The role of the teacher at Central is unclear to the role incumbents, and they would like to have that situation changed, although it may be that it is the lack of role clarity which enables the teacher to creatively act on his own.

There emerges what may be a new emphasis in the teacher's role on the importance of helping the individual in his or her personal development, and while this remains undefined in terms of research, it fits very well into the role that the schools are expected to perform in our highly mobile society.

## References

Fromm, Erich. *Escape from Freedom.* New York: Avon, 1968.

Herzberg, Frederick, Mausner, Bernard and Snyderman, Barbara Bloch. *The Motivation to Work.* New York: John Wiley and Sons, 1967.

Katz, Daniel and Kahn, Robert. *The Social Psychology of Organizations.* New York: John Wiley & Sons, 1966.

Kendall, Maurice. *Rank Correlation Methods.* New York: Hafner, 1962.

Woodward, Joan. *Industrial Organizations: Theory and Practice.* New York: Oxford University Press, 1965.

# BIBLIOGRAPHY

## The Evaluation of Individualized Instruction

America, R.P. *et al.* "Individual Versus Co-operative Learning," *Educational Research,* Vol. 11, February 1969, pp. 95-103.

Anastasiow, W.J. *et al.* "Use of an Evaluation Model to Individualize Learning: CIPP Model," *Viewpoints,* Vol. 46, November 1970, pp. 119-127.

Askov, Eunice N. "Assessment of Teachers' Attitudes Toward an Individualized Approach to Reading Instruction," Wisconsin University, Madison, February 1971, 19pp., ERIC No. ED048349.

Askov, Eunice N. "An Instrument for Assessing Teachers' Attitudes Toward Individualizing Reading Instruction," *Journal of Experimental Education,* Vol. 39, No. 3, Spring 1971, pp. 5-10.

Bolvin, John O. "The Use of Field Data for Improving IPI Materials and Procedures." Paper presented at the Annual Meeting of the American Educational Research Association, Los Angeles, February 1969.

Boozer, Robert F. "Evaluation of the Variability Among Students in Total Number of Units Mastered Per Year." Unpublished paper, Pittsburgh: Learning Research and Development Center, University of Pittsburgh, Summer 1968.

Bosco, James. "Individualization—Teacher's Views," *The Elementary School Journal,* December 1971, pp. 125-131.

Buchanan, A. and others. "Monitoring the Progress of the Group in an Individualized Reading Program Based on Behavioral Objectives," American Educational Research Association, February 1971, 15pp., ERIC No. ED047925.

Cray, Douglas W. "What's Happening in Gary?" *School Management,* May 1971.

Dionne, Joseph. "Future of Testing: A Look at the Trends," Paper presented at the American Personnel and Guidance Association Convention, New Orleans, Louisiana, March 1970, pp. 1-3, ERIC No. ED043669.

Dovoky, Diane. " 'Too Elaborate,' Critics Say, But IPI Keeps on Growing," *Nation's Schools,* Vol. 84, No. 5, November 1969, pp. 44-46 and 50.

Duda, Mary Jane. "A Critical Analysis of Individually Prescribed Instruction," *Educational Technology*, Vol. 10, No. 12, December 1970, pp. 47-51.

Edling, J.V. and Buck, J.E. *An Interpretative Study of Individualized Instruction Program Phase I—Analysis and Interpretation*. U.S. Dept. of Health, Education and Welfare, Oregon State System of Higher Education, 1969.

Gallagher, J.J. "A Comparison of Individual and Group Instruction in Science: Effects on 3rd Grade," *Journal of Research in Science Teaching*, Vol. 7, No. 3, 1970, pp. 253-263.

Geis, George L. and Chapman, Reuben. "Knowledge of Results and Other Possible Reinforcers in Self-Instructional Systems," *Educational Technology*, Vol. 9, No. 4, April 1971, pp. 38-40.

Gibb, E. Genadine. "Through the Years: Individualizing Instruction in Mathematics," *The Arithmetic Teacher*, May 1970.

Grobman, Hulda. "Educational Packages—Panacea?" *Educational Leadership*, Vol. 27, No. 8, May 1970, pp. 781-783.

Hausen, Duncan N. and Johnson, Barbara F. "Measurement Techniques for Individualized Instruction in CAI," Florida State University, Tallahassee, May 1971, 28pp., ERIC No. ED053550.

*Individualizing Learning Bibliographies*, Research for Better Schools, Inc., Philadelphia, Penn. 1970, 37 pp.

Lindvall, C. Mauritz. "The IPI Evaluation Program." Paper presented at the Annual Meeting of the American Association for the Advancement of Science, Dallas, December 1968.

Lindvall, C. Mauritz and Cox, Richard C. "Evaluation as a Tool in Curriculum Development: The IPI Evaluation Program." Unpublished paper, Pittsburgh: Learning Research and Development Center, University of Pittsburgh, July 1968.

Miller, Jack W. and Miller, Haroldine W. "Individualizing Instruction Through Diagnosis and Evaluation," *Childhood Education*, Vol. 4, May 1970, pp. 417-421.

Morrison, Donald E. "Innovative Teaching," *Today's Education*, March 1972, pp. 23-28.

Nevjaho, James L. "An Analysis of Teacher-Pupil Interactions When Instruction is Individualized," Columbia University, New York, 1970, 217pp.

Novak, J.D. "Relevant Research on Audio-Tutorial Methods," *School Science and Mathematics*, Vol. 70, December 1970, pp. 777-784.

O'Hanian, Vera. "Educational Technology: A Critique," *The Elementary School Journal*, Vol. 71, January 1971, pp. 182-197.

O'Toole, R.J. "Review of Attempts to Individualize Elementary School Science," *School Science and Mathematics*, Vol. 68, May 1968, pp. 385-390.

Ott, Jack M. and others. "Individualization and Needed Research." Paper presented at Annual Meeting of AERA, 1971, 10pp., ERIC No. ED048106.

Quirk, Thomas J., Steen, Margaret T. and Lipe, Dewey. "Development of the Program for Learning in Accordance with Needs Teacher Observation Scale; a Teacher Observation Scale for Individualized Instruction," *Journal of Educational Psychology,* Vol. 62, No. 3, June 1971, pp. 188-200.

Rahmlow, Harold, F. and Dunn, James A. "Some Results of Using Student Performance Data for Improvement of Individualized Instructional Units. The Development of Procedures for the Individualization of Educational Programs." Paper presented at the American Psychological Association Convention, Miami, Florida, September 1970, 24pp., ERIC No. ED043044.

Sartain, H.W. "What Are the Advantages and Disadvantages of Individual Instruction?" *International Reading Association Conference Proceedings,* Part 2, 1969, pp. 328-356.

Scharf, E. "Implementation of Individually Prescribed Instruction: Summary of Problem Areas, Fall 1966-Spring 1968, and Possible Solutions." Unpublished paper, Philadelphia: Research for Better Schools, Inc., 1968.

Schoeller, Arthur W. "First Steps to Individualization," *Instructor,* January 1972, pp. 53-55.

Schubert, J.G. and others. "Development and Evaluation of an Experimental Curriculum for the New Quincy, Mass. Vocational-Technical School. The Social Studies Curriculum." Office of Education, September 1970, 177pp., ERIC No. ED047157.

Seidel, Robert, J. "Theories and Strategies Related to Measurement in Individualized Instruction," *Educational Technology,* Vol. 11, No. 8, August 1971, pp. 40-46.

Steen, Margaret J. and Lipe, Dewey. "Teacher Behavior in PLAN and Control Classrooms Using the PLAN Teacher Observation Scale." Albuquerque, New Mexico: Westinghouse Learning Corporation, 1970, 41pp. ERIC No. ED045586.

Taylor, Gary. "The Lone Learner," *Audiovisual Instruction,* Vol. 16, No. 4, April 1971, pp. 54-55.

Tillman, Rodney. "Do Schools Need IPI? No!" *Educational Leadership,* Vol. 29, No. 6, March 1972, pp. 495-498.

Turnbull, William W. "The Uses of Measurement in Individualized Education," *Bulletin of the National Association of Secondary School Principals,* Vol. 54, No. 346, May 1970, pp. 80-87.

Turner, William E. "A Plan to Appraise Individual Progress for Continuous Learning," *The Elementary School Journal,* Vol. 96, May 1969, pp. 426-430.

White, Beverly L. "The Package and the Supervisor," *Educational Leadership*, Vol. 27, No. 8, May 1970, pp. 788-791.

Wright, Calvin E. "Evaluation Data and Their Uses in an Individualized Education Program." Palo Alto, California: American Institutes for Research, September 1970, 17pp., ERIC No. ED045724.

Yeager, J.L. and Lindvall, C.M. "Evaluating an Instructional Innovation Through the Observation of Pupil Activities; Individually Prescribed Instruction (IPI) Project," *High School Journal*, Vol. 51, March 1968, pp. 248-253.

Yeager, J.L. and Wang, M.C. "Evaluation Under Individualized Instruction," *The Elementary School Journal*, Vol. 71, May 1971, pp. 448-452.

Yetter, Clyde C. "Do Schools Need IPI? Yes!" *Educational Leadership*, Vol. 29, No. 6, March 1972, pp. 491-494.

# APPENDIX I

## Annotated Bibliography of
## Textbooks on Individualized Instruction

Drumheller, Sidney J. *Handbook of Curriculum Design for Individualized Instruction—A Systems Approach.* Englewood Cliffs, New Jersey: Educational Technology Publications, 1970. $8.95.

Describes a comprehensive design model for preparing curriculum materials for individualized instruction based on rigorously defined behavioral objectives. Procedures are given in the text, reader exercises and foldouts.

Edling, Jack V. *Individualized Instruction: A Manual for Administrators.* Corvallis, Oregon: State University, 1970. $7.50.

Describes forty-six case studies of schools throughout the country that have been chosen as having exemplary individualized instruction programs. Each study emphasizes a particular strength or a unique contribution made by that school.

Esbensen, Thorwald. *Working with Individualized Instruction: The Duluth Experience.* Belmont, California: Fearon Publishers, 1968. $2.75.

Describes the Duluth, Minnesota, individualized instruction project, paying particular attention to the three elementary school projects with widely varying student populations.

Gibbons, Maurice, *Individualized Instruction.* New York: Teachers College Press, 1971.

Analyzes the concept of individualized instruction and proposes a taxonomy for classifying the many varieties of individualized programs. Also described is an observational instrument for profiling the major curricular features of individualized programs.

Howes, Virgil M. *Individualization of Instruction: A Teaching Strategy.* New York: Macmillan Company, 1970. $3.50.

A book of twenty-five readings on individualized instruction related to three topics: Why individualize? What is individualization? and Individualized Instruction Programs and Practices.

Johnson, Stuart R. and Johnson, Rita B. *Developing Individualized Instructional Material.* Palo Alto, California: Westinghouse Learning Press, 1970. $3.75.

A self-instructional handbook designed to help teachers prepare individualized materials.

Kapfer, Philip G. and Ovard, Glen F. *Preparing and Using Individualized Learning Packages for Ungraded, Continuous Progress Education.* Englewood Cliffs, New Jersey: Educational Technology Publications, 1971. $8.95.

A manual for teachers written in the form of nine self-instructional Individualized Learning Packages (ILPs). Explains the procedures for designing and preparing Individualized Learning Packages.

Lewis, James, Jr. *Administering the Individualized Instruction Program.* West Nyack, New York: Parker Publishing, 1971. $9.95.

Describes a model for preparing individualized study units. Each chapter provides a detailed information section about the components of the model. The appendix includes samples of individualized instruction packages developed by a variety of educational institutions.

Lewis, James, Jr. *Differentiating the Teaching Staff.* West Nyack, New York: Parker Publishing, 1971. $9.95.

Clearly and concisely describes procedural guidelines for implementing differentiated staffing in individualized instruction programs. Defines nine positions for differentiating the teaching staff and outlines the duties and responsibilities for each position. Also includes procedures for training school personnel and evaluating the effectiveness of a differentiated program.

Postlethwait, Samuel N., Novak, J. and Murray, H.T., Jr. *The Audio-Tutorial Approach to Learning.* Third Edition. Minneapolis, Minnesota: Burgess Publishing Company, 1972. $4.75.

A thorough explanation of the Audio-Tutorial Approach used to teach botany at Purdue University. The Audio-Tutorial system combines small and large group instruction centering around a supervised self-instructional lab.

Smith, James E. *The Activity Package.* Fort Lauderdale, Florida: Edutronics Corporation, 1971.

A position paper explaining the rationale and components of an individualized instruction learning package. The role of a teacher and a student as well as the implication for the future are explained.

Stahl, Dona K. and Anzalone, Patricia M. *Individualized Teaching in Elementary Schools.* West Nyack, New York: Parker Publishing, 1970. $8.95.

Describes procedures for implementing an individualized instruction curriculum on the elementary level. Attention is devoted to the development of materials and the integration of media.

Weisgerber, Robert A. *Developmental Efforts in Individualized Learning.* Itasca, Illinois: Peacock Publishers, 1971. $8.50.

A book of readings concerned with the operational approaches of large-scale individualized learning programs, packaged learning units and current developments in the field at the local school and college levels.

Weisgerber, Robert A. *Perspectives in Individualized Learning.* Itasca, Illinois: Peacock Publishers, Inc., 1971. $8.50.

A book of readings concerned with the fundamental aspects of the process of individualized learning. The text considers theoretical aspects and then analyzes specific educational components of individualized learning.

# APPENDIX II

## Annotated Bibliography of Media on Individualized Instruction

*Aiding IPI.* Filmstrip and audio cassette, 17 minutes, color, produced by Research for Better Schools, 1700 Market Street, Philadelphia, Penn. 19103, 1970. $3.00.

Describes the role of the teacher's aide in the IPI approach to individualized instruction. Shows several aides performing various duties in an actual school situation.

*Apollo: School Without Failure.* Filmstrip and audiotape, 18 minutes, color, produced by the Center for Advanced Study of Technology of the U.S. International University in San Diego, California 98124, 1972. Free to state agencies.

Excellent description of an open plan individualized instruction school in Louisiana. Shows the school building and explains how the school has been successful in achieving objectives, full student participation and strong community support.

*Audio-Tutorial System.* 16mm film, 24 minutes, color, produced by Purdue University Audio Visual Dept., 1968. $8.00 rental.

Describes the audio-tutorial system for teaching botany developed at Purdue University by Professor Samuel Postlethwait. Explains the component parts of the system: the lab, the small group discussion and the general assembly.

*Children as People.* 16mm film, 35 minutes, black and white, produced by Polymorph Films, 1970, ERIC NO. ED045612.

Describes a school in Cambridge, Massachusetts, in which children are free to move about and to plan and direct their own work. Shows

*363*

children of different ages engaged in group and individual work in art, math, science, reading and English.

*Continuous Progress Learning.* 16mm film, 22 minutes, color, distributed by the Institute for the Development of Educational Activity, Box 446, Melbourne, Florida 32901. $200.00 purchase, $11.00 rental.

Describes the transition of a graded program into a continuous progress system. Designed for school systems that have already nongraded their programs or are considering doing so in the future.

*How to Provide Personalized Education in a Public School.* A series of five 16mm films, black and white, produced by Special Purpose Films, 26740 Latigo Shore Drive, Malibu, California 90265, 1966.

Titles include:
   *Can Individualization Work in Your School System?*
   John I. Goodlad, narrator, 41 minutes.
   *How Can You Make Individualization Work in Your School System?*
   Madeline Hunter, narrator, 35 minutes.
   *Why Are Team Teaching and Nongrading Important?*
   John I. Goodlad, narrator, 49 minutes.
   *How Can You Apply Team Teaching and Nongrading to Your School?*
   Madeline Hunter, narrator, 35 minutes.
   *How Can the Curriculum for Individualized Education Be Determined?*
   John I. Goodlad, narrator, 35 minutes.

A series of filmed lectures on individualized instruction concentrating on the topics listed above.

*Individualized Instruction.* A series of six filmstrips with accompanying audio tapes and printed scripts, 20 minutes each, color, produced for the Association of Educational Communications and Technology, Washington, D.C., 20036, 1971. $10.00 each.

Titles include:
   *Individualized Instruction: Its Nature and Effects*
   *Individualized Instruction: Its Problems and Some Solutions*
   *Individualized Instruction: Diagnostic and Instructional Procedure*
   *Individualized Instruction: Materials and Their Use*
   *Individualized Instruction: Recommendations for Implementation*

*Individualized Instruction: Its Objectives and Evaluative Procedure*

A visual survey with accompanying explanations of various approaches to individualized instruction.

*Individualized Instruction.* Filmstrip and audio cassette, 15 minutes, color, produced by General Programmed Teaching, San Rafael, California 94903. $24.95.

Discusses the basic components of an individualized instruction system, including the role of the student and the teacher. Also, includes an overview of a state-wide application now being used in kindergarten through grade six.

*Individualized Instruction, Student Freedom and Educational Technology.* Audio cassette produced by Educational Technology Cassettes, 140 Sylvan Avenue, Englewood Cliffs, New Jersey 07632, 1971. $7.50.

An interview with Charles W. Slack, conducted by Gabriel D. Ofiesh, concerning individualized instruction. Cassette was recorded at the 1971 National Educational Technology Conference in New York.

*Make a Mighty Reach.* 16mm film, 45 minutes, color, distributed by the Institute for the Development of Educational Activity, Box 446, Melbourne, Florida 32901, 1967. $300.00 purchase, $15.00 rental.

Explores various innovations in education including ungraded programs of study, computer teaching, flexible scheduling and new building designs.

*More Different than Alike.* 16mm film, 36 minutes, color, produced by Capital Films for the National Commission on Teacher Education and Professional Standards, Washington, D.C. 20036, 1967. $125.00 purchase, $10.00 rental.

Describes several school systems throughout the U.S. which have adopted methods to provide individualized instruction. Discusses the objective and rationale behind each program and shows them in action.

*My Name Is Children.* 16mm film, 60 minutes, black and white, distributed by the Indiana University Audio Visual Center, Bloomington, Indiana 47401, 1967. $200.00 purchase, $12.00 rental.

Describes how the Nova Elementary School at Fort Lauderdale, Florida, is employing an individualized instruction approach. Shows children working on various projects and shows teachers coordinating plans and discussing individual student problems.

*The Oakleaf Project.* 16mm film, 31 minutes, black and white, produced by William Matthews, Inc., 130 Seventh Street, Pittsburgh, Penn. 15222, 1968. $125.00.

Describes the first attempt in implementing the IPI approach at Oakleaf School in Philadelphia. Shows a six-year-old who goes through a normal day of activities in an IPI school. Dr. Robert Glaser presents the philosophy behind the program.

*Project PLAN.* 16mm film, 30 minutes, black and white, produced by the Far West Laboratory for Educational Research and Development, Berkeley, California, 94705. Free loan.

A panel discussion describing the development and implementation of Project PLAN. The panel includes Dr. John C. Flanagan, founder of Project PLAN, and his associates at the American Institute for Research in Palo Alto, California.

*Rx For Learning.* 16mm film, 35 minutes, color, produced by William Matthews, Inc., 130 Seventh Street, Pittsburgh, Penn. 15222, 1969. $175.00.

Excellent description of the IPI concept of individualized instruction. Explains the IPI process and shows its implementation in an actual school. Curriculum organization, the role of the teacher's aide and evaluation procedures are also explained.

# APPENDIX III

## Sample Individualized
## Instruction Packages

Individualized Instruction Package


by

Russ Mouritsen


entitled

<u>TWO-WAY COMMUNICATION</u>


Subject Area:   Communications

Level: Grades 9 to 12

## RATIONALE

In this lesson you will learn about the importance of proper two-way communication and how it affects your ability to get along with people. You will discover the various components of the art of communicating properly and in so doing find that effective listening is an often neglected but very integral skill. You will find that learning to provide feedback or listen properly will be an asset to you in your daily communications.

## CONTENT

This individualized instruction package will cover the concept of communications models with emphasis on two related subconcepts, feedback and hindrances affecting proper feedback. The student will learn the basic theory of the communications model and its applications on the practical level. The communications model has several integral and necessary working components which will be covered in a discussion of the basic concept. The two subconcepts include listening as a form of proper feedback and hindrances affecting proper feedback.

## BEHAVIORAL OBJECTIVES

After completing this package, you will be able to:

1. Diagram a basic communications model and explain each component.

2. Determine accurately after reading and listening to conversations
   if proper feedback has occurred. In those cases where proper feedback

has not occurred the student will also be able to determine at least
one cause of hindrance for improper feedback.


## PRE-TEST


The pre-test is given to determine how much of the lesson you are

familiar with and what materials you should be required to study.

1. Diagram a basic communications model with all integral parts.
   Define the terms feedback, channel, sender, receiver and noise.


2. List several factors which may hinder a successful communication
   experience.


## ALTERNATIVE LEARNING ACTIVITIES


It is important for you to understand that listening and giving proper

feedback is an important part of understanding everyday conversations and

communications.  The following model is the basic communications model.

To understand how relevant this model is, several learning activities have

been outlined for you.  They have been organized in a very practical way

which will allow you to understand the communications components well.  The

activities will not only be advantageous to your learning processes but

will be enjoyable to implement.  You will be asked to utilize various

communication experiments with your friends which will prove to be eye openers

for them about how poorly we communicate.  You will find that your under-

standing of this model will increase as you perform the various tasks sug-

gested in your learning options.  The model can be expressed several ways.

If after you try the learning activities, you might decide to rewrite the model. Please do so in a way that will be relevant to you. Note how your model, completed in the pre-test and the model on this page compare. Good luck!

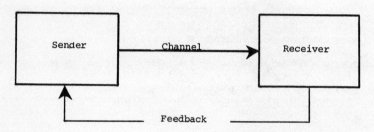

BASIC COMMUNICATIONS MODEL

If you are not familiar with the communications model and its components, it is suggested that alternative learning activity number 1 be completed.

After completion of number 1, proceed through as many alternative activities as necessary to achieve the specified objectives.

ALTERNATIVE LEARNING ACTIVITY NO. 1. View the film A COMMUNICATIONS MODEL at the Media Center. This 29-minute film presents a way of looking at the problems involved with communicating with others. A visual explanation is made about the importance of proper feedback as an integral part of the communications model. View the film with another student and discuss the material which has been presented.

ALTERNATIVE LEARNING ACTIVITY NO. 2. Contained in this packet is an exercise in one-way and two-way communications. It is necessary that a small group be present to utilize this exercise.

This activity includes two charts. In using chart one, stand with your back to the group and instruct members of the group to draw the squares as you have them drawn on the paper. No questions are allowed.

In using chart two, you are to face the group and instruct the members to draw this group of figures. Begin with the top square and describe each in succession, taking particular note of the relation of each to the preceding one. Answer all questions from participants and repeat if necessary. The group should not be permitted to see the groups of squares.

Chart one is an example of one-way communication and its shortcomings. Chart two is an example of two-way communications as questions are answered. Note how much more effective two-way communications are.

ALTERNATIVE LEARNING ACTIVITY NO. 3. This activity is a demonstration of how poorly we listen. It shows that feedback or listening is a very important part of the communications model.

Assemble a group of people and indicate that you will be administering a short test. It will only take two minutes of their time. The only rule you give them is that they are to read all instructions before doing anything. Hand them the following question sheet.

1. Write your name in the upper right-hand corner of this sheet.

2. Circle the word "name" in direction number two.

3. Draw five small squares in the upper left hand corner of this sheet.

4. Place an X in the lower left hand corner of this sheet.

5. On the bottom of this sheet multiply 706 by 56.

6. Place a square around the first letter of each sentence.

7. Now that you have finished don't feel silly that you didn't listen
   to the directions as they indicated you should read all questions first
   and you are to do nothing. Ignore the first 6 questions.

ALTERNATIVE LEARNING ACTIVITY NO. 2 - <u>CHART NO. 1</u>

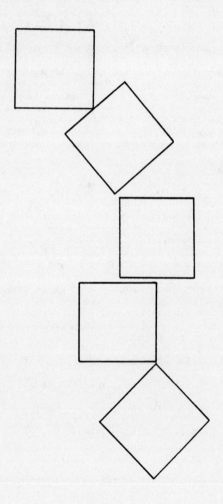

ALTERNATIVE LEARNING ACTIVITY NO. 2 - CHART NO. 2

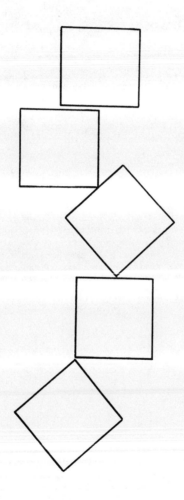

## SELF - TEST

The purpose of the self-test is to allow you to check your own progress. After you have completed one of the activities try to answer the following questions.

1. Where on the communications model is feedback placed?

2. How can feedback be improved?

3. Write a brief conversation incorporating feedback.

## Key for Self-Test

1. Feedback is placed on the model as a connecting line from the receiver to the sender. This indicates that the receiver always provides some type of feedback.

2. Feedback can be improved by a better process of listening.

3. Conversation should be checked by the instructor. Please ask him to do so.

ALTERNATIVE LEARNING ACTIVITY NO. 4. This exercise should prove to be valuable in understanding why different people misunderstand each other. It handles the basic communications model from the receiver standpoint.

You should read the booklet COMMUNICATIONS by Don Fabun, which describes in a very refreshing way the model of communicating. Also read S. I. Hayakawa's HOW WORDS CHANGE OUR LIVES. This is a definitive work on mis-interpretation of words and meanings. It describes in a different way why we do not listen effectively.

Fabun's booklet and Hayakawa's article are included with this package.

WHEN YOU FEEL YOU HAVE SUCCESSFULLY COMPLETED THIS UNIT, ASK FOR THE POST-TEST.

## OPTIONAL QUEST ACTIVITIES

Instructions:

The following activities are designed to help you gain further under-standing of the art of communicating.

QUEST NO. 1 Carry out a study which could eventually be used by your school administrator to help him in his job. In this case you will be in a better position to do it than he will as you have been on the receiving end of his communications and will be able to provide a different perspective.

Make a determination of the various communication models that are in use in your school. For example, the telephone, intercom, students as senders, teachers as receivers and vice versa, administration to faculty, etc. Suggest ways for improvement based on your understanding of the communications model. Suggest ways in which new channels for feedback might be instigated and ways in which hindrances might be overcome.

QUEST No. 2    This quest activity can also be done in your school and will have practical applications.

Make an analysis of a particular communications problem within your school and determine a solution or solutions to the problem. Analyze the problem within your school and determine a solution or solutions to the problem. Analyze the problem in this way:

1.  Analyze the causes of the problem.

2.  Determine a plan of action for solving the problem.

3.  Carry out your procedure for solving the problem (it might be necessary to suggest your solution to an administrator and let him carry it out).

4.  Evaluate the results. Consider time expended to results obtained.

## TEACHERS' GUIDE

This package has been created to be a practical exercise in learning the communications model. The exercises are practical attempts to describe real life situations.

It will be necessary for the student to work with groups of other students for two of the activity options. He can make the exercise valuable for them by explaining why listening and feedback is important, especially in alternative learning activities number 2 and 3.

The necessary equipment for the package includes a 16mm projector.

The cost of the package is $2.25, not including the rental of the film. This includes handouts and pamphlets.

There are no pre-requisite courses for this package.

## RESOURCE MATERIALS REQUIRED FOR THE PACKAGE

Film, A COMMUNICATIONS MODEL, Available from the U. of U. Media Center, 16mm, 29 min., produced by Dr. Max Carruth, 1963, Rental $10

Pamphlets, COMMUNICATIONS: THE TRANSFER OF MEANING, Fabun, Don, Glencoe Press, Beverly Hills, California, 1965, $1.25

Handouts, HOW WORDS CHANGE OUR LIVES, Hayakawa, S. I., Curtis Publishing Co., 1958

## Pre-Test Key

1.

BASIC COMMUNICATIONS MODEL

Definitions

Feedback - information returned to sender

Channel - the method by which the information is sent, i.e., TV, voice, etc.

Sender - the person who presents the original information

Receiver - the person who listens and provides the feedback

2. Factors which hinder successful communications include:

    1. poor attitude

    2. judgment

    3. excessive talking

    4. semantics

    5. lack of attention


### POST-TEST

If you have not already read page 43 in the COMMUNICATIONS pamphlet by Don Fabun, in alternative learning activity number 4, please diagram the communications model, filling in all integral parts. Indicate who was sending and receiving. Explain how the receiver listened or did not listen properly. If he did not listen properly indicate what hindrances might have been present to prevent him from doing so.


Post-test Key

1. Refer to the BASIC COMMUNICATIONS MODEL diagramed in the Pre-test answer key.

2. The receiver did not listen properly because there was a misunderstanding of words. Ted thought George meant something different than what he said. The main hindrance in this case was a semantic hindrance. Note the explanation on page 42.

Individualized Instruction Package


by

Boyd Bronson


entitled

"LOOK MA, NO BATTERIES!"

AN INTRODUCTION TO THE SLIDE RULE


Subject Area:  Math

Level: Grades 10 to 12

## RATIONALE

There will be numerous times in your everyday activities that you will want to multiply and divide numbers, and you will not be excited about doing so by "hand." This unit introduces you to a computing device called a "slide rule." The unit will teach you how to properly hold a slide rule, locate a number, multiply and divide.

Having facility in slide rule use will permit you to solve quickly many of the complicated multiplication and division problems encountered in areas such as physics, chemistry, home economics, accounting, mathematics, and others.

## CONTENT

Content of this unit includes the proper physical handling of the slide rule, location of numbers on the scales, proper set up of the scales for multiplication and division, and proper set up of the scales for problems involving both multiplication and division simultaneously.

Let's be more specific, shall we? Let's state exactly what you will be able to do at the end of this unit. Bear in mind that the level and complexity is such that you should have a good background in decimal fractions and multiplication of powers before starting.

## BEHAVIORAL OBJECTIVES

After completing this package, you will be able to:

1. Hold the slide rule in your hands so as to operate the slide and cursor.

2. Locate any 3 digit number on the C or D scale with the hairline 100% of the time.

3. Multiply any two numbers consisting of one, two or three digits and be accurate to 3 significant figures at least 90% of the time.

4. Divide any two numbers consisting of one, two, or three digits and be accurate to 3 significant figures at least 90% of the time.

5. Multiply and divide in the same problem any two or more numbers consisting of one, two, or three digits and be accurate to 3 significant figures at least 80% of the time.

Now just in case you may have had some experience in using a slide rule, please take the following Pre-test to determine whether or not you should skip this unit and go on to the next one.

PRE-TEST

Perform the following indicated operations with a 10" or longer slide rule, and express your answers with 3 significant digits:

1. 65 X 8

2. 6.2 X 34

3. 2.95 X 7.3

4. 65 ÷ 40

5. 895 ÷ 18

6. 47.2 ÷ 5.7

7. $\dfrac{3.5 \text{ X } 480}{62}$

What number is indicated by the hairline in each of the following:

8.

9.

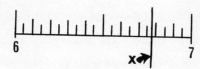

10. Let your teacher watch you operate the slide rule to determine whether or not you can do so smoothly and without binding.

    After you have completed the test, take it to your teacher's assistant for correction and then to your teacher for consultation. You and he will then decide whether or not you should complete the unit. If it is decided that you will complete the unit, proceed!

### ALTERNATIVE LEARNING ACTIVITIES

Introduction:

    During the next 5 or 10 minutes you will need the following materials:

        stop watch
        pencil
        paper
        boyfriend or girlfriend (whichever is preferable)

Obtain the stop watch from the media center and take your friend to a convenient table. Have your friend time you while you work the following

problem using only the pencil and paper (of course, you may also use your
brain if you like):

$$\frac{67.8 \times 356 \times 2.9}{3.85 \times 197}$$

If you are of average speed, you should have finished the calculation
in about 10 to 13 minutes. You may not have even finished; you may have
given up. It really wasn't very exciting to do that long drawn out problem,
was it?

HOW WOULD YOU LIKE TO DO THE SAME PROBLEM IN 90 SECONDS WITH 3 PLACE
ACCURACY? What's more, you will be able to do even more complicated problems
in only seconds without a complex device that doesn't need to be plugged into
electricity and doesn't even use batteries; it's completely portable.

This device is known as a "slipstick", or slide rule, to be correct.
It is ancient yet modern, but easy to learn and use!!! Why spend the time
to learn to use such an instrument? Just think, you'll be the envy of
all your physics buddies: you'll work those D A R N physics problems in one-
third the time. Your chemistry teacher won't believe how fast you can get
the answers, and they'll be correct too! You will be able to carry in your
shirt pocket or purse a small 1" X 6" substitute for hundreds of pages of
complicated mathematical tables. In your Home Economics class you can decide
which can of corn is the best buy in just a few seconds by using your
"slipstick."

You may choose one or more of the following activities in order to
complete the package objectives.

ACTIVITY NO. 1    This is a fun activity! Almost everyone enjoys making a
slide rule that really works. In fact, the one you are about to make will

work every bit as well as rules costing $10 or more.

Obtain the following materials from your teacher's lab assistant, or from your own source:

1.  two 5 x 8 unlined index cards

2.  two narrow strips cut from logarithmic ruled paper   (these will be used for the scales)

3.  glue

4.  masking or scotch tape

5.  scissors

6.  pencil or pen

Step 1.  Fold one index card in half lengthwise and cut a window in one half as shown in the diagram.  The dimensions of the cutout  should be about 7-5/8 inches X 1-1/4 inches.  Tape the lower edges together.

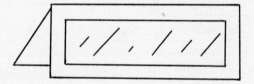

Step 2.  Glue or tape one of the scale strips against the lower edge of the window.  Number the scale from one to ten placing the numerals on the major divisions.

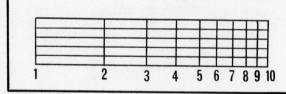

Step 3.  Cut a piece from the other card that will fit inside the "envelope" you have just made.  Don't make it too snug nor too loose.  This will be the slide of the slide rule.  Tape or glue the remaining scale strip to the slide so that it matches up with the scale on the front of the envelope (body

of the rule). Number this new scale in exactly the same way as you did the other one.

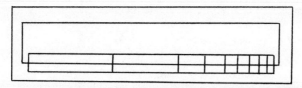

Step 4.  Now make a hairline indicator (cursor or indicator of the rule). Cut a piece of heavy paper or stock similar to the body and slide so that it measures 5-1/2" X 3/4".  Cut a window in this that measures 4" X 3/8". Tape a piece of hair (dog, horse, girl, cow) lengthwise exactly in the center of this window.  Be sure to stretch it tightly before you firm it in place. Incidentally, a piece of fine thread will suffice also.

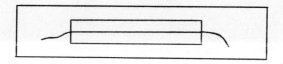

Next, fold and tape this cursor around the slide rule as shown below.

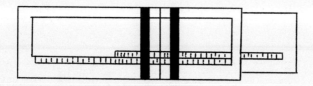

GUESS WHAT?  YOU ARE NOW READY TO TRY IT.

Make arrangements with the media center to view the filmstrip entitled, SLIDE-RULE:  AN INTRODUCTION.  Also, view another filmstrip entitled, THE SLIDE-RULE:  C and S SCALES.

After you have viewed the two filmstrips, use your newly made slide rule to work the problems below (answers given in parentheses):

1. 3 x 45                    (135)

2. 7 X 65                    (455)

3. 2.8 X 37.5                (105)

4. 34 X 86                   (2,920)

5. 15 X 95                   (1,420 or 1,430)

Since a longer slide rule is inherently more accurate and easier to use than a shorter one, you may wish to supply your own commercially made slide rule of 10 inches or longer or you may obtain one from your teacher or his assistant. In either case it is advisable that you use one of these longer ones for the remaining exercises in this activity.

ACTIVITY NO. 2   Go to the media center and check out the filmstrip entitled SLIDE RULE - AN INTRODUCTION. View this filmstrip in one of the carrels. Now, check out a second filmstrip entitled, THE SLIDE RULE:  C and D SCALES. View the filmstrip and do the exercises on pages 9, 12, 13, 14, 15 in the book, SLIDE RULES, by Maurice L. Hartung. You may check your answers with those on page 60.

ACTIVITY NO. 3   If you are a good reader and prefer a more challenging approac then try this activity. Locate the lab assistant and sign out for the booklet entitled, A TEACHING GUIDE FOR SLIDE RULE INSTRUCTION, by Maurice L. Hartung. Study pp. 5 through 16, and be sure to perform the activities which are indicated in this reading. When you finish, do the exercises in NO. 2 above.

ACTIVITY NO. 4   Are you the daring type? Are you inquisitive, self-reliant, and the kind who likes to figure things out for yourself? If so, then this one is for--------YOU! This activity is somewhat more difficult and requires more thinking and originality. It should be attempted immediately after ACTIVITY NO. 1. If you complete this one legitimately, your teacher will graciously supply you with a special reward! Tempting? OK, here's what you do. Obtain from the media center, the cassette tape entitled, LOOK MA, NO BATTERIES. Listen to the tape no more than twice. THREE TIMES OR MORE VIOLATES CONSIDERATION FOR THE REWARD. Follow the directions on the tape, and when you finish, do the exercises as listed in ACTIVITY NO. 2.

How are you doing? Would you like to check yourself against the behavioral objectives? If so, then take the Self-Test.

## SELF-TEST

Perform the following indicated operations with a 10 inch or longer slide rule, and express your answers with 3 significant digits:

1. 85 X 7

2. 7.8 X 56

3. 3.85 X 6.4

4. 75 ÷ 30

5. 865 ÷ 23

6. 49.2 ÷ 5.4

7. 450 X 98

8. 85 ÷ 257

9. $\dfrac{6.5 \ X \ 560}{43}$

10. $\dfrac{23 \ X \ 13}{6 \ X \ 19}$

Demonstrate smooth handling of the slide rule by letting your teacher observe you.

The answers to the Self-Test are given below. Correct your paper, and immediately see your teacher if you did not score 90%.

ANSWERS TO SELF-TEST:   (1) 595   (2) 437   (3) 24.6   (4) 2.50   (5) 37.6

(6) 9.11   (7) 44,000   (8) .331   (9) 84.7   (10) 2.62

If you are like most people, this unit has been fun and rewarding.
Perhaps you wish to consider doing some in-depth quest activities?

## OPTIONAL QUEST ACTIVITIES

The following Quest Activities may be pursued at your discretion.  They
are most interesting and are designed to broaden your outlook on the content
of this unit and create a smooth transition to the next unit.  They are of
varying difficulty, and one or two of them may require some strategic hints
from your teacher.  Solicit these hints only if you are stuck.

QUEST NO. 1  From sufficient reference sources of your choice, familiarize
yourself with the meaning of "scientific notation."  Choose a dozen or so
numbers at random and express these in "scientific notation."  When you are
satisfied that you can do so without difficulty, then concentrate your efforts
on the following activity:

How can you incorporate the notion of "scientific notation" in locating
the decimal point in any slide rule multiplication or division problem?
The culminating aspect of this Quest will be a short written essay not more
than one-half page in length which presents your theory or answer.  When
your essay is in finished form, take it to your teacher for critique.

QUEST NO. 2  Locate from your friends, family, or acquaintances several slide
rules which have been manufactured from different types of materials.  Some
of the materials to look for are:

    1.  metal

2. redwood

3. bamboo

4. plastic

5. wood (other than redwood)

Evaluate these rules using as your criteria such characteristics as
smooth operation of the slide and cursor, glare, ease of reading the numerals,
weight, alignment, ease of adjusting alignment, closeness of the hairline
to the body of the rule, durability of the finish, and any others you may wish
to add.

After this evaluation, submit a short paper of one page or less indicating
which type slide rule in a given price range you would personally buy.  Base
your decision on the above criteria and not necessarily on the number of
scales offered.


QUEST NO. 3  This activity is for those of you who have successfully passed
a course in Advanced Algebra.  This is a challenging and very intriguing
pursuit.  Once you get involved you won't want to quit until you have ------
found the SECRET.

To prepare yourself for the main problem it will probably be necessary
to review a few concepts.  These are:  meaning of exponents, multiplication
of powers, multiplication of two numbers using logarithms and antilogarithms.
You may do this by obtaining the filmstrip, EXPONENTS AND LOGARITHMS, from
the media center.  View the filmstrip in one of the carrels.

If you feel that you need more review than the filmstrip offers, secure
from the media center two filmstrips with their accompanying cassettes,
entitled, EXPONENTIAL AND LOGARITHMIC FUNCTIONS, and COMPUTATION WITH LOGARITHMS.
These filmstrips will provide more in-depth information.

You may also study pp. 408-426 in the book, <u>MODERN SCHOOL MATHEMATICS</u>, by Dolciani, Wooten, Beckenbach, and Sharron.

After you have established familiarity with these concepts, you will be prepared to tackle the problem, which is:

What is the basic theory of operation underlying the design of a slide rule? Prepare a one page or less paper on your own theory. Support your theory with mathematical concepts using those you have just reviewed as hints. Turn your paper in to your teacher for evaluation and discussion.


<u>TEACHERS' GUIDE</u>

In order to utilize this package effectively, the teacher should make some preliminary preparations. These are:

1. Perform activity number 2

2. Familiarize himself with all the media called for

3. Establish a filing system for the answer sheets to the Pre-test and Post-test so they can be located quickly

4. Make available all the materials needed and ensure that they can be located in the specified areas or as amended by him


<u>MATERIALS NEEDED FOR THIS PACKAGE</u>

pencil

paper

stop watch (optional)

5 x 8 unlined cards

masking tape or scotch tape

logarithmic ruled paper (Dietzgen no. 340-1210, semi-logarithmic, 2 cycles with 10 divisions per inch)

Filmstrip, SLIDE RULE: AN INTRODUCTION, color, 39 frames, silent, produced by Popular Science Pub. Co. Inc., 1968

Filmstrip, THE SLIDE RULE: C and D SCALES, b&w, 53 frames, silent, produced by US Office of Education, 1943

Filmstrip, EXPONENTS AND LOGARITHMS, color, 45 frames, silent, produced by Popular Science Pub. Co. Inc., 1962

Filmstrip, EXPONENTIAL AND LOGARITHMIC FUNCTIONS, color, 45 frames, accompanied by cassette, produced by Eye Gate House Inc., 1970

Filmstrip, COMPUTATION WITH LOGARITHMS, color, 47 frames, accompanied by cassette, produced by Eye Gate House Inc., 1970

Book, A TEACHING GUIDE FOR SLIDE RULE INSTRUCTION, by Maurice L. Hartung, Pickett Inc., 1960

Cassette, LOOK MA, NO BATTERIES, 14 min., 1 7/8 ips, produced by West High School Media Center, Salt Lake City, Utah, 1971

EQUIPMENT AND FACILITIES NEEDED

Filmstrip projector, manual, for use in student carrel

Cassette tape recorder

Film projector, 16mm

Earphones

Carrels equipped with 110 volt electrical outlets

screen or equivalent provision for using the projector

Pre-test Key

| | | | |
|---|---|---|---|
| 1. | 520 | 6. | 8.28 |
| 2. | 211 | 7. | 27.1 |
| 3. | 215 | 8. | 3.50 |
| 4. | 1.63 | 9. | 6.77 |
| 5. | 49.7 | | |

Post-test Key

| | | | |
|---|---|---|---|
| 1. | 115 | 6. | 12.0 |
| 2. | 361 | 7. | 2,860 |
| 3. | 26.8 | 8. | .286 |
| 4. | 1.93 | 9. | 83.7 |
| 5. | 31.4 | 10. | 5.79 |

POST-TEST

Perform the following indicated operations with a 10 inch or longer slide

rule, and express your answers with 3 significant digits:

1.  23 x 5
2.  8.6 x 42
3.  5.83 x 4.6
4.  27 ÷ 14
5.  972 ÷ 31
6.  46.7 ÷ 3.9
7.  325 x 88
8.  57 ÷ 199

9.  $\dfrac{4.3 \times 720}{37}$

10. $\dfrac{32 \times 19}{5 \times 21}$

Individualized Instruction Package

by

Steven Streadbeck

entitled

EMOTIONS AND YOUR BODY

Subject Area:  Health Education

Level:  Grades 5 and 6

## RATIONALE

The purpose of this packet is to help you understand different emotions that you experience and their effect on your health.

Many body changes take place when any form of emotion is experienced. When you are growing up emotionally, you increase your ability to handle fears, face your problems squarely, and solve them through correct planning.

There are many undesirable habits annoying to other people and harmful to your health.

Developing your emotional maturity signifies your ability to face reality and progress toward desirable goals.

## CONTENT

This package is designed to help you as a student in understanding and knowing what the emotions are that you may experience and how they may affect your health. It is designed to be informative as well as beneficial. You will learn the skills for good mental health, including ways to overcome objectionable habits such as smoking, drinking, and drug addiction. It allows different ways for you, as a fifth grade student, to develop your interests.

## BEHAVIORAL OBJECTIVES

After completing this package you will be able to:

1.  Define the meaning of emotion and give examples of both pleasant and unpleasant emotions.

2.  Explain how the adrenal glands in the body are equipped to handle situations involving strong emotions and how they do this.

3.  Describe the effects that harmful, long-term emotional conditions may have on your physical condition and describe how they affect your health.

4.  Define the meaning of "defense mechanisms" and be able to cite an example.

5.  Identify several harmful habits and explain how these habits are harmful to your health.

PRE-TEST

Instructions:  Choose the best answer.

1.  The word emotion

    a.  means to move your body
    b.  is taken from the latin word Emovere
    c.  means only unpleasant things

2.  All emotions, pleasant and unpleasant

    a.  result in some physical change
    b.  can be entirely eliminated
    c.  are always helpful

3.  If an unpleasant emotion comes and goes quickly

    a.  there is usually a lasting effect on your general health
    b.  there are no physical changes in the body
    c.  there is not likely to be any lasting effect upon your general health

4.  Your personality is

    a.  the sum total of your appearance and usual actions as they impress other people
    b.  measured entirely by your emotions shown to others
    c.  unimportant to success

5.  Some psychologists believe that all other emotions stem from

    a.  fear, anxiety, and love
    b.  fear, anger, and love
    c.  anxiety, anger, and love

6.  An individual does not always recognize either his emotions or their cause

    a.  because the body and the personality have needs and cravings which remain far below the level of the conscious mind
    b.  because emotional patterns may be connected with events which have occurred long ago and have been forgotten
    c.  both

7.  There are in general two groups of emotions caused by two types of situations

    a.  happy and joyful
    b.  upset and frustrated
    c.  pleasant and unpleasant

8.  What is meant by a "defense mechanism?"

    a.  a mechanism used by psychologists to help them understand your problems
    b.  avoiding your problems, or hoping they will clear up of their own accord
    c.  another way of saying you have a good sense of humor

9.  If emotion lasts long or is strong enough, what body changes may take place?

    a.  your adrenals put out a greater amount of adrenalin
    b.  your kidneys seal off, preventing sugars from entering your blood
    c.  your gastro-intestinal tract secretes bile salts to give greater energy by means of better digestion
    d.  all of the above

10. It has been scientifically proven that which of the following is harmful to your health?

    a.  smoking
    b.  drinking alcohol
    c.  drug addiction
    d.  all of the above


ALTERNATIVE LEARNING ACTIVITIES


In this package we will find out how the emotions we experience affect body changes. There is a good filmstrip on emotional health along with possible work in small group discussions, interesting reading, reports, interviews, dictionary work, collecting and assembling pictures, research from the encyclopedia, and experiments. Read through the following activities and decide which one you would like to try.

ACTIVITY NO. 1   Read pages 174-199 in your text UNDERSTANDING YOUR NEEDS and answer the questions under "Let's Review" on page 200. This should be answered on a separate sheet of paper and turned in.

ACTIVITY NO. 2   You should do all of the following to complete this activity.
1. Look up the following words in the dictionary and write definitions of each on a sheet of paper.

      a.  emotion
      b.  fear
      c.  adrenal glands
      d.  anger
      e.  love
      f.  habit

After you have written all of the definitions, study each word and see if it means what you thought it did.

2. You should now view the two films entitled CONTROL YOUR EMOTIONS and THE COLOR OF HEALTH. Notice that the films stress that well-balanced emotions create a well rounded personality. Also notice the interaction of each of the characters in the film.

3. Get together with two or three other students and discuss the following topics in relation to emotions:

      a.  how children differ in their abilities to do various things, and how they set up "defense mechanisms"
      b.  the harm of keeping emotional tension, such as worry, anxiety, and fear bottled up inside. In the discussion, consider the need for friends to talk to, hobbies for outlets and how to face your problems
      c.  how planning can help avoid many of your problems
      d.  unhealthful habits such as smoking, alcohol, and drugs

ACTIVITY NO. 3  You are to view the filmstrip <u>YOUR FEELINGS</u> (note the harmful emotional effects).  You can find it along with the projector and individual viewer in the back of the room.

Read the article in the World Book Encyclopedia on <u>Emotion</u>. (Be sure and note what "defense mechanism" means and what functions the adrenal glands have.)  You can get this information from the teacher or from the library.

Collect two or more pictures for each of the following emotions: fear, anger, and love.  Collect three pictures showing some harmful habits.

SELF-TEST

1. Do you know what the word emotion means?  What are the three basic emotions from which all others originate?

2. Do you know the bodily changes which take place under emotional strain?

3. Do you know what some unhealthy habits people have which are harmful to their health?

4. Do you know what is meant by "defense mechanism?"

5. Do you know what are some harmful effects of prolonged emotional stress?

6. Do you know what the adrenals are and how they function?

<u>Self-Test Key</u>

6. The adrenal glands are the keys to emotional changes.  Their purpose is to keep circulation, blood sugars, and blood pressure regulated.

5. Prolonged emotional stress can lead to physical illness.

4. A type of activity which is engaged in to avoid a particular problem is a "defense mechanism."  An example is daydreaming.

3. Some unhealthy habits include: drinking, smoking, taking drugs, glue sniffing, etc.

2. Under emotional strain your adrenal glands put out a greater than normal amount of adrenalin.

1. Emotion means feelings such as joy, excitement, love, anger, and fear. The three basic emotions are fear, anger, and love.

## OPTIONAL QUEST ACTIVITIES

QUEST NO. 1. Look up in the encyclopedia further information on emotion, habits, use of alcohol, smoking of cigarettes and drugs. This may be turned in as an extra report.

QUEST NO. 2. Interview a member of the Police Department to learn more about the effect of poor habits on delinquency. Report to the class on your findings.

QUEST NO. 3. Have the school psychologist explain the experiments on developing the "defense mechanism" in the Rhesus Monkey. Prepare a demonstration, if possible, using the monkey, or assist the psychologist in a demonstration for the class.

TEACHERS' GUIDE

Basic Instructions:  Stimulate the class by discussing the picture in the text UNDERSTANDING YOUR NEEDS on page 174.  Allow the students to choose alternative learning activities and supervise the small group discussion.

MEDIA NEEDED:

COLOR OF HEALTH, color, 11 min. 16mm.  Rental available from Indiana University Film Library, No. HSC-659, $2.00.

CONTROL YOUR EMOTIONS, color, 14 min. 16mm, Coronet Films, Inc. $125. purchase, $6.75 rental.

UNDERSTANDING YOUR NEEDS, Textbook, McGraw Hill, Inc., 1965, Unit 8, pp. 174-200

WORLD BOOK ENCYCLOPEDIA, Vol. E, World Book Publishing Company, 1959, pp. 154-156

YOUR FEELINGS, Filmstrip, Jam Handy Corp.  Detroit, Michigan

EQUIPMENT AND MATERIALS NEEDED:

Filmstrip Viewer

16mm Film Projector

Dictionary

Stack of old magazines

Paper

Pre-test key:

1.  b            6.  c
2.  a            7.  c
3.  c            8.  b
4.  a            9.  a
5.  b           10.  d

# POST-TEST

1. What does the word emotion mean?

2. How can the emotion of fear affect your body?

3. Are all emotions unpleasant?  What are some of the pleasant ones?

4. What parts of the body are keys to emotional changes?

5. What is the work of the adrenal glands?

6. How can you control your fears?

7. How can your emotions affect your health?

8. When do we develop many of our fears and prejudices?

9. What is meant by "facing your problems?"

10. What is the main value of planning?

11. What is meant by "defense mechanism?"

12. How can proper planning help you to control your emotions?

13. What are the steps in forming a habit?

14. What are some habits that wreck health?

Post-test key:

1. Feelings such as joy, excitement, love, anger, and fear.

2. It can cause a rapid heartbeat, dry feeling in the mouth; and the body may
   tremble and break out in a cold sweat.

3. No.  Joy, excitement, love, and contentment are pleasant emotions.

4. The adrenal glands.

5. They keep circulation, blood sugars, and blood pressure normal.  They help
   the body adjust to emergency situations.

6. An unpleasant emotion that stays with you over a long period of time can
   cause physical illness.  Happiness, contentment, peacefulness, and
   satisfaction with what you have done are among the emotions which bring
   health to the body and mind.

7. By trying to understand the reasons behind them. By not allowing your imagination to build little fears into big ones.

8. Many fears and prejudices come to us when we are very small.

9. Realizing that you have a problem, trying to understand the reasons for it, and doing something definite to overcome it.

10. Hoping the problem will clear up of its own accord; perhaps using certain defense mechanisms, such as daydreaming, as excuses for not tackling the problem.

11. By understanding what defense mechanisms are; that they are crutches and should not be leaned upon too heavily in order to minimize the disappointment.

12. It helps to avoid worries and fears that come about because of unaccomplished tasks.

13. You begin a habit for a reason. If it brings what you want, you may use it again and again. The more you use it, the more it becomes a part of you.

14. Smoking, use of habit-forming drugs, use of alcoholic drinks.

Individualized Instruction Package

by

Kristeen Fjeldsted

entitled

WHAT IS A LUNAR ECLIPSE?

Subject Area: Science

Level: Grades 3 and 4

## RATIONALE

Have you ever really wanted to show up a buddy or a friend?  Well, next time you see a friend, ask him how much he knows about a lunar eclipse. Chances are he may not know what you are talking about.  You will know once you have completed this package.

Actually, it's an easy package and you should go right through it. The package contains all kinds of activities including reading, film viewing and the creation of shadows.  All the activities are about a lunar eclipse.

Have fun and see if you can't out-smart that other guy!

## CONTENT

This package develops concepts and skills related to the formation of a lunar eclipse.

Since a lunar eclipse occurs very seldom, this package will allow you to study what an eclipse is like so that you will be able to discuss an eclipse with other students when it occurs.  This package will describe the formation of an eclipse and discuss the principles behind that formation. You will, at the end of this package, be able to create your own basic eclipse with the skills you acquire.

Before taking this package, you should know the location of the sun, moon, and the planets.  You should be able to describe the orbit in which each one travels.

## BEHAVIORAL OBJECTIVES

After completing this package, you will be able to:

1. Identify and create a shadow using a light source and a common object.

2. Draw a diagram showing the movement of the earth in relation to the sun.

3. Draw a diagram showing the movement of the moon in relation to the earth.

4. Describe the steps involved in creating a lunar eclipse.


## PRE-TEST

In order to take this test, you will need to obtain from the reference center:

1. a book called, MY PICTURE BOOK

2. a flashlight

3. a large ball

4. a small ball

5. a square piece of cardboard

6. a plastic sheet with a sun in the middle

7. a black crayon

Write all answers on a separate sheet of paper.

1. Look at the 12 pictures in MY PICTURE BOOK. On your piece of paper make two columns, one titled Shadows and the other No Shadows. Under each title list the pictures that fit that category.


2. Create a shadow using:

   1. a ball

   2. a square piece of cardboard

3. a large ball

4. a small ball

5. a square piece of cardboard

6. a plastic sheet with a sun in the middle

7. a black crayon

When you have created the shadow, show it to your teacher or the teacher's aide. Now move on to the next questions.

3. Using the big ball and the little ball, show the movement of the earth in relation to the sun. Which ball is the sun, which is the earth?

When you know you have the right answer, show your teacher or teacher's aide.

4. Again using the big ball and the little one, show the movement of the moon in relationship to the earth.

When you have completed this, show it to your teacher or teacher's aide.

5. Using the plastic covered sheet and the black crayon, draw a lunar eclipse.

Take your completed test to the teacher or her aide to correct. After she has done this, consult with your teacher as to what you should do next. If you and your teacher decide to go on, proceed to the reference center to get the rest of the material you will need for the package.

## ALTERNATIVE LEARNING ACTIVITIES

All the activities that follow have materials which are found in the reference center. For any help you might need in acquiring these materials, ask your teacher or teacher's aide.

Make sure you follow directions clearly and if there is some part you don't quite understand, be sure to ask for help.

Choose the activity which you feel is the best one for you. When you have a desire to find out where you stand on the subject of a lunar eclipse, ask your teacher or the aide for the self-test.

ACTIVITY NO. 1    Look through the book THE SHADOW BOOK by B. D. de Regniers and point out the pictures of shadows. Describe how you think they are formed.

Read the book THE MOON SEEMS TO CHANGE by Franklin M. Branley, See if you can see why the moon changes. Draw a picture of the movement of the moon in relation to the earth.

Read pages 1-13 in the book SHADOWS by Irving and Ruth Adler. Draw a picture of the lunar eclipse the Adlers talk about.

ACTIVITY NO. 2    View the film LIGHT FOR BEGINNERS. After seeing it, describe on a sheet of paper how a shadow is made.

Read pages 106-111 in the book LET'S SEE WHY. Describe, by use of the plastic sheet and a black crayon, the movement of the moon in relation to the earth.

Read the section in TARGET APOLLO by Michael Chester, pages 103-107. See if you can clearly describe an eclipse of the moon.

ACTIVITY NO. 3    Read chapter one of the book YOU AND YOUR SHADOW by Bill Severn. See if you can explain how a shadow is made.

View the film THE MOON AND HOW IT AFFECTS US. After viewing it, describe the way the moon moves in relation to the earth.

Watch the film THE MOON. See if you can describe a lunar eclipse by use of a drawing or a story about the moon.


SELF-TEST

1. Draw a shadow.



2. What do you need to make a shadow?

   a. strong light source
   b. object
   c. house
   d. all of the above

3. The movement of the earth in relation to the sun is

   a. it goes around the sun
   b. it stands still
   c. the sun goes around the earth
   d. none of the above

4. The moon goes in an orbit

   a. around the earth
   b. around the sun
   c. out in space
   d. a and c

5. A lunar eclipse is really

   a. sinking of the moon
   b. a shadow on the moon
   c. a big bluff
   d. a loss of the moon's power

Self-test Key

2) d, 3) a, 4) d, 5) b          1)

## OPTIONAL QUEST ACTIVITIES

This section of the package is for all those who believe in a little extra fun.

QUEST NO. 1   Make a shadow play, using materials suggested in YOU AND YOUR SHADOW by Bill Severn, or materials created by yourself.   After you have worked it out, give it in front of the class or to a small group of friends.

QUEST NO. 2   Prove that the earth does revolve around the sun.   Use Irving Adler's book called the SUN AND ITS FAMILY, as one of your reference sources. Also the film called THE EARTH IN MOTION is a good reference.

QUEST NO. 3   List the superstitions that a culture had about a lunar eclipse. A good source of reference is TARGET APOLLO by Michael Chester and also an encyclopedia.

## TEACHERS' GUIDE

This package was developed so a child may learn more about a lunar eclipse than he already knows. The teacher and teacher's aide need to become familiar with the activities and the optional quests. They should be able to do all of them. This is so that if a child needs help, he may come to any one of you and receive an answer to his question.

Most of the instructions for the tests are found on the test keys. Any instruction on the equipment is on the list of equipment. Activity Number 1 is the simplest of the three; the rest are of equal ability. It is hoped that you will guide those who can into a set of activities that will best fit their abilities.

The best advice is to let the child proceed at his own rate with as much help from you as he may want but do not offer assistance when it is not necessary. He should be able to complete the package on his own, except for the times during the tests when he needs a question corrected. This is explained in the test key.

Hopefully, the package is put together well enough that any resource you may wish to add will increase the benefit of the package, especially on the optional quest activities.

EQUIPMENT NEEDED

16mm film projector

two balls--one the size of a baseball and the other the size of a ping pong ball

a standard flashlight

a plastic covered piece of paper with the sun in the center

a square piece of cardboard, about 2" by 2"

a plastic covered piece of paper with a model of the earth in the center.

The plastic covered piece of paper with the sun in the center and the paper with a model of the earth in the center can be made by purchasing two plastic covers for the paper. The teaching assistant can then draw a circle of the earth and the sun on a piece of paper and place them in the covers.


BOOKS NEEDED

Adler, Irving and Ruth. SHADOWS. New York: John Day Co., 1961

Adler, Irving. SUN AND ITS FAMILY. New York: John Day Co., 1968

Branley, Franklin M. THE MOON SEEMS TO CHANGE. New York: Thomas Y. Crowell Co., 1960

Chester, Michael and McClinton, David. TARGET FOR APOLLO. New York: G. P. Putnams and Son, 1963

Mandell, Muriel. SCIENCE FOR CHILDREN. New York: Sterling Publishing Co., 1960

Platt and Munk, MY PICTURE BOOK. Platt and Munk Deluxe Cloth Book.

de Regniers, B. B. THE SHADOW BOOK. New York: Harcourt, Brace and Co., 1960

Severn, Bill. YOU AND YOUR SHADOW. New York: David McKay Co., Inc., 1961

Thorn, Samuel A. and Duman, Carl D. LET'S SEE WHY. New York: Benefic's Press, 1961


FILMS NEEDED

The main purpose for the films used in this package will be underlined. This is the key information the child needs to acquire from each film.


THE MOON, Encyclopedia Britannica Film Corporation, 11 min. black and white

Demonstrates using animation the concept of tides and the phases of the moon. Photographically illustrates a sunrise and a sunset on the moon and describes the moon's orbit. Both lunar and solar eclipses are also diagrammed.

LIGHT FOR BEGINNERS, color, 11 min., produced by Cornella Films, 1960.

Uses simple observations to demonstrate the basic properties of light. The effects of sunlight are compared with artificial light. Also discusses shadows, reflections, and the straight path of light.

THE MOON AND HOW IT AFFECTS US, b&w, 11 min., produced by Cornella Films, 1968.

Uses telescopic photography to show the seas, craters, and mountains of the moon. Eclipses, the moon's phases and the moon's effect on the earth's tides are explained as well as the moon's size, movement, and distance in relation to the earth.

Pre-test Key

1.

| Shadows | No Shadows |
|---|---|
| shovel and bucket | zipper |
| cups | gloves |
| spoon | |
| house | |
| umbrella | |
| telephone | |
| clock | |
| balls | |
| cookies | |
| pencils | |

2. The child is to create a shadow. He is then to come to you or your aide to be checked off. The shadow he creates does not have to be perfect but it does have to be there. He should also be able to give a reason why, although it is not necessary.

3. and 4. These two questions are essentially the same. The child is told to use the big and small ball to demonstrate the movement of the earth around the sun and the moon around the earth. He must bring it to you to pass this part of the test. Make sure he can tell you which ball represents which planet.

5. If his picture looks something like this,

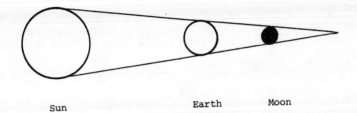

Sun                        Earth       Moon

then he should not have to do anything in this package.

## POST-TEST

In order to take this test, you will need to obtain from the reference center

    1. a plastic covered sheet with the earth in the center

    2. a flashlight

    3. an object of any type

    4. a piece of art paper

    5. your crayons

1. On the plastic sheet of paper with the earth in the middle, draw, using your black crayon, the movement of the moon in relation to the earth.

2. A shadow is created by using what? Create a shadow. Show it to your teacher.

3. Using your piece of art paper and your crayons, draw a lunar eclipse. Make sure you label all parts. Be able to describe your picture to your teacher, if she asks you to do so.

Post-Test Key

1. This illustration is all that is required to get the question correct. If he has added more information, make sure the added material is correct.

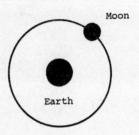

2. In creating a shadow, make sure he knows about the light source and the object. Look to see that he does know how to create a good shadow.

3. His picture should look something like this.

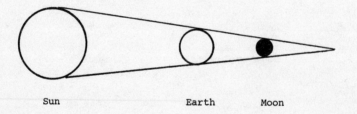

When you ask him to describe it, make sure he points out that the moon has moved into the shadow of the earth. If he does, he has successfully completed this package.